Statistical Tragedy in Africa?

T0314847

What do we know about economic development in Africa? The answer is that we know much less than we would like to think. This collection assesses the knowledge problem present in statistics on poverty, agriculture, labour, education, health and economic growth. While diverse in origin, the contributors to this book are unified in two conclusions: that the quality and quantity of data needs to be improved; and that this is a concern not just for statisticians. Weaknesses in statistical methodology and practice can misinform policy-makers, international agencies, donors, the private sector and the citizens of African countries themselves. This is also a problem for academics from various disciplines, from history and economics, to social epidemiology and education policy. Not only does academic work on Africa regularly use flawed data, but many problems encountered in surveys challenge common academic abstractions. By exploring these flaws, this book will provide a guide for scholars, policy-makers, and all those using and commissioning surveys in Africa.

This book was originally published as a special issue of *The Journal of Development Studies*.

Morten Jerven is an Associate Professor in the School for International Studies at Simon Fraser University, Vancouver, Canada and Associate Professor in Global Change and International Relations at Norwegian University of Life Sciences in Ås, Norway. He is an economic historian, publishing widely on patterns of African economic development, including recent books, *Africa. Why Economists Get It Wrong* (2015) and *Poor Numbers: How We Are Misled by African Development Statistics and What to Do About It* (2013).

Deborah Johnston is a Reader in Development Economics at SOAS, University of London, UK. She has published widely on poverty, HIV, nutrition and labour in African countries, including a recent book, *Economics and HIV: The Sickness of Economics* (Routledge, 2013).

Statistical Tragedy in Africa?

Evaluating the database for African economic development

Edited by

Morten Jerven and Deborah Johnston

LONDON AND NEW YORK

First published 2016
by Routledge
2 Park Square, Milton Park, Abingdon, Oxon, OX14 4RN, UK

and by Routledge
711 Third Avenue, New York, NY 10017, USA

First issued in paperback 2017

Routledge is an imprint of the Taylor & Francis Group, an informa business

British Library Cataloguing in Publication Data
A catalogue record for this book is available from the British Library

ISBN 13: 978-1-138-29492-9 (pbk)
ISBN 13: 978-1-138-94582-1 (hbk)

Typeset in Times
by RefineCatch Limited, Bungay, Suffolk

Publisher's Note
The publisher accepts responsibility for any inconsistencies that may have
arisen during the conversion of this book from journal articles to book chapters,
namely the possible inclusion of journal terminology.

Disclaimer
Every effort has been made to contact copyright holders for their permission to
reprint material in this book. The publishers would be grateful to hear from any
copyright holder who is not here acknowledged and will undertake to rectify
any errors or omissions in future editions of this book.

Contents

Citation Information   vii
Notes on Contributors   ix

Foreword: Africa's Statistical Tragedy: Take 2   xi
Morten Jerven

Introduction: Statistical Tragedy in Africa? Evaluating the Data Base for African
Economic Development   1
Morten Jerven & Deborah Johnston

1. The Political Economy of Bad Data: Evidence from African Survey and
   Administrative Statistics   6
   Justin Sandefur & Amanda Glassman

2. From Tragedy to Renaissance: Improving Agricultural Data for Better Policies   23
   Calogero Carletto, Dean Jolliffe & Raka Banerjee

3. The Invisibility of Wage Employment in Statistics on the Informal Economy in Africa:
   Causes and Consequences   39
   Matteo Rizzo, Blandina Kilama & Marc Wuyts

4. Poverty in African Households: the Limits of Survey and Census Representations   52
   Sara Randall & Ernestina Coast

5. The Making of the Middle-Class in Africa: Evidence from DHS Data   68
   Abebe Shimeles & Mthuli Ncube

6. Random Growth in Africa? Lessons from an Evaluation of the Growth Evidence on
   Botswana, Kenya, Tanzania and Zambia, 1965–1995   84
   Morten Jerven

7. GDP Revisions and Updating Statistical Systems in Sub-Saharan Africa: Reports
   from the Statistical Offices in Nigeria, Liberia and Zimbabwe   105
   Morten Jerven, Yemi Kale, Magnus Ebo Duncan & Moffat Nyoni

Index   119

Citation Information

The following chapters were originally published in *The Journal of Development Studies*, volume 51, issue 2 (February 2015). When citing this material, please use the original page numbering for each article, as follows:

Introduction

Statistical Tragedy in Africa? Evaluating the Data Base for African Economic Development
Morten Jerven & Deborah Johnston
The Journal of Development Studies, volume 51, issue 2 (February 2015) pp. 111–115

Chapter 1

The Political Economy of Bad Data: Evidence from African Survey and Administrative Statistics
Justin Sandefur & Amanda Glassman
The Journal of Development Studies, volume 51, issue 2 (February 2015) pp. 116–132

Chapter 2

From Tragedy to Renaissance: Improving Agricultural Data for Better Policies
Calogero Carletto, Dean Jolliffe & Raka Banerjee
The Journal of Development Studies, volume 51, issue 2 (February 2015) pp. 133–148

Chapter 3

The Invisibility of Wage Employment in Statistics on the Informal Economy in Africa: Causes and Consequences
Matteo Rizzo, Blandina Kilama & Marc Wuyts
The Journal of Development Studies, volume 51, issue 2 (February 2015) pp. 149–161

Chapter 4

Poverty in African Households: the Limits of Survey and Census Representations
Sara Randall & Ernestina Coast
The Journal of Development Studies, volume 51, issue 2 (February 2015) pp. 162–177

Chapter 5

The Making of the Middle-Class in Africa: Evidence from DHS Data
Abebe Shimeles & Mthuli Ncube
The Journal of Development Studies, volume 51, issue 2 (February 2015) pp. 178–193

Chapter 7

GDP Revisions and Updating Statistical Systems in Sub-Saharan Africa: Reports from the Statistical Offices in Nigeria, Liberia and Zimbabwe
Morten Jerven, Yemi Kale, Magnus Ebo Duncan & Moffat Nyoni
The Journal of Development Studies, volume 51, issue 2 (February 2015) pp. 194–207

The following chapter was originally published in *The Journal of Development Studies*, volume 46, issue 2 (February 2010). When citing this material, please use the original page numbering for each article, as follows:

Chapter 6

Random Growth in Africa? Lessons from an Evaluation of the Growth Evidence on Botswana, Kenya, Tanzania and Zambia, 1965–1995
Morten Jerven
The Journal of Development Studies, volume 46, issue 2 (February 2010) pp. 274–294

For any permission-related enquiries please visit:
http://www.tandfonline.com/page/help/permissions

Notes on Contributors

Raka Banerjee is the Project Coordinator for the Living Standards Measurement Study team in the Development Research Group at the World Bank. Her research interests are in the areas of poverty, food security, gender, and agriculture and rural development, as well as data collection and measurement issues.

Calogero Carletto is the Lead Economist for the Development Research Group for the World Bank. He co-ordinates a large methodological research program on the improvement of productivity measurement in agriculture, as well as a new research program on poverty and food security measurement.

Ernestina Coast is Associate Professor of Population Studies at the London School of Economics, London, UK. Her work focuses on relationships, including union formation, sexual behaviour and HIV/AIDS. She is the co-editor of *Fertility, Living Arrangements, Care and Mobility* (with Stillwell and Kneale, 2009).

Magnus Ebo Duncan is a Macro Economist and Financial Sector Specialist at the Economic Section of the Swiss Embassy in Accra, Ghana.

Amanda Glassman is Director of Global Health Policy, and Senior Fellow, at the Center for Global Development in Washington DC, USA. She leads work on priority-setting, resource allocation, and value for money in global health, with a particular interest in vaccination. She is the co-author of the books *From Few to Many: A Decade of Health Insurance Expansion in Colombia* (2010) and *The Health of Women in Latin America and the Caribbean* (2001).

Morten Jerven is an Associate Professor in the School for International Studies at Simon Fraser University, Vancouver, Canada and Associate Professor in Global Change and International Relations at Norwegian University of Life Sciences in Ås, Norway. He is an economic historian, publishing widely on patterns of African economic development, including recent books, *Africa. Why Economists Get It Wrong* (2015) and *Poor Numbers: How We Are Misled by African Development Statistics and What to Do About It* (2013).

Deborah Johnston is a Reader in Development Economics at SOAS, University of London, UK. She has published widely on poverty, HIV, nutrition and labour in African countries, including a recent book, *Economics and HIV: The Sickness of Economics* (Routledge, 2013).

Dean Jolliffe currently works at the World Bank on the Poverty and Inequality team in the Research Group (DECRG). He also holds appointments as a Research Fellow with the Institute for the Study of Labor in Bonn, Germany, and as a Research Affiliate with the National Poverty Center at the Gerald R. Ford School of Public Policy at the University of Michigan, Ann Arbor, MI, USA.

Yemi Kale is Statistician General of the Federation and Chief Executive Officer for the National Bureau of Statistics in Nigeria.

Blandina Kilama is a Senior Researcher with Policy Research for Development (REPOA), based in Dar es Salaam, Tanzania. She has over ten years of practical experience in research and policy analysis particularly in the areas of poverty, public policy, value chains, and service delivery.

Mthuli Ncube is a Senior Research Fellow and Project Leader at the Blavatnik School of Government, University of Oxford, UK, leading a multi-disciplinary project on the Economics of HIV (Rethink HIV), sponsored by the Rush Foundation. He previously served as Chief Economist and Vice President, African Development Bank Group.

Moffat Nyoni is based at the National Statistics Agency in Harare, Zimbabwe.

Sara Randall is Professor of Anthropology at University College London, UK. Most of her research experience is in francophone West Africa (Mali, Burkina Faso, Senegal) and she is generally interested in all aspects of fertility, reproduction and health in this region and how they interplay with migration and development.

Matteo Rizzo is a Lecturer in Development Research Methods, and the Economics of Africa, at SOAS, University of London, UK. His research interests are the economics of Africa, and the political economy of development, with a focus on the present as well as on African economic history, with a focus on Eastern Africa.

Justin Sandefur is a Research Fellow at the Center for Global Development in Washington DC, USA. His expertise is in legal empowerment of the poor, education, African development and evaluating the effectiveness of aid.

Abebe Shimeles is Acting Director of the Development Research Department for the African Development Bank, based in Tunis, Tunisia. He is the co-editor of *Urbanization and Socio-Economic Development in Africa: Challenges and Opportunities* (with Steve Kayizzi-Mugerwa and Nadège Désirée Yaméogo, Routledge, 2014).

Marc Wuyts is a Professor in the International Institute of Social Sciences at Erasmus University of Rotterdam, The Netherlands. His most recent book is *Making the International: Economic Interdependence and International Political Order* (with Bromley, Mackintosh and Brown, 2004).

Foreword: Africa's Statistical Tragedy: Take 2

MORTEN JERVEN

School for International Studies, Simon Fraser University, Vancouver, Canada and Norwegian University of Life Sciences, Ås, Norway

In 2011 the then Chief Economist for the World Bank Africa region, Shanta Devarajan declared Africa's Statistical Tragedy (Devarajan, 2011, 2013). It was in part responding to the news of the GDP revision in Ghana in 2010 (Jerven & Duncan, 2012), and in part reacting to new research that laid bare some of the shortcomings of the data reported in international databases (Jerven, 2012, 2013c, 2013b). More recent news, such as the GDP rebasing in Nigeria, and elsewhere in sub-Saharan Africa in 2014 would seem to reaffirm this statistical tragedy.

As recent publications show, including this volume, 'Africa's Statistical Tragedy' is and was a bit of a misnomer. When the journal special issue was launched at the Centre for Global Development on April 6, 2015,[1] the point was made that the real statistical failure occurred in Washington, and that perhaps the real tragedy was that we did not know how little we knew (Jerven, 2015b). If there was a tragedy in African statistics it did occur some time ago, and it was particularly pronounced in the 1980s and 1990s (Jerven, 2013c).[2] That many were so late to discover that a statistical catastrophe may have had unfolded is symptomatic of how many researchers, institutions and analysts depend on what they hope to be hard facts, but what turns out to be numbers that really are quite soft guesstimates (Jerven, 2015a).

Since 2011, a range of important publications have helped galvanize international attention to the gaps in the development data. *Poor Numbers: How We Are Misled by African Development Statistics and What to Do about It* was launched in April 2013 at a conference organized at Simon Fraser University in Vancouver, Canada.[3] The first set of papers were published in the *Canadian Journal of Development Studies* (Jerven, 2014b), and are available as an edited volume published by Routledge (Jerven, 2015a). The papers included in the edited volume were all part of *The Journal of Development Studies*, with the exception of the article "Random Growth in Africa? Lessons from an Evaluation of the Growth Evidence on Botswana, Kenya, Tanzania and Zambia, 1965–1995" which was published in 2010 in *The Journal of Development Studies*, before the big GDP rebasings in Ghana and Nigeria drew the attention of international media to the serious problems in the international datasets on economic growth.[4]

While it may be too early to call Africa's Statistical Renaissance, the last population census round is the most successful on record (in terms of countries participating) and there is better raw data available to calculate many social development indicators than a decade ago. Yet, progress has been uneven, and particularly, economic statistics have been neglected. It is symptomatic that recent papers on manufacturing, labour and structural change in Africa makes use of data from the Demographic Health Surveys in lieu of comparable labour and GDP data (MacMillan & Hartgren, 2014), and similarly a paper in this volume uses the same dataset to get an idea of what the income distribution may look like in African economies (Shimeles & Ncube, 2015).

The GDP rebasing in Ghana, Nigeria and elsewhere reflects how long economic statistics have been neglected in African economies, but perhaps the attention to the knowledge problem may start a healthy broader discussion of production of statistics with scholars, statisticians, international organizations and other stakeholders. Recent debates on economic statistics in Africa certainly show that the stakes are high. In February 2013, *Poor Numbers: How We Are Misled by African Development Statistics and What to Do about It* was reviewed in the *Financial Times* under the title "Africa Counts the Cost of its Miscalculations" to which the Chief Economist and Vice President of African Development Bank Group responded, "Africa's rise is real. Come and see for yourselves" (Jack, 2013). In order to diagnose the problem, and seeking to appease worries from investors and other stakeholders, both African Development Bank and the IMF's African Regional Economic Outlook issued reports on the status of economic statistics in the region, as well as replicating the studies on base years first conducted in *Poor Numbers*. The reports were published in May and April, and contain conflicting findings on methods and sources in economic statistics, showing that the problem of incomparable and unreliable estimates extends to the metadata as well (IMF, 2013; African Development Bank, 2013).

That credibility of official statistics may be a sensitive topic was well displayed during the summer of 2013. Directors of statistics in South Africa and Zambia made public statements reacting to *Poor Numbers*, including an intervention to stop an address at a UNECA conference in September 2013 (Taylor, 2013). A public exchange in the media followed (York, 2013), and the incident was commented upon in an editorial "Africa at Dawn" (*Financial Times*, 2013):

> "Too often, the continent's leaders have punished western scholars for questioning government numbers. Critical voices have even been excluded from regional economic forums by means of informal bans. Taking criticism on board would be one worthwhile step. Granting independence to national statistics agencies would be another. Official statistics can only be credible if governments are willing to voice inconvenient truths."

With this volume, Deborah Johnston and I wanted to do a follow-up on the special issue of the *Journal of Development Economics* in 1994 by Srinivasan – reflecting on the challenges for scholars that had access to all those new global datasets (Jerven & Johnston, 2015). The contributions display different ways of quizzing and contesting statistics. One way of questioning measurement is by comparing different numbers achieved through different methods and surveys that are supposed to measure the same phenomena, like GDP before and after rebasing, GDP growth in different databases (Jerven, 2010, 2011), health and education (Sandefur & Glassman, 2015), labour (Bardasi et al,. 2010), agriculture (Carletto, Jolliffe, & Banerjee, 2015; Jerven, 2014). For some areas the issue may not be conflicting data, but missing data. Serajuddin et al. (2015) show that for the countries where the World Bank is monitoring poverty as many as 77 out of 155 countries measured do not have adequate poverty data. Relating to comparing results in different datasets, using different methodologies, is to questioning categories and definitions. It is of utmost importance who and what gets counted and why. In this volume this is displayed by looking at the suitability of the household as an accounting unit in measuring poverty (Randall & Coast, 2015) and the suitability of employment and labour categories (and the translation of these from English to Kiswahili) in questions of labour in Tanzania (Rizzo, Kilama, & Wuyts, 2015). Fundamentally, the volume underlines the importance of approaching statistics as products and not as facts. We need to worry more about the politics and economics of how indicators and statistics of economic development are produced and used.

Notes

1. Many thanks to Amanda Glassman and the Center of Global Development for making that possible.
2. Thus, when Devarajan modified the title of Easterly's 1997 paper, "Africa's Growth Tragedy", he may have done better using the title from a 2001 paper, "The Lost Decades".
3. The conference and the publication of these two volumes have been possible due to funding and support from the School for International Studies at Simon Fraser University, the Social Sciences and Humanities Research Fund, the International Development Research Center, the African Development Bank, the Global Venture Fund and the African Economic History Network.
4. See Jerven (2014a).

References

African Development Bank. (2013). *Situational Analysis of Economic Statistics in Africa: Special focus on GDP measurement*. Tunis: African Development Bank.

Bardasi, E., Beegle, K., Dillon, A., & Serneels, P. (2010). Do labor statistics depend on how and to whom the questions are asked? Results from a survey experiment in Tanzania. *The World Bank Economic Review, 25*(3), 418–447.

Carletto, C., Jolliffe, D., & Banerjee, R. (2015). From tragedy to Renaissance: Improving agricultural data for better policies. *The Journal of Development Studies, 51*, 133–148. doi: 10.1080/00220388.2014.968140.

Devarajan, S. (2011, October 6). *Africa's statistical tragedy. Africa Can End Poverty: A blog about the economic challenges and opportunities facing Africa*. Retrieved from http://blogs.worldbank.org/africacan/africa-s-statistical-tragedy.

Devarajan, S. (2013). Africa's statistical tragedy. *The Review of Income and Wealth, 59*, S9–S15.doi: 10.1111/roiw.12013.

Easterly, W. (2001). The lost decades: Developing countries' stagnation in spite of policy reform 1980–1998. *Journal of Economic Growth, 6*, 135–157. doi: 10.1023/A:1011378507540.

Easterly, W., & Levine, R. (1997). Africa's growth tragedy: Policies and ethnic divisions. *Quarterly Journal of Economics, 112*, 1203–1250.

Financial Times (2013, October 28). Africa at dawn: Continent will gain by putting investors in the picture. Retrieved from http://www.ft.com/cms/s/0/3bb87da0-3fce-11e3-8882-00144feabdc0.html#axzz3ZPyTDRGU.

International Monetary Fund. (2013). *Regional Economic Outlook: Sub-Saharan Africa: Building momentum in a multi-speed world*. Washington DC: International Monetary Fund.

Jack, A. (2013). 'Africa counts the cost of miscalculations'. *Financial Times*, 24 February. http://www.ft.com/cms/s/2/0168741a-7c4d-11e2-91d2-00144feabdc0.html#axzz2fieCV9p3.

Jerven, M. (2012, November 20). Lies, damn lies and GDP. *The Guardian*. Retrieved from http://www.theguardian.com/business/2012/nov/20/economics-ghana.

Jerven, M. (2013a). Comparability of GDP estimates in sub-Saharan Africa: The effect of revisions in sources and methods since structural adjustment. *Review of Income and Wealth, 51*, S16–S36. doi: 10.1111/roiw.12006.

Jerven, M. (2013b). For richer, for poorer: GDP revisions and Africa's statistical tagedy. *African Affairs, 112*, 138–147. doi: 10.1093/afraf/ads063.

Jerven, M. (2013c). *Poor Numbers: How we are misled by African Development Statistics and what to do about it*. Ithaca: Cornell University Press.

Jerven, M. (2014a). *Economic Growth and Measurement Reconsidered in Botswana, Kenya, Tanzania and Zambia, 1965–1995*. Oxford: Oxford University Press.

Jerven, M. (2014b). Measuring African development: Past and present. *Canadian Journal of Development Studies, 35*, 1–8. doi: 10.1080/02255189.2014.876617.

Jerven, M. (2014c). The political economy of agricultural statistics and input subsidies: Evidence from India, Nigeria and Malawi. *Journal of Agrarian Change, 14*, 129–145. doi: 10.1111/joac.12025.

Jerven, M. (2015a). *Africa: Why Economists Get it Wrong*. London & New York: Zed Books.

Jerven, M. (2015b, April 6). *Africa's Statistical Tragedy: Take 2*. Presentation at Center for Global Development, Washington, DC.

Jerven, M. (2015c). *Measuring African Development: Past and Present*. Oxford: Routledge.

Jerven, M., & Duncan, M.E. (2012). Revising GDP estimates in sub-Saharan Africa: Lessons from Ghana. *African Statistical Journal, 13*, 12–24.

Jerven, M., & Johnston, D. (2015). Statistical tragedy in Africa? Evaluating the data base for African economic development. *The Journal of Development Studies, 51*, 111–115. doi: 10.1080/00220388.2014.968141.

Jerven, M., Kale, Y., Duncan, M.E., & Nyoni, M. (2015). GDP revisions and updating statistical systems in sub-Saharan Africa: Reports from the Statistical Offices in Nigeria, Liberia and Zimbabwe. *The Journal of Development Studies*, *51*, 194–207. doi: 10.1080/00220388.2014.968139.

McMillan, M.S., & Harttgen, K. (2014). What is driving the 'Africa Growth Miracle'?. *NBER Working Paper No. 20077*. doi: 10.3386/w20077.

Ncube, M. (2013). Africa is on the rise – come see for yourselves. *Financial Times*. http://www.ft.com/intl/cms/s/0/da7121ba-8802-11e2-8e3c-00144feabdc0.html?siteedition=intl#axzz2fieCV9p3.

Randall, S., & Coast, E. (2015). Poverty in African households: The limits of survey and census representations. *The Journal of Development Studies*, *51*, 162–177. doi: 10.1080/00220388.2014.968135.

Rizzo, M., Kilama, B., & Wuyts, M. (2015). The invisibility of wage employment in statistics on the informal economy in Africa: Causes and consequences. *The Journal of Development Studies*, *51*, 149–161. doi: 10.1080/00220388.2014.968136.

Sandefur, J., & Glassman, A. (2015). The political economy of bad data: Evidence from African survey and administrative statistics. *The Journal of Development Studies*, *51*, 116–132. doi: 10.1080/00220388.2014.968138.

Serajuddin, U., Uematsu, H., Wieser, C., Yoshida, N., & Dabalen, A.L. (2015). Data deprivation: another deprivation to end, Volume 1. *World Bank Policy Research Working Paper No. WPS 7252*.

Shimeles, A., & Ncube, M. (2015). The making of the middle-class in Africa: Evidence from DHS Data. *The Journal of Development Studies*, *51*, 178–193. doi: 10.1080/00220388.2014.968137.

Taylor, M. (2013, September 19). Poor numbers: Why is Morten Jerven being prevented from presenting his research at UNECA? *African Arguments*. Retrieved from http://africanarguments.org/2013/09/19/poor-numbers-why-is-morten-jerven-being-prevented-from-presenting-his-research-at-uneca-by-magnus-taylor/.

York, G. (2013). 'B.C. professor ruffles feathers by spotlighting Africa's data problems'. *The Globe and Mail*, 13 November. http://www.theglobeandmail.com/news/world/bc-professor-ruffles-feathers-by-spotlighting-africasdata-problems/article15434240/.

Statistical Tragedy in Africa? Evaluating the Data Base for African Economic Development

MORTEN JERVEN & DEBORAH JOHNSTON

School for International Studies, Simon Fraser University, Vancouver, Canada, Department of Economics, SOAS University of London, UK

ABSTRACT *Measurement is increasingly at the centre of debates in African economic development. Some remarkable upward revisions of GDP, which are signs of statistical systems improving, caused the declaration of a statistical tragedy in Africa. This special issue evaluates the database for African economic development with articles on the quality of the data on GDP, health and education, poverty, labour, agriculture and income distribution.*

Measurement matters. This is true for any scholarly inquiry. However, increasingly measurement is at the forefront of debates in development. The 'data revolution' meme has been central in the post-2015 Millennium Development Goals (MDG) debates, and data quality has been the main focus in recent debates on development in Africa.[1] The remarkable upward revision of GDP in Ghana in 2010 generated plenty of discussion (Jerven & Duncan, 2012), which was re-ignited with Nigeria's GDP revision (Jerven 2013b, Jerven 2014a). These statistical events are good news. Not only are some countries richer than previously thought, but the updating of benchmarks is tangible evidence of improved statistical systems.

1. Introduction

There are indications of a significant knowledge problem. The chief economist for Africa at the World Bank, Shanta Devarajan, declared a statistical tragedy in Africa,[2] reflecting the scholarly debate over the appropriateness of current indicators. Are trends in growth and poverty properly represented, particularly over the past two decades? The political and financial importance of the numbers has drawn in scholars, international financial institutions, journalists and also public officials, with exchanges in financial newspapers, blogs and at international conferences (see Jerven [2013d] for an overview).

In 1989, Nicholas Stern noted that the newly published Penn World Tables was 'a major public good and an important statistical event' (1989, p. 600). He added that the third and fourth editions of the World Tables (1983, 1987) 'are now available on magnetic tape'. Only a few years later, in 1994, T. N. Srinivasan edited a special issue of the *Journal of Development Economics*, which surveyed the knowledge problems presented by the use of these new statistical databases. Srinivasan raised the 'concern that analyses based on unreliable and biased data could result in seriously distorted, if not altogether wrong, analytical and policy conclusions' (1994, pp. 4–5). The instigation, then, was the sheer increase in data on economic development. Several decades on, things have changed, but many of the statistical challenges remain neglected.

This collection of articles goes beyond problems of harmonisation in international databases, and digs deeper into statistical concepts, survey methodology and data collection. We have contributions from academics, researchers from leading development institutions and by officials from African statistical offices. While diverse in origin, they are unified in two conclusions: the quality and quantity of data need to be improved; and this is a concern not just for statisticians.

Weaknesses with statistical methodology and practice can misinform policy-makers, international agencies, donors, the private sector and citizens of African countries generally. This is also a problem for academics from various disciplines, from history and economics to social epidemiology and education policy. Much academic work on Africa regularly uses flawed data, but not all researchers demonstrate awareness of the flaws. Many problems encountered in surveys challenge common academic abstractions. As we will see below, for example, the difficulties in collecting poverty data illuminate weaknesses in the way the household is conceptualised.

2. Knowledge Problems

At the macro level, development is conventionally measured by trends in GDP and GNP, either in total or on a per capita basis.[3] However, the problems with these data are widespread, requiring improvement in national accounts data (Jerven, 2013c). The report from the statistical offices in Nigeria, Liberia and Zimbabwe suggest that GDP is under-reported in each country, yet the causes and dimension of this problem differ, and so does the statistical capacity of each statistical office. The implications of our lack of understanding of GDP run deep – not only do we know less than often portrayed about performance denominated in GDP in many African countries, we also know less about the structure of most African economies.

The article by Carletto et al. suggests that we know less about the size, productivity and contribution to welfare made by the agricultural sector. While problems in assessing agricultural output have been long recognised (Jerven, 2014b; Svedberg, 1999), Carletto et al. differentiate the problem by farmers of various sizes and a variety of crops. At the same time, Rizzo, Kilama and Wuyts suggest that we know less about informal activity and use Tanzania as case study to illustrate specific limitations in the data. Specifically, they argue that we know almost nothing about informal employment, with forms of wage employment being widely mistaken for self-employment. This lack of knowledge about labour has been discussed for agricultural employment (Cramer, Johnston, Mueller, Oya, & Sender, 2014). Given the evidence of huge gaps in our understanding of the use of labour in both informal and agricultural activity, it is easy to conclude that we may know very little indeed about how people work in African countries.

The issue of what constitutes an appropriate poverty measure has been debated long and hard,[4] but the basic data collection problems are sometimes forgotten in debates around the global poverty headcount. Randall and Coast show what a poor picture statistics provide of the basic unit of society: the household. As a result, we then misunderstand the profile of poverty because we do not understand how resources are shared, or how people are absorbed by new households at times of stress. Specifically, they argue that our rigid application of narrow and inappropriate household definitions means that poverty data will usually produce a misleading picture.

Sandefur and Glassman suggest a significant problem with health and education data. To make their case, they compare administrative data and survey data. Looking at school enrolment and vaccinations, they show not only that there are gaps between survey and administrative data, but that these gaps widened when financial incentives exist to over-report performance. These systematic measurement errors in administrative data may only worsen as pay-for-performance schemes increase incentives to mis-report. The key message is not that survey data are faultless, while administrative data are flawed,

2

but rather that statistical systems are endogenous. This undermines the notion of evidence-based policy. What is observed here (and elsewhere: Jerven [2013a, 2014b]) is the opposite – policy-driven evidence.

Thus, the very basics of development data seem flawed for many African countries. For some readers, this will be depressing in its familiarity. After all, the articles here often refer to problems that have been long-standing.[5] What are the implications for data users? One view is that the researcher has to make the most of what data are available, because the alternative is silence.

Ncube and Shimeles attempt to shed light on an issue where official statistics yield little guidance – income distribution. The key questions in the recent debates on African economic development are whether Africa is rising, and if so, how fast? Ncube and Shimeles sidestep conventional income data and use DHS asset data to guesstimate the way in which distribution of income is changing in a subsample of countries. Their conclusions face the same kind of questions and problems that other scholars have met. The first question is whether the proxy they are using is appropriate (assets ownership compared to income). The second is whether it is defensible to extrapolate across time periods and countries without data using econometric methods to estimate parameters for years and countries not covered in the dataset.[6]

What of those who still use official statistics? The contribution of this special issue is not only to elaborate and clarify well-known knowledge problems, but also to give guidance on questions of governance – how can statistical capacity be improved?

3. More Money, Better Data?

The articles in this special issue consider the implications for the future – can the problem raised be solved, and if so, how? The present interest in the use of evidence for policy-making provides momentum for improvement. Of course, it is not that there was a wholesale disinterest in statistics before – simply that the interest in data changes over time reflect the complex dynamics of policy-making, theory, ideology and necessity. Certainly, the development of the MDGs has launched a raft of statistical exercises to collect data on the progress towards MDG targets. After the onslaught of structural adjustment programmes in the 1980s and 1990s seriously reduced the capacity and output of official statistical offices in African countries (Jerven 2013a), this expansion of data has to be cautiously welcomed.

These newer, ad hoc, MDG-focused survey instruments have increased the evidence base available for African countries. They also create particular kinds of opportunities. For example, Sandefur and Glassman compare census, survey and administrative data to understand data quality. Ad hoc surveys can improve other sources of data by road-testing new survey methods or approaches, as Carletto et al. point out for agricultural data. Here, new methods developed in ad hoc Living Standards Measurement Study (LSMS) surveys promise some improvement for regular agricultural surveys.[7]

New technology promises an improvement in cost-effectiveness. Indeed, lack of money and people are major factors in improving statistical capacity, as Jerven, Kale, Duncan, and Nyoni suggest. However, the new ad hoc surveys are not without blame on this score. There is often a trade-off between ad hoc donor-funded surveys and regular national undertakings (Jerven, 2013a; Sandefur & Glassman, this issue), with resources, people and attention diverted from regular national surveys and censuses. Rizzo et al. note the way that labour force surveys have fallen out of fashion, with funds and attention drawn to other instruments.[8]

The need for resources is clear, but the picture is uneven. Some African statistical departments have stronger capacity and experience than others. Similarly, the depredations on statistics department have arisen for varied and complex reasons, but certainly conflict, economic upheaval and fiscal restrictions have all played their role. International donor support (in terms of finances and capacity-building) will have a role in improving the situation. Indeed, Sandefur and Glassman notes how extensively many African statistical offices depend on donor funding. Going forward, it is important to bear in mind that this is not only a problem of funding – but the incentives that current donor data needs create.

4. Concluding Remarks

While human and financial resources might set the possibility frontier for the production of statistics, there are other issues of quality. The political economy of data is crucial. The article by Sandefur and Glassman suggests that it is often incentives that are at fault. Governments have incentives to misreport data in certain situations, but can also be fooled, as well, when they consume the data of line ministries or local departments. The political meaning and sensitivity of data is always at issue and has been discussed elsewhere (Jerven, 2013b).

Indeed, data are products of over-layered meaning. Between the conceptual framework set by theory, the approach of researchers and the understanding of research subjects, the potential for misunderstanding, ideology and bias are rife. Rizzo et al. clearly show how disciplinary bias, poorly-worded questions and loaded local meanings lead to flawed labour force data in Tanzania. Conceptual limitations are at the heart of the problems identified by Randall and Coast. When households are understood in overly reductionist ways during surveys, the complex interlinkages between individuals who may or may not live and eat together are missed. It is a challenge for academics as well as statisticians. How to produce approaches that allow abstract theoretical concepts to be applied in concrete complex situations?

The weaknesses in the development data base for Africa raise particularly acute issues. This special issue links empirical problems with their theoretical and policy implications by looking at both thematic issues and particular case studies. Some readers may be surprised to learn just how little confidence we can have in key development data. At both the micro and macro level, for analysis of short- or long-term change, the absence of adequate data on economic development continues to be a serious challenge for researchers and policymakers.

Notes

1. See, for example, the discussion at http://www.copenhagenconsensus.com/.
2. In his keynote address to the 2011 IARIW-SSA Conference on Measuring National Income, Wealth, Poverty, and Inequality in African Countries, 28 September–1October 2011.
3. The problems of estimating population size have also been discussed by Carr-Hill (2014), suggesting that our most widely used indicator of growth, GNP per capita, may contain errors in both the numerator and denominator.
4. See, for example, on African countries, Green and Hulme (2005) and Hanmer, Pyatt, and White (1999).
5. While the general lack of a robust development database was discussed by Srinivasan (1994), African data was the focus of the review by Sender (1999).
6. See the debate between Young (2012), Harttgen, Klasen, and Vollmer (2013) and also Sala-i-Martin and Pinkovskiy (2010).
7. In a similar example, the use of mobile technology to gather data in smaller ad hoc surveys suggests promising avenues for future national data collection (Hoogeveen, Croke, Dabalen, Demombynes, & Giugale, 2014)
8. See also Johnston (in press) on this issue for southern Africa.

References

Carletto, Gero, Jolliffe, Dean and Banerjee, Raka. "From Tragedy to Renaissance: Improving Agricultural Data for Better Policies." *Journal of Development Studies*, doi:10.1080/00220388.2014.968140.

Carr-Hill, R. (2014). Measuring development progress in Africa: The denominator problem. *Canadian Journal of Development Studies*, 35(1), 136–154.

Cramer, Christopher, Johnston, Deborah, Mueller, Bernd, Oya, Carlos, & Sender, John. (2014). How to do (and how not to do) fieldwork on Fair Trade and rural poverty. *Canadian Journal of Development Studies*, 35(1), 170–185.

Green, M., & Hulme, D. (2005). From correlates and characteristics to causes: Thinking about poverty from a chronic poverty perspective, *World Development*, 33(6), 867–879.

Hanmer, L., Pyatt, G., & White, H. (1999). Poverty in sub-Saharan Africa. What can we learn from the World Bank's poverty assessments? *Development and Change*, 30(4), 795–823.

Harttgen, K., Klasen, S., & Vollmer, S. (2013). An African growth miracle? Or: what do asset indices tell us about trends in economic performance? *Review of Income and Wealth*, 59(Issue Supplement S1), S37–S61. doi:10.1111/roiw.12016.

Hoogeveen, Johannes, Croke, Kevin, Dabalen, Andrew, Demombynes, Gabriel, & Giugale, Marcelo. (2014). Collecting high frequency panel data in Africa using mobile phone interviews. *Canadian Journal of Development Studies*, 35(1), 136–154.

Jerven, M. (2013a). *Poor numbers: How we are misled by African development statistics and what to do about it.* Ithaca, NY: Cornell University Press.

Jerven, M. (2013b). For richer, for poorer: GDP revisions and Africa's statistical tragedy. *African Affairs, 112*(446), 138–147.

Jerven, M. (2013c). Comparability of GDP estimates in sub-Saharan Africa: The effect of revisions in sources and methods since structural adjustment. *Review of Income and Wealth, 51*(Issue Supplement S1), S16–S36.

Jerven, M. (2013d). Poor numbers: The politics of improving GDP statistics in Africa. African Arguments, 26 September. Retrieved from http://africanarguments.org/2013/09/26/poor-numbers-the-politics-of-improving-gdp-statistics-in-africa-by-morten-jerven/

Jerven, M. (2014a). The political economy of agricultural statistics and input subsidies: Evidence from India, Nigeria and Malawi. *Journal of Agrarian Change, 14*(1), 129–145.

Jerven, M. (2014b). What does Nigeria's new GPD number actually mean? African Arguments, 8 April. Retrieved from http://africanarguments.org/2014/04/08/what-does-nigerias-new-gdp-number-actually-mean-by-morten-jerven/.

Jerven, M., & Duncan, M, Ebo. (2012). Revising GDP estimates in sub-Saharan Africa: Lessons from Ghana. *African Statistical Journal, 15*, 12–24.

Johnston, Deborah. (in press). 'Disguised employment? Labour market surveys, migration and rural employment in southern Africa. In C. Oya & N. Pontara (Eds.). Rural wage employment in developing countries: Theory, evidence and policy. *Routledge ISS Studies in Rural Livelihoods.*

Sala-i-Martin, Xavier, & Pinkovskiy, Maxim. (2010). *African poverty is falling ... much faster than you think!* (Working Paper No. 15775). Cambridge, MA: NBER.

Sender, J. (1999). Africa's economic performance: limitations of the current consensus. *Journal of Economic Perspectives, 3*, 89–114.

Srinivasan, T. N. (Ed.). (1994). *Data base for development analysis:* An overview. Journal of Development Economics, *44*(1).

Stern, N. (1989). The economics of development: A survey. *The Economic Journal, 99*, 597–685.

Svedberg, P. (1999). 841 million undernourished? *World Development, 27*(12). 2081–2098.

Young, A. (2012). The African growth miracle. *Journal of Political Economy, 120*(4), 696–739.

The Political Economy of Bad Data: Evidence from African Survey and Administrative Statistics

JUSTIN SANDEFUR & AMANDA GLASSMAN

Center for Global Development, Washington DC, USA

ABSTRACT *Across multiple African countries, discrepancies between administrative data and independent household surveys suggest official statistics systematically exaggerate development progress. We provide evidence for two distinct explanations of these discrepancies. First, governments misreport to foreign donors, as in the case of a results-based aid programme rewarding reported vaccination rates. Second, national governments are themselves misled by frontline service providers, as in the case of primary education, where official enrolment numbers diverged from survey estimates after funding shifted from user fees to per pupil government grants. Both syndromes highlight the need for incentive compatibility between data systems and funding rules.*

1. Introduction

There is a growing consensus among international observers that official statistics in many sub-Saharan African countries are woefully inadequate and unreliable (Jerven, 2013), what Devarajan (2013) calls a 'statistical tragedy'. In response to this tragedy, the UN High Level Panel on post-2015 development goals has called for a 'data revolution' to improve tracking of economic and social indicators in Africa and the rest of the developing world (United Nations, 2013). The agenda emerging around these discussions has tended to assume that more money and better technology will solve the problem, focusing on an expansion of survey data collection efforts, and a push for national governments to disseminate information under open data protocols (Caeyers, Chalmers, & De Weerdt, 2012; Demombynes, 2012).

Do these solutions address the underlying causes of bad statistics? Relatively less attention has been paid to understanding why national statistics systems became so badly broken in the first place, or to analysing the perverse incentives which any data revolution in sub-Saharan Africa must overcome. We attempt to fill this gap by documenting systematic discrepancies between data sources on key development indicators across a large sample of countries. By necessity, we focus on cases where multiple independent sources report statistics on ostensibly comparable development indicators.[1] For this, we draw on cross-national data within Africa on primary school enrolment and vaccination rates taken from the Demographic and Health Surveys (DHS), and contrast it with data from education and health management information systems maintained by line ministries.[2]

The core hypothesis to be tested in this article is that misrepresentation of national statistics does not occur merely by accident or due to a lack of analytical capacity – at least, not always – but rather that systematic biases in administrative data systems stem from the incentives of data producers to over-state development progress. The administrative data we analyse are designed to be part of management information systems in health and education ministries. It should be no surprise, then, that misrepresentations in the data reflect the incentives provided by the governance and funding structures of these ministries, particularly in the low-income, highly aid-dependent countries which dominate our sample.[3]

The article is organised around two interlinked principal–agent problems: in the first, national governments can be seen as agents of international aid donors and domestic constituencies; in the second, governments act as principals seeking to motivate civil servants to simultaneously provide public services and report truthful data on the same.

In the first case, an international aid donor (the principal) seeks to allocate resources between and evaluate the performance of a national government (the agent). The principal requires data to monitor agents' performance. Recognising the risks inherent in 'self- reported' official statistics, international donors invest heavily in the collection of survey data on households, farms and enterprises. Notably, these surveys involve considerable foreign technical assistance paid for directly by donors. In the extreme case of the DHS data sponsored by the US Agency for International Development (USAID) and other partners – on which much of the analysis below relies – the donor insists on a standardised questionnaire format in all countries, donor consultants train the data collectors and oversee fieldwork, and all or most raw data is sent back to the donor country for analysis and report writing.[4]

Donors can't always rely on such carefully controlled data products like the DHS, though, and Section 3 shows the predictable results when donors link explicit performance incentives to administrative data series managed by national governments. In 2000, the Global Alliance for Vaccines and Immunisation (GAVI) offered eligible African countries a fixed payment per additional child immunised against DTP3, based on national administrative data systems. Building on earlier analysis by (Lim, Stein, Charrow, &Murray, 2008), we show evidence that this policy induced upward bias in the reported level of DTP3 coverage amounting to a 5 per cent overestimate of coverage rates across 41 African countries.

In short, pay-for-performance incentives by a donor directly undermined the integrity of administrative data systems. To invert the common concern with incentive schemes, 'what gets measured gets managed', in the case of statistics it appears that what gets managed gets systematically mismeasured, particularly where few checks and balances are in place.

In the case of immunisation statistics, national governments mislead international donors and their citizens, whether by accident or design. Previous analysis of African statistics has focused on this dynamic in which central governments are the producers of unreliable statistics (Jerven, 2011). But in other cases national governments themselves are systematically misled, creating an important obstacle to domestic evidence-based policy-making.

In this second accountability relationship discussed in Section 4, national governments and line ministries (the principal) seek to allocate resources between and evaluate the performance of public servants such as nurses and teachers (the agents). By and large, the information the principal relies on in such settings comes from administrative data systems based on self-reports by the very agents being managed. The result is systematic misreporting, undermining the state's ability to manage public services, particularly in remote rural areas.

Section 4 illustrates this problem in primary school enrolment statistics. Comparing administrative and survey data across 46 surveys in 21 African countries, we find a bias towards over-reporting enrolment growth in administrative data. The average change in enrolment is roughly one-third higher (3.1 percentage points) in administrative than survey data – an optimistic bias which is completely absent in data outside Africa. Delving into the data from two of the worst offenders – Kenya and Rwanda – shows that the divergence of administrative and survey data series was concomitant with the shift from bottom–up finance of education via user fees to top–down finance through *per pupil* central government grants. This highlights the interdependence of public finance systems and the integrity of administrative data systems. Difference-in-differences regressions on the full sample confirm that the gap between administrative and survey of just 2.4 percentage points before countries abolished user fees grew significantly by roughly 10 percentage points afterwards.

This dual framework relating the reliability of statistics to the accountability relationships between donors (and citizens), national governments and frontline service providers clearly abstracts from certain nuances, as does any useful model. Household survey data are not *only* used by international donors as a tool to monitor aid recipients. Donor agencies also use survey data for research purposes, and recipient governments frequently cite survey reports in planning documents and incorporate survey data into the construction of macroeconomic aggregates like GDP which are key indicators in domestic policy-making. Conversely, international donors are far from apathetic about administrative data systems, and indeed invest heavily in education and health management information systems in the region. Nevertheless, we believe the political economy dynamics suggested by this framework, however simplistic, help make some sense of the seemingly chaotic data discrepancies documented in the article.

Seen through the lens of this framework, the agenda for a data revolution in African economic and social statistics clearly must extend beyond simply conducting more household surveys to help donors circumvent inaccurate official statistics – to avoid, as we label it, being fooled by the state. If donors are genuinely interested in promoting an evidence-based policy-making process, they must assist government to avoid being systematically fooled itself by administrative data systems built on perverse incentives. Aid resources must be directed in a way that is complementary to, rather than a substitute for, statistical systems that serve governments' needs.

2. Seeing like a Donor versus Seeing Like a State

The different needs of donors and government present trade-offs between the comparability, size, scope and frequency of data collection. Given that donors finance a large share of spending on statistics, these differing needs can imply that national statistical systems aren't built to produce accurate data disaggregated for use by domestic policy-makers and citizens. In stylised form, this creates a choice between (1) small-sample, technically sophisticated, possibly multi-sector, infrequent surveys designed to facilitate sophisticated research and comparisons with other countries,[5] and (2) large sample surveys or administrative data sets providing regional- or district-level statistics on relatively fewer key indicators at higher frequency, designed for comparisons across time and space within a single country.[6]

International aid donors must make allocation decisions across countries, and in many cases they are bound to work solely with national governments as their clients. Due to this focus, donors' preferences often (but far from always) skew toward statistics based on standardised international methodologies and homogenised questionnaire formats.[7] At times this desire for international comparability is directly at odds with comparability over time within a single country. A second key implication of donors' concern with international comparisons is less attention to domestic, subnational comparisons. Household survey data reflects this preference.

Consider the case of primary education in Kenya. The DHS provides comparable information across countries and time on both health and schooling outcomes and is designed to provide provincial estimates, with most analysis focusing on a single set of national or rural and urban statistics. At the time of the last DHS, Kenya had eight provinces. This allowed at least limited correspondence between survey estimates and units of political accountability. In neighbouring Tanzania, the mainland was at the time of the last survey divided into 21 regions, but the survey reported results for just seven aggregate zones corresponding to no known political division. To stress the point, we might say that the structure of the DHS meets the needs of a donor sitting in Washington, allowing them to evaluate, say, Kenyan and Tanzanian performance in primary schooling on a comparable basis.

But national governments need to make subnational resource allocation decisions. To be useful, data are often required at relatively low levels of disaggregation that coincide with units of political accountability. Ministries of health require up-to-date information on clinics' stocks to manage their supply chain; ministries of education require school-level enrolment statistics to make efficient staffing decisions. In Kenya, the education ministry obtains this information from the country's Education Management Information System (EMIS), three times a year, for all 20,000 government schools in the country.[8]

Arguably, citizens' interests are better aligned with the preferences of their own government's EMIS than donors in this case. In order for citizens to exert bottom–up accountability of public service providers, they require data in an extremely disaggregated form. Kenya's national trends in literacy rates are likely of limited interest to citizens of rural Wajir, but the local primary school's performance on national exams relative to neighbouring villages may be of acute interest. Thus, appropriately, the Kenyan government's 'open data portal' provides access to the disaggregated administrative data EMIS system. Unfortunately, as we show in Section 4, the reliability of this data is questionable.

Kenya may not be unique in this respect, as we show, but the situation is far from uniform across the region. While quality measures in statistics are few and far between, and indeed measuring discrepancies is a key contribution of this aftricle, the World Bank's Bulletin Board of Statistical Capacity provides some indication.[9] On average, sub-Saharan Africa scores below all other regions, with an overall score of 58 compared to a global average of 64. But the variance within Africa is enormous, ranging from the very bottom of the rankings (Somalia with a score of 24) to Malawi with a score of 79 (just above the 75th percentile globally). These numbers should be treated with caution though: while it is no surprise to see Mauritius score highly (76), it is perhaps surprising to see it tied with Nigeria, where Jerven (2013) documents considerable challenges in data reliability.

Viewed from the perspective of national governments' data needs for policy planning and management purposes, household surveys perform poorly in terms of geographic representativeness and frequency. Many surveys provide only national estimates, offering little guidance to domestic policy-makers allocating resources and attention between subnational units. Few surveys are able to provide statistics at the district or equivalent level, and many are unable to provide even regional or provincial estimates. Furthermore, surveys of household income, health outcomes, agricultural production and other key indicators typically occur only once every several years, often with long lags between data collection and the publication of statistics.

The overwhelming strength of household surveys in sub-Saharan Africa, however, is that they provide information that is likely to be more reliable, as it is better documented and collected with much higher levels of international technical assistance and oversight.

While this section has focused on outlining the theoretical advantages of administrative data sources, the following two sections turn to the core task of the article, documenting the deep flaws with administrative data systems in practice and diagnosing the causes of these ills. In the conclusion, we turn to the question of whether administrative and survey data could be better integrated for purposes of cross-validation to prevent or correct the discrepancies we document.

3. Fooled by the State:Immunisation Rates across 41 Countries

In this section, we turn to the role of national statistics in holding national governments accountable to international donors, as well as their own citizens. Relative to other government functions, the production of national statistics in sub-Saharan Africa is highly dependent on foreign aid.[10] Donors demand statistics for a variety of purposes including, but not limited to, the allocation of aid resources across countries and the evaluation of specific programmes, as well as recipient governments' overall economic management. We study these dynamics in the case of an explicit donor incentive scheme to promote vaccinations.

The health sector provides an important case study of the tension between more reliable, smaller-sample, less-frequent survey data and the high-frequency administrative data with limited quality controls which purports to cover the entirety of the population. Like EMIS databases in education examined below, many countries' health management information systems (HMIS) databases rely on self-reported information from clinic and hospital staff, which is aggregated up by district and regional health officers, each with potentially perverse incentives.

There are a number of reasons why HMIS and survey sources may disagree. Numerators in administrative data can be inaccurate due to incomplete reporting, reporting on doses distributed rather than administered, repeat vaccination or omission of the private sector and non-governmental organisations. Denominators can be inaccurate due to migration, inaccurate or outdated census estimates or projections, inaccurate or incomplete vital registration systems, among others. Indeed, Brown (2012) notes that denominators are frequently estimated by programme managers in each country for the WHO's Expanded Programme on Immunisation, based on counts or estimates by local programme staff or health workers. Finally, in countries where immunisation card distribution, retention and utilisation are suboptimal and mothers report vaccination coverage from memory to enumerators, survey-based coverage estimates can also be biased, particularly for multi-dose vaccines that can be under-reported (WHO & UNICEF, 2012).

One additional layer of perverse incentives for accurate reporting in the health context is the policy of aid donors to link payments to progress on HMIS indicators. Starting in 2000, the Global Alliance on Vaccines and Immunisations (GAVI) offered low-income countries cash incentives for every additional child immunised with the third dose of the vaccine against diphtheria, tetanus and pertussis (abbreviated as DTP3) based on HMIS reports. Lim et al. (2008) compare survey-based DTP3 immunisation rates and their growth over time with HMIS or administrative rates reported to the WHO and UNICEF, finding that survey-based coverage has increased more slowly or not at all when compared to administrative reports.

We extend this analysis with a particular focus on establishing the causal role of the GAVI performance incentives on misreporting in a sample of African countries. Our primary innovation is the use of 'placebo' regressions that test for an effect of GAVI on a vaccination (that is, measles) for which GAVI created no incentive to misreport. This allows us to construct a more plausible counter-factual for what would have happened in the absence of the GAVI ISS scheme, and thus go beyond noting the growing discrepancies as in past analyses, to identifying the impact of GAVI through the creation of perverse incentives.[11] Interestingly, we are also able to document a significant decline in misreporting since publication of the Lim et al. (2008) study, which suggests GAVI was able to partially rectify the perverse incentives it helped create – though largely by reducing payouts under the incentive scheme.

3.1. Vaccination Data

We focus on two childhood vaccinations: DTP3, which was the target of the incentive scheme; and the vaccine against measles, which was not included in the scheme. Data are drawn from two sources: household surveys; and administrative data on vaccination rates.

Our benchmark is the vaccination rate for a given disease in a given country and year, based on harmonised household survey data, that is, the Demographic and Health Survey (DHS) indicators. The DHS data are sponsored by the United States Agency for International Development (USAID), and is collected with a high level of technical assistance from USAID contractors based in the United States. For African countries participating in the DHS, international technical assistance frequently covers sample design and selection, enumerator training, questionnaire development and all data cleaning and analysis. From the perspective of country ownership, capacity building and sustainability, this heavy-handed approach to foreign technical assistance may be regrettable. For the narrow purposes of this study, however, DHS provides us with a more reliable, fairly independent benchmark against which to judge administrative data.

From 1990 to 2011, the pooled DHS data set contains 181 surveys spanning 70 countries with data on both DTP3 and measles coverage, of which 93 surveys were conducted across 41 African countries. We focus on this sample of African countries here, though note below where results differ from the broader global sample. For the 44 African surveys in the period 1990–2000 (that is, pre GAVI), the average rate of DTP3 vaccination in our sample was 59 per cent and 63 per cent for measles. For the 49 African surveys from 2001–2011, this rose to 70 per cent for DTP and 72 per cent for measles. In both periods, there was enormous heterogeneity across countries, with the lowest performer recording vaccination rates below 25 per cent for both diseases (that is, Chad) and the highest performers above 90 per cent coverage for both diseases (for example, Rwanda and Malawi).

To test hypotheses about misreporting, we compare this household survey data to administrative data as recorded by the WHO. The primary data series we use consists of the estimates of vaccination coverage posted online by the WHO.[12] Based on personal communication with WHO staff, our understanding is that from 2000 onwards (but not before) these figures do not reflect countries' raw reports, but have been modified by the WHO – often with the specific goal of ensuring greater consistency with survey data. Clearly, any such correction would cause us to understate the effect of GAVI on misreporting. To overcome this problem, we extract the original, uncorrected 'official' vaccination rates submitted by countries in their country reports.[13] We rely on the WHO web data as our primary data source, but also test the robustness of our results to using the raw, uncorrected reports from countries which we have extracted from the PDFs. On the whole, we find discrepancies between survey and administrative data are larger when using the uncorrected reports, but the sample of PDFs from which we draw is quite small ($N = 42$) to make confident inferences.

Finally, a number of differences between our sample and that used by Lim et al. (2008) bear emphasis. We rely on a single set of harmonised household surveys believed *ex ante* to be as comparable as possible, both across countries and – more importantly, given our estimation strategy – over time within countries. In contrast, Lim et al. (2008) use a variety of survey sources including vaccination rates based on maternal self-reports and drop observations they define as outliers *ex post*, though there is no sign this affects results. Additionally, Lim et al. (2008) rely on fairly ambitious imputation of survey data for years in which it is not available, expanding their apparent sample size several fold and inducing a risk of overly confident statistical inferences. We eschew imputation, preferring to restrict ourselves to the most reliable available survey data for the years in which it is available.

3.2. Estimation and Results: GAVI and Vaccination Rates

Our estimation strategy amounts to a quadruple-difference estimate of the effect of GAVI's incentive scheme, comparing (1) changes over time (2) in survey versus administrative data, (3) before and after 2000 (4) for DTP3 versus measles.

Let c index countries, d diseases (DTP3 or measles), and t years. We regress changes over time within the same country in vaccination rates as measured in administrative data, ΔV_{cdt}^{WHO}, on the equivalent change in survey data, ΔV_{cdt}^{DHS}.

$$\Delta V_{cdt}^{WHO} = \beta_0 + \beta_1 \Delta V_{cdt}^{DHS} + \beta_2 I[t \geq 2000] + \beta_3 I[t \geq 2008] + \beta_4 I[d = DTP3]$$
$$+ \beta_5 I[t \geq 2000] \times I[d = DTP3] + \beta_6 I[t \geq 2008] \times I[d = DTP3] + \varepsilon_{cdt} \tag{1}$$

We alternate between estimating Equation (1) in levels rather than differences, and running separate regressions for DTP3 and measles. Here, the coefficient of interest is β_2, which measures whether discrepancies increased after the GAVI scheme was introduced (that is, when $I[t \geq 2000]$ takes a value of 1). We then pool the data so that each country-year reports two observations. In the pooled specification, the parameter of primary interest is β_4, the coefficient on the interaction between a dummy variable for observations in 2000 or later and a dummy variable for observations of DTP3 rather than measles vaccination ($I[t \geq 2000] \times I[d = DTP3]$). Our estimate of $\hat{\beta}_5 > 0$ measures the degree to which the discrepancy between administrative and survey data grew more rapidly over time for DTP3 vaccinations relative to measles vaccinations after the onset of the GAVI scheme in 2000. The β_3 and β_6 terms are included to test whether any observed discrepancies have improved in more recent years.

Starting with the simplest single-difference comparison, Table 1 reports regression estimates of DTP3 and measles immunisation coverage before and after the onset of GAVI incentive scheme (essentially, estimating β_2 in isolation). The dependent variable in each case is the immunisation rate from the administrative HMIS reported to the WHO. Without controlling for other variables, average DTP3 rates in our sample of 93 observations spanning 41 countries increased by 11 percentage points from 2000 onward (column 1), while measles coverage increased by roughly 8 percentage points (column 4). Column 7 pools the data from both diseases to compute the difference-in-differences (the

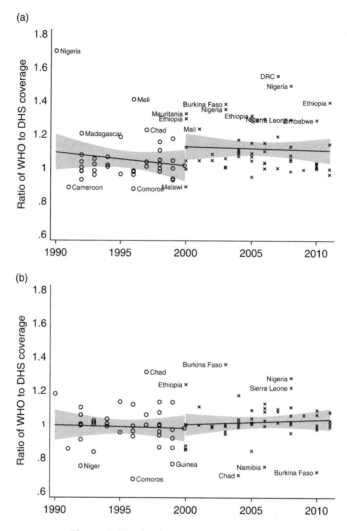

Figure 1. Vaccination rates: WHO vs DHS.

shift after 2000 in administrative data for DTP3 relative to measles) and shows that this divergence in immunisation rates of 11 versus 8 points is statistically significant at the 5 per cent level.

Controlling for the coverage rate reported by the DHS puts the focus directly on discrepancies between administrative and survey data. When including this control, DTP3 coverage rates in the administrative data rose by 5.6 percentage points after 2000 (column 2, statistically significant at the 1% level) while measles coverage rose by only 2.3 points (column 4, insignificant). Column 8 shows that this triple-difference is again significant (now at the 5% level). Finally, we look at changes over time immunisation rates before and after 2000 to produce a quadruple-difference comparison. As see in column 9, discrepancies in administrative data on DTP3 coverage accelerated significantly (by 4.7 percentage points, significant at the 10% level) relative to measles rates.[14]

So far, we have focused on establishing a casual effect of GAVI's ISS programme on misreporting of DTP3 data (that is, the post-2000 dummies). While we would argue that comparison to a control group (in this case, measles vaccinations) is necessary to draw causal inferences, the existence of discrepancies was highlighted prominently several years ago by Lim et al. (2008). An obvious question then arises: did awareness of these problems, at least since 2008, lead to any improvements? We can answer this question using the coefficient on the dummy variable for 2008 and thereafter (as well as it's interaction with DTP3). Both DTP3 and measles coverage continued to grow after 2008, as

Table 1. Immunisation rates: Regression results

	DTP3			Measles			Pooled		
	Level		Change	Level		Change	Level		Change
	(1)	(2)	(3)	(4)	(5)	(6)	(7)	(8)	(9)
Year ≥ 2000	11.03	5.55	5.84	7.75	2.25	2.60	7.75	2.48	1.75
	(3.99)***	(1.30)***	(2.38)**	(3.42)**	(1.66)	(3.07)	(3.43)**	(1.65)	(2.89)
Year ≥ 2008	11.61	-.62	-6.15	12.16	-.64	-3.93	12.16	-.12	-4.75
	(3.69)***	(2.16)	(3.59)*	(3.34)***	(2.75)	(3.47)	(3.35)***	(2.76)	(4.01)
DHS rate		.87	.95	.94	.66	.90	.82		
		(.03)***	(.08)***	(.04)***	(.19)***	(.03)***	(.12)***		
DTP3							-.24	2.35	-2.39
							(.99)	(.85)***	(1.79)
(Year ≥ 2000) × DTP3							3.28	2.90	4.67
							(1.54)**	(1.12)***	(2.27)**
(Year ≥ 2008) × DTP3							-.55	-.88	-1.12
							(3.16)	(3.12)	(3.85)
Const.	61.11	9.38	-2.29	61.34	3.06	.23	61.34	5.44	.31
	(4.08)***	(2.16)***	(2.30)	(3.90)***	(2.47)	(2.28)	(3.91)***	(2.03)***	(2.28)
Observations	93	93	57	93	93	57	186	186	114
Countries	41	41	26	41	41	26	41	41	26

The sample is restricted to African countries. Each column shows a separate regression. The dependent variable is the immunisation rate reported in administrative data via the WHO. The unit of observation is a country-year for a given disease. Each regression in columns 1-6 includes one observation per country-year, while the pooled regressions in columns 7-9 include two observations per country-year: one for DTP3 and one for measles. 'Year ≥ 2000' is a dummy variable for the years 2000 and beyond; DTP3 is a dummy variable that takes the value of one for DTP3 rates and zero for measles rates. For the first two columns under each disease, both the dependent variable and the DHS rate are measured in levels; in the third column under each disease both of these variables are measured in changes (that is, first differences between survey rounds). All standard errors are clustered at the country level. Asterisks (*, **, ***) denote coefficients that are significantly different from zero at the 10, 5 and 1 per cent levels, respectively.

seen in columns 1 and 3. The good news is that it appears this growth in coverage was genuine, in the sense that administrative and survey sources agree. Furthermore, there is suggestive evidence that the discrepancies induced by the GAVI ISS programme have ameliorated since 2008. Column 3 shows a larger and marginally significant (at the 10% level) reduction in DTP3 discrepancies since 2008 compared to a smaller and insignificant improvement in measles coverage in column 6.[15]

The last point suggests that GAVI, the WHO and national governments may have successfully responded to the Lim et al. (2008) findings. How was this achieved? The short answer is that GAVI disbursements through the ISS programme declined rapidly from 2008 onwards.[16] From a peak of $90 million disbursed in 2007, the spending rate declined to roughly $10 million per annum from 2009 to 2011, and fell even further in subsequent years. So while misreporting may have been ameliorated, this was achieved by curtailing payment-for-performance payments. An important outstanding question is whether this reflected (a) better monitoring of data quality, leading to fewer payments, or (b) a quiet scale-back of the programme in the face of irresolvable data issues. The former would suggest such data problems are fixable with proper due diligence. The latter would suggest that the perverse incentives created by a payment-for-performance scheme were corrected only by effectively removing the scheme. As of now, we cannot distinguish these hypotheses.

To summarise, in the case of both DTP3 and measles, we find over- and under-reporting of vaccination coverage by administrative sources. On average, over-reporting of DTP3 coverage was about 5 per cent prior to the GAVI scheme, and non-existent for measles. But this changed over time. When comparing trends in discrepancies, DTP3 discrepancies accelerated when GAVI introduced its ISS incentives in the early 2000s, and this acceleration significantly outpaced similar trends for measles vaccination. This analysis confirms and updates the findings of Lim et al. (2008); without greater verification of self-reported administrative data, financial incentives from donors may affect the accuracy of data used by the vaccination programme by making it vulnerable to political interference. This finding is not a general feature of survey versus administrative data (as we rely on changes over time) and is not a general feature of periods where vaccination rates are increasing rapidly, as we find misreporting that is specific to the diseases incentivised by GAVI.

This lack of accuracy has knock-on effects for the impact of programmes. GAVI, for example, uses coverage data to forecast vaccine procurement. While over-procuring inexpensive vaccines such as measles (at 3 cents a dose) does not imply large additional costs or major trade-offs with other health system priorities, newer vaccines donated by the GAVI Alliance cost about $3.50 per dose, and require several doses. As a result, every vaccine purchased that is not used due to inaccuracy in vaccination coverage implies significant expense and opportunity cost, both in lives and money.

Not all, or perhaps even most, of the discrepancies in HMIS data are the result of the incentives to misreport provided by the GAVI ISS programme. The issue of weak state capacity to monitor front-line service providers discussed in Section 4 is likely crucial here as well. We note this to caution against interpreting the analysis here to imply that health systems suffer from one type of malaise, while education systems suffer from another. We do not believe this is the case; rather, the health data provide the opportunity to identify one specific problem, and the education data another.[17]

4. Fooling the State: School Enrolment across 21 Countries

Having focused in the previous section on the role of national governments as suppliers of statistics, we return to the challenges facing national governments as users of statistics for evidence-based policy-making.

We discuss the pitfalls of the principal–agent relationship between central governments and front-line service providers scattered across the country. Rather than managing a single agent, line ministries require data on thousands of schools, clinics, police stations, water points and road maintenance activities across the country. Given many African states' historical weakness in terms of their ability to exert control over or provide government services to remote populations (Herbst, 2000), it is perhaps unsurprising that they struggle to collect reliable data on these same activities.

We draw lessons from the education sector, but similar examples exist in the agriculture and other sectors. What these cases share in common is that administrative data systems are based on self-reports by low-level public servants. The resulting biases are disproportionately in the direction one might expect given the inherent conflicts of interest in data collection, and they help point to lessons about (a) how public finance systems and administrative data systems must be designed in tandem to avoid compromising the integrity of the evidence base for policy-making, and (b) how surveys could be designed to complement and correct rather than substitute for administrative data sets.

4.1. Enrolment Data

We compare two independent sources of information on primary school enrolment: administrative records and household surveys. Administrative records are drawn primarily from the Education Monitoring and Information System (EMIS) databases sponsored by UNESCO and maintained by ministries of education throughout the region. EMIS data is typically compiled from reports submitted by school officials and aggregated up. We compare these records to survey-based estimates of school enrolment, focusing both on levels at a point in time and trends over time. Surveys data are taken from Demographic and Health Surveys (DHS) sponsored by DHS and collected by national statistics offices, usually in collaboration with ministries of health.

The full sample of the 21 country-year periods for which comparable administrative and survey data are available is listed in Table 2. Of the twenty-one spells, fifteen show discrepancies in the direction of greater optimism in the administrative data relative to household surveys. This tendency appears to be particularly pronounced in sub-Saharan Africa: the average gap between enrolment growth in

Table 2. Changes in primary school net enrolment

Country	Years Start	End	Admin. data Start	End	Δ	Survey data Start	End	Δ	Gap	FPE
Kenya	1998	2003	56.4	74.2	17.8	82.3	78.7	−3.6	21.4	2003
Rwanda	2005	2010	81.9	98.7	16.9	85.4	87.3	1.9	15	2003
Ethiopia	2000	2005	40.3	61.9	21.6	30.2	42.2	12	9.6	2002
Cameroon	1991	2011	70	93.8	23.7	63.7	78.3	14.6	9.1	1999
Burkina Faso	1993	1999	26.9	33.3	6.4	26.6	25	−1.6	8	2007
Kenya	2003	2008	74.2	82	7.8	78.7	78.7	0	7.8	2003
Benin	1996	2006	62	87.1	25.1	41.8	60.1	18.3	6.8	2006
Burkina Faso	2003	2010	36.5	58.1	21.5	28	44.4	16.4	5.1	2007
Eritrea	1995	2002	26.5	43.2	16.7	36.6	50.3	13.7	3	2005
Niger	1992	2006	22.3	43.2	20.9	13.6	32.1	18.5	2.4	2009
Ethiopia	2005	2011	61.9	86.5	24.6	42.2	64.5	22.3	2.3	2002
Guinea	1999	2005	43.2	68.3	25.1	21.6	45	23.4	1.7	
Senegal	2005	2010	72.2	75.5	3.3	52	54.3	2.3	1	2001
Namibia	1992	2000	82.6	88.1	5.5	76.5	81.3	4.8	0.7	2013
Burkina Faso	1999	2003	33.3	36.5	3.2	25	28	3	0.2	2007
Tanzania	1999	2004	49.3	86.2	36.9	35	73.1	38.1	−1.2	2001
Tanzania	1992	1996	50.6	48.7	−1.9	26.2	27.3	1.1	−3	2001
Nigeria	1999	2003	61.3	65.6	4.3	56.7	64.2	7.5	−3.2	1999
Nigeria	2003	2008	65.6	58.8	−6.8	64.2	62	−2.2	−4.6	1999
Tanzania	1996	1999	48.7	49.3	0.6	27.3	35	7.7	−7.1	2001
Lesotho	2004	2009	73.9	71.9	−2	80.9	88.8	7.9	−9.9	2000
Ave.: Africa					12.9			9.8	3.1	
Ave.: Other					3.8			4.5	−0.8	

Table reports the starting and ending rates (%) of net primary enrolment in the administrative data reported in the WDI data base and attendance rates in the DHS survey data, and their respective changes over time. The 'gap' measures the difference between the rise in the admin data and the rise in the survey data. The FPE column lists the date that the country removed user fees for public primary education.

administrative versus survey data (that is, the degree of over- optimism in administrative data) was 3.1 percentage points in the African sample, but was slightly in the pessimistic direction at –0.8 for the 15 observations available from non-African countries.

There are multiple reasons why EMIS records may exhibit systematic biases. The first is under-reporting of private schools. There is evidence from household surveys of a rapid increase in private schooling in at least some countries (Bold, Kimenyi, Mwabu, & Sandefur, 2011a), and even where theoretically required to report to EMIS, unregistered schools may have little incentive to do so. The second, potentially more damaging bias stems from the incentives for public school officials to report accurately. The abolition of school fees for primary education in much of the region has brought a shift, in many cases, to a system of central government grants linked to the headcount of pupils. In Tanzania, for instance, enrolment rates in the EMIS database suggest the country is on the verge of reaching the Millennium Development Goal of universal primary enrolment. Yet household survey estimates show that one in six children between ages 7 and 13 are not in school (Morisset and Wane, 2012).

We explore the second hypothesis by examining two cases from Table 2 which exhibit large discrepancies and where survey data span the abolition of user fees in primary education: Kenya and Rwanda.

Kenya abolished user fees in government primary schools beginning with the 2003 school year. Figure 2a shows the trend in net primary education spanning this reform as reported by the Ministry of Education's (MOE) administrative data, as well as two independent household survey data sources: two rounds of the DHS conducted in 2003 and 2008, and two successive surveys conducted by the Kenyan National Bureau of Statistics (KNBS) in 1997 and 2006.[18] The striking feature of Figure 2a is the steady upward trend in enrolment, including a sharp jump with the introduction of free primary education, juxtaposed with absolutely no change in enrolment measured by either household survey.

Rwanda, which also abolished user fees for primary education in 2003, presents a similar, if slightly less stark picture in Figure 2b. Administrative data from the Ministry of Education (MINEDUC) show steady enrolment growth spanning the abolition of fees. The DHS rounds from 2000 to 2005 confirm this general growth trend, but the 2005 to 2010 rounds of the DHS show a very modest increase from 85 to 87 per cent net enrolment, while the administrative data shows a huge leap over the same period from 82 to 99 per cent.

How comparable are the data in these Kenyan and Rwandan examples? Are surveys and adminis-trative data sets measuring the same thing? Note that while administrative statistics are typically defined in terms of net and gross enrolment, the DHS fields two distinct question types, both of which focus on school *attendance*. In theory, attendance rates may be higher or lower than enrolment rates, for reasons above and beyond the main hypotheses of this article: for instance, children may enrol but rarely attend; on the other hand, Ministry of Education enrolment statistics may omit attendance at private and non-recognised schools which is reported in survey data. In practice, Kenya reported DHS primary attendance rates well above official enrolment numbers prior to the introduction of free primary education, as seen in Figure 2a. Beyond Kenya, though, on average the discrepancy goes the other way: DHS attendance rates are about 13 per cent lower than official enrolment rates in our regression sample.

The relevant question for our analysis is how these differences in definitions might affect the evolution of enrolment and attendance rates over time, before and after the abolition of user fees. One clear pattern observed in Kenya after free primary education (FPE) was a large increase in private school enrolment (Bold, Kimenyi, Mwabu, & Sandefur, 2011b; Lucas & Mbiti, 2012). This would, if anything, tend to increase survey statistics relative to official statistics, causing us to understate any effect of FPE in exacerbating data discrepancies. It is also possible that fee abolition led to enrolment of pupils with little intention of actually attending school, leading to a genuine and widening discrepancy between enrolment and attendance rates. This alternative hypothesis should be kept in mind when interpreting our results below. We note, however, that while the mechanism is different, the public finance implications of this story are very similar: a change in the way schools are funded leads to discrepancies in data between how many pupils are counted and how many are actually in school.

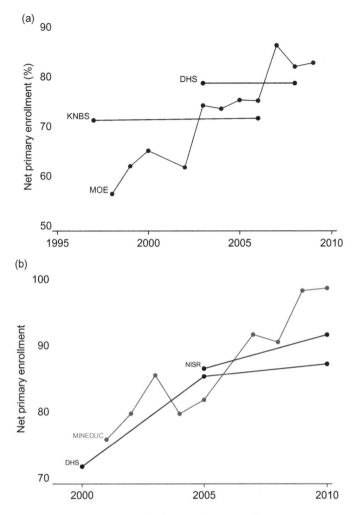

Figure 2. Trends in net primary enrolment.
Sources: See text.

Note that we focus our analysis (and report all numbers in the tables) using net enrolment and attendance rates, which provide the best available apples-and-apples comparison across data sources and time periods. We should note, however, that there are often anecdotal reports of a surge in gross enrolment relative to net enrolment after fee abolition, as older children enter school who were previously excluded. This should in no way affect our results, but merits exploration.[19] These anecdotes find limited corroboration in administrative data from the WDI which include both gross and net numbers: in our sample of African countries with data spanning the abolition of fees, average net enrolment before and after FPE rose by 41 per cent or about 30 percentage points (from 74% to 104%), while net enrolment rose by 44 per cent or about 24 percentage points (from 54% to 78%).

Unfortunately, it is not possible to construct comparable gross attendance rates spanning fee abolition from the DHS data. While more recent DHS data also includes both a gross and net rate, older DHS data sets only report rates by age group. We use these older numbers to construct a rough estimate of net attendance using the 6 to 10 age range (valid assuming no children in this age range attend secondary school; otherwise an over-estimate), but are unable to construct a gross figure using these DHS data.

To test whether the patterns observed in Kenya and Rwanda represent a systematic pattern in the data, we draw on the full sample of African countries for which comparable administrative and survey data are available. This includes 46 spells spanning 21 countries, of which 35 spells are drawn from the 14 countries in Table 2 with more than one data point over time. All of these countries, with the exception of Guinea, previously imposed user fees for primary education and repealed those fees during the period covered here. We record the year of fee abolition for each country in the final column of Table 2, based on information reported in Riddell (2014).[20] This staggered abolition of user fees across countries creates the quasi-experiment we exploit in the following subsection.

4.2. Estimation and Results: User Fees and Net Enrolment Statistics

Using a methodology similar to the vaccination regressions in Section 3, we regress changes in primary school enrolment from administrative data (ΔE_{ct}^{WDI}, as reported in the World Bank's World Development Indicators) on changes in enrolment in survey data (ΔE_{ct}^{DHS}).

$$\Delta E_{ct}^{WDI} = \gamma_0 + \gamma_1 \Delta E_{ct}^{DHS} + \gamma_2 \Delta FPE_{ct} + \gamma_3 t + \upsilon_{cdt} \qquad (2)$$

We estimate equation (2) both in levels and in changes. In both cases, the parameter of interest is γ_2, which measures the extent to which the gap between administrative and survey-based enrolment rates diverged after the introduction of free primary education.

As a preliminary step, columns 1 and 2 of Table 3 use the DHS enrolment rates as the dependent variable, showing that enrolment rates were nearly 16 percentage points higher for observations in our sample after fees were abolished, though when comparing like with like (that is, in the first-difference specification in column 2), this change falls to just 6 percentage points and is statistically insignificant. Columns 3 and 4 repeat this exercise for the WDI administrative data, which rose by 15 per cent on average and remained at 15 per cent when comparing changes within the same country, significant at the 1 per cent level in both cases. Finally, columns 5 and 6 estimate the full specification shown in Equation (2), with the administrative data as the dependent variable and the survey data as a control. Our estimate of $\hat{\gamma}_2$ is 4 percentage points (statistically insignificant) in the levels specification in column 5, but rises to 10.3 per cent (significant at the 1% level) when

Table 3. Primary school net enrolment rates: Regression results

DHS	Level (1)	Change (2)	WDI Level (3)	Change (4)	Level (5)	Change (6)
Free primary educ	15.81	6.46	15.30	14.89	4.93	10.25
(dummy)	(7.48)**	(5.66)	(6.79)**	(4.90)***	(4.82)	(3.59)***
Time trend	1.38	.34	.96	.49	.06	.25
	(.66)**	(.43)	(.53)*	(.43)	(.45)	(.42)
DHS enrolment (%)					.66	.72
					(.12)***	(.18)***
Const.	42.40	4.79	56.81	5.84	29.00	2.40
	(7.71)***	(2.25)**	(7.79)***	(2.75)**	(7.14)***	(2.77)
Obs.	46	21	46	21	46	21
Countries	21	14	21	14	21	14

The sample is restricted to African countries. Each column shows a separate regression. The dependent variable is the primary school enrolment rate as measured by either the WDI (primarily administrative data) or DHS (survey data). The unit of observation is a country-year. In columns labeled 'Change', the dependent variable as well as both the FPE dummy and the DHS enrolment variable are measured in first-differences, as shown in equation (2). The time trend is a year variable set to zero in 2000. All standard errors are clustered at the country level. Asterisks (*, **, ***) denote coefficients that are significantly different from zero at the 10, 5 and 1 per cent levels, respectively.

comparing changes within the same country in column 6. In all cases, standard errors are clustered at the country level.

As an additional placebo test, we can run the same regression from Table 3 using sec- ondary instead of primary data. If our hypothesis is correct, and discrepancies are driven by the incentives to misreport created by the abolition of user fees at the primary level, we should see no effect at the secondary level. Unfortunately, data are extremely limited, as many countries do not report secondary net enrolment administrative statistics in the WDI. For the handful of countries with comparable data, it is notable that discrepancies between administrative and survey data *declined* by about 8 per cent, while they increased at the primary level for this same set of countries by about 15 per cent.[21] To summarise, we find that administrative data sources claim enrolment increases that are more than twice as fast after FPE than comparable survey sources – a differential of roughly ten percentage points.

While the patterns in Kenya and Rwanda, and even from the econometric results for the broader sample of countries, are far from definitive proof of a causal chain from top– down funding for education to the production of unreliable enrolment statistics, they are suggestive of an important link between funding systems and data systems. EMIS in much of the region appear to have been designed with little regard for the incentives faced by teachers and education officials to report accurately. With the onset of free primary education, these incentives changed radically, and the data systems have failed to keep up. The resolution to overcoming these perverse incentives is not immediately obvious, but in Section 5 we discuss possible ideas for how survey and administrative data collection efforts could be better integrated so that the former could act as a check on misreporting in the latter.

5. Discussion and Conclusion

While recognising the different uses and timing of administrative and survey data, our analyses of the discrepancies between administrative data and household survey-based estimates in education and health suggest that – in some African countries – there are significant inaccuracies in the data being published by national and international agencies. These inaccuracies appear to be due in part to perverse incentives created by connecting data to financial incentives without checks and balances, and to competing priorities and differential funding associated with donor support.

Further, in spite of international declarations to support statistical capacity in Busan and a concerted effort by the World Bank's International Development Association (IDA) and Paris21 to support national statistical strategies, indices prepared by the World Bank and the United Nations Economic Commission for Africa (UNECA) suggest that performance has not improved much over time, in large part because statistical agencies in the region – particularly those in Anglophone Africa – lack functional independence, fail to attract and retain high-quality staff, depend on external funders for the majority of their spending and experience significant volatility and unpredictability in their year-to-year budgets. Plans are often divorced from budget realities, thus forcing National Statistics Offices (NSOs) to prioritise 'paying customers' rather than national priorities and core statistical activities as articulated in country developed plans.

Together, these inaccuracies, perverse incentives and lack of functional independence mean that public and private investment decisions based on poor data can be deeply flawed, with major implications for wellbeing and public expenditure efficiency. Further, pressure to open data can result in 'garbage in, garbage out' if measures are not taken to strengthen underlying source data.

There are clear opportunities to redesign accountability relationships in ways that can serve all kinds of data clients, whether national governments, donors or citizens. Getting administrative and survey data to 'speak to each other' is one strategy, where household surveys can be used to provide regular checks on administrative data at different levels. This analysis has shown that a system to identify perverse incentives currently operating within various sectors including the NSO and line ministries' statistics units could provide a valuable measure of the statistical capacity that matters, and can suggest alternative policy or measurement arrangements. This would be one way to deliberately assess the extent to which administrative data contain avoidable biases and to understand where the introduction of additional checks and balances would be needed to correct the accuracy issues within that data.

Both the main case studies examined in this article involved data misrepresentations that resulted from pay-for-performance initiatives (that is, the GAVI ISS or capitation grants to primary schools). Such schemes appear to be spreading in the region, both due to the widespread roll-back of user fees and to donor enthusiasm for results-based aid. For instance, Huillery and Seban (2013) notes 18 ongoing impact evaluations of payment-for-performance in the health sector within African countries. In future, new pay-for-performance initiatives must seek to avoid the pitfalls documented here. One potential example of how to do this is provided by pay-for-performance agreements between national governments and providers under the World Bank's Health Results Innovation Trust Fund (HRITF). The HRITF uses survey data in small, local samples to cross-validate and improve the accuracy of the administrative data used to report performance. HRITF verifies data reported by participating facilities using a representative sample, visited unannounced, while also including penalties for over-reporting measured using the micro-household survey. A clear and relatively rapid jump in the accuracy of self-reported data on quantity of services delivered has been observed. In Cameroon, for example, independent verification of administrative data helped reduce over-reporting of outpatient consultations by over 90 per cent in less than a year (World Bank, 2013). Still, there remains much to learn about the optimal strategy for measuring and verifying data quality.

These kinds of mutually reinforcing administrative plus survey data verification arrangements will make all kinds of results-based funding work better, whether between a national government and subnational providers, or between donors and recipient country governments.

Acknowledgements

Thanks to Morten Jerven, Oliver Morrissey, two anonymous referees, and the members of CGD's Data for Africa Development working group (http://www.cgdev.org/page/data-african-development) for comments and suggestions. Denizhan Duran, Sarah Dykstra, and Yuna Sakuma provided excellent research assistance. All viewpoints and remaining errors are ours.

Notes

1. This approach has parallels to the approach used by Jerven (2010) to examine discrepancies in GDP data for several African countries. While in that case Jerven calculates margins of error based on disagreement between multiple sources – all of which contain some element of signal and noise – for social statistics we have access to a 'gold standard' measure in the form of independent household surveys, and can study not only the magnitude but also the direction of the bias in official data.
2. It is important to acknowledge that household surveys – which we treat as our gold standard to assess errors in administrative data – have their own imperfections, including both sampling and non-sampling errors discussed by other articles in this special issue. Because our focus here is on bureaucratic and political incentives that are unique to administrative data systems, household surveys remain a very useful benchmark. Our argument ultimately requires only that errors in household surveys are *independent* of, not necessarily smaller than, the errors in administrative data systems.
3. It should be noted that our statistical methodology lends itself to focusing on averages; for example, how the mean discrepancy between administrative and household data changed after a certain policy change. This masks considerable heterogeneity across countries that is difficult to study econometrically in samples of this size, but should not be taken to imply that Africa's 'statistical tragedy' is a uniform phenomenon.
4. While we focus on the role of external aid donors, national governments are ideally accountable first and foremost to national citizens. Statistical literacy in the region is low, and the role of economic data in public discourse is limited, but there are exceptions to this rule, particularly for the highly visible phenomenon of rising consumer prices. Sandefur (2013) illustrates the potential pitfalls of politically salient data series with the case of the measurement of inflation in consumer prices in a panel of African countries.

5. In the first category, several internationally comparable survey programmes are very active in sub-Saharan Africa since 2000:; the Demographic and Health Surveys (DHS); LSMS; Global Findex; and Multiple Indicator Cluster Surveys (MICS) are main examples.

6. We ignore, for present purposes, a third category which is likely quite large but not directly relevant to our analysis here: one-off survey projects that ignore both time-series and cross-country comparisons, and often produce redundant data due to a lack of coordination between donors or government agencies. At times, such one-off, bespoke surveys may be fully justified for, say, specific project evaluation purposes, but again this falls outside our scope here.

7. Note again that this is an aspiration for some, not all, donors and often not the reality. An independent evaluation of the Integrated Household Survey Network (Thomson, Eele, & Schmieding, 2013) notes that 'IHSN has not been effective in improving the coordination of surveys' and '[s]ome international organisations have committed considerable amounts of their own resources to developing survey formats and questions which are not always mutually compatible' (p. 20). Furthermore, '[t]he duplication of both actors and products in the data management field as well as feedback from countries obtained during the evaluation indicate that effective coordination remains a serious challenge.' We would endorse the conclusion of the evaluation, that is, '[w]ith resources for global public goods in statistics often in very limited supply, what is done is largely driven by agency-specific budgets and decision-making processes (p. 33).'

8. Although we argue that household surveys can be of limited utility to domestic policy-makers and citizens, we recognise that international standards and comparability also serve these groups – where standards don't already exist, or as a way to enhance quality of estimates and shield statistical activities from political interference, or to provide a framework for comparing, assessing and learning experiences globally. Indeed, household surveys also allow us to assess the quality of more disaggregated administrative data that are the main subject of this article.

9. http://data.worldbank.org/data-catalog/bulletin-board-on-statistical-capacity.

10. McQueston (2013) shows that in Ethiopia (2007–2008) and Malawi (2007–2011) over 80 per cent of funding for the national statistics office came from direct donor support, while national statistics offices in Tanzania (2008–2014) and Kenya (2008–2009) received 36 per cent and 54 per cent from aid donors respectively.

11. The implicit counterfactual used by Lim et al. (2008) is simply the past; that is, that without GAVI ISS, the *absolute* gap between survey and administrative data in the 2000s would have looked exactly like the 1990s, despite the rapid growth in immunisation and health aid over this period, as well as improvements in both survey and administrative data coverage.

12. These data are available for download at http://apps.who.int/immunization monitoring/globalsummary/timeseries/tscover-agedtp3.html.

13. These official country reports are available only in PDF format, which we converted to machine-readable data. The PDFs are available at http://apps.who.int/immunizationmonitoring/globalsummary/wucoveragecountrylist.html.

14. As noted in the previous subsection, all of these results can be replicated using the data on the WHO website, rather than the raw reports submitted by countries to the WHO in PDF format which we have used here. When we re-run the regressions with the web data, the findings are strikingly robust. The size of the discrepancies is slightly smaller for both diseases, but the divergence in discrepancies between DTP3 and measles after 2000 is almost identical; that is, the point estimates in columns 1–6 are mostly smaller but retain statistical significance, while those in columns 7–9 are virtually unchanged. For brevity, we do not reproduce an alternate version of the table here. Results are available upon request.

15. This relative improvement for DTP3 compared to measles since 2008 is not itself significant, as seen in columns 7–9. Sample sizes since 2008 may simply be too small to detect real changes. A more optimistic reframing of the same regression result would note that since 2008 there is no significant tendency for discrepancies in DTP3 administrative data relative to measles; that is, while we have no definitive proof the problem has been fixed since 2008, nor is there definitive proof it still exists.

16. http://www.gavialliance.org/results/disbursements/.

17. Note also that vaccination coverage is only one of many essential indicators of health system performance that are affected by weak institutional capacity to collect and analyse data. For example, even in countries where vital registration systems are almost complete in terms of coverage, the quality of reporting remains an important problem. In South Africa, where 89 per cent of adult deaths are reported via the vital registration system, a death certificate audit found errors in 45 per cent of all records (Bradshaw et al., 2006; Burger, Van der Merwe, & Volmink, 2007; Nojilana, Groenewald, Bradshaw, & Reagon, 2009; Yudkin et al., 2009). A 2009 study found that 43 out of 46 countries in the World Health Organization, Regional Office for Africa (WHO/AFRO) region had no population-level data on cause of death (Mathers, Boerma, & Fat, 2009).

18. These are the 1997 Welfare Monitoring Survey and the 2006 Kenyan Integrated Household Budget Survey, which measured comparable indicators of primary school enrolment. For further discussion of these surveys and the effect of Kenya's free primary education policy on enrolment, see Bold et al. (2011b).

19. An exception, whereby gross enrolment trends could be driving our results, would be a case in which (a) gross and net enrolment are conflated in the data, (b) this conflation is unique to administrative data and not found in the survey data, and (b) worsens over time after FPE. We know of no reason to suspect this is happening, but cannot rule it out as a potential mechanism to explain the data discrepancies we document.

20. For countries that abolished user fees after the publication date of Riddell (2014), we rely on a variety of UN, NGO and media reports: for example, UNICEF (2012) for Burkina Faso, Brandt (2013) for Namibia, and Scan News (2013) for Nigeria.

21. The countries included are Burkina Faso, Eritrea, Guinea, Kenya and Lesotho. Note that while both the increase in discrepancies at primary level and decrease at secondary level are statistically significant, the regression in changes (as opposed to levels) includes only seven data points; thus, we do not report tables here. Full results are available upon request.

References

Bold, T., Kimenyi, M., Mwabu, G., & Sandefur, J. (2011a). *The high return to private schooling in a low-income country* (Working Paper no. 279). Washington DC: Center for Global Development.

Bold, T., Kimenyi, M., Mwabu, G., & Sandefur, J. Can free provision reduce demand for public services? evidence from Kenyan education. *The World Bank Economic Review* (2014): lht038.

Bradshaw, D., Groenewald, P., Bourne, D. E., Mahomed, H., Nojilana, B., Daniels, J., & Nixon, J. (2006). Making COD statistics useful for public health at local level in the city of Cape Town. *Bulletin of the World Health Organization, 84*, 211–217.

Brandt, E. (2013). Namibia: Free primary education starts. http://allafrica.com/stories/201301090299.html.

Brown, David W., Burton, Anthony H., Gacic-Dobo, Marta, & Karimov, Rouslan I. (2014). A comparison of national immunization programme target population estimates with data from an independent source and differences in computed coverage levels for the third dose of DTP containing vaccine. *World Journal of Vaccines, 4*, 18–23.

Burger, E. H., Van der Merwe, L., & Volmink, J. (2007). Errors in the completion of the death notification form. *South African Medical Journal, 97*, 1077–1081.

Caeyers, B., Chalmers, N., & De Weerdt, J. (2012). Improving consumption measurement and other survey data through CAPI: Evidence from a randomized experiment. *Journal of Development Economics, 98*(1), 19–33.

Demombynes, G. (2012). Opening up microdata access in Africa. World Bank 'Development Impact' Blog. http://blogs.worldbank.org/impactevaluations/opening-up-microdata-access-in-africa.

Devarajan, S. (2013). Africa's statistical tragedy. *Review of Income and Wealth, 59*, S9–S15.

Herbst, J. (2000). *States and power in Africa: Comparative lessons in authority and control.* Princeton, NJ: Princeton University Press.

Huillery, E., & Seban, J. (2013). Performance-based financing for health: Experimental evidence from the Democratic Republic of Congo. http://federation.ens.fr/ydepot/semin/texte1314/ELI2014PER.pdf.

Jerven, M. (2010). Random growth in Africa? Lessons from an evaluation of the growth evidence on Botswana, Kenya, Tanzania and Zambia, 1965–1995. *Journal of Development Studies, 46*, 274–294.

Jerven, M. (2011). Users and producers of African income: Measuring the progress of African economies. *African Affairs, 110*, 169–190.

Jerven, M. (2013). *Poor numbers: How we are misled by African development statistics and what to do about it.* Ithaca, NY: Cornell University Press.

Lim, S., Stein, D., Charrow, A., & Murray, C. (2008). Tracking progress towards universal childhood immunisation and the impact of global initiatives: A systematic analysis of three-dose diphtheria, tetanus, and pertussis immunisation coverage. *The Lancet, 372*, 2031–2046.

Lucas, A. M., & Mbiti, I. M. (2012). Access, sorting, and achievement: The short-run effects of free primary education in Kenya. *American Economic Journal: Applied Economics, 4*(4), 226–253.

Mathers, C. D., Boerma, T., & Fat, D. M. (2009). Global and regional causes of death. *British Medical Bulletin, 92*(1), 7–32.

McQueston, K. (2013). *Autonomy, independence, and capacity of national statistics offices.* Background paper for the Data for African Development Working Group: Center for Global Development, Washington D.C., and the African Population and Health Research Council, Nairobi.

Morisset, J., & Wane, W. (2012). Tanzania: Let's think together. World Bank. http://blogs.worldbank.org/africacan/tanzania-lets-think-together/.

Nojilana, B., Groenewald, P., Bradshaw, D., & Reagon, G. (2009). Quality of cause of death certification at an academic hospital in Cape Town, South Africa. *SAMJ: South African Medical Journal, 99*(9), 648–652.

Riddell, A. (2014). The introduction of free primary education in sub-Saharan Africa. UNESCO background paper prepared for the Education for All Global Monitoring Report 2003/4. http:// unesdoc.unesco.org/images/0014/001469/146914e.pdf.

Sandefur, J. (2013). *Africa rising? Using micro surveys to correct macro time series.* Center for Global Development, mimeo.

Scan News. (2013). Niger spends n15bn on free education. http://scannewsnigeria.com/news/niger-spends-n15bn-on-free-education/.

Thomson, A., Eele, G., & Schmieding, F. (2013). Independent evaluation of the International Household Survey Network (IHSN) and Accelerated Data Programme (ADP) – final report. Oxford Policy Management. http://adp.ihsn.org/sites/default/files/IHSN%20ADP%20Evaluation%20-%20Final%20report.pdf.

UNICEF. (2012). Schools for Burkina Faso: Investing in the future. http://www. schoolsforafrica.com/results/Burkina%20Faso%20Story.pdf.

United Nations. (2013). Communiqué. meeting of the High-Level Panel of Eminent Persons on the Post-2015 Development Agenda in Bali, Indonesia, 27 March 2013.

WHO & UNICEF. (2012). Users reference to country reports of WHO and UNICEF estimates of national infant immunization coverage. WHO and UNICEF working group for monitoring immunization coverage. http://www.childinfo.org/files/Immunization WUENIC guide and mark-up.pdf.

World Bank. (2013). Using results-based financing to achieve maternal and child health – progress report 2013. http://rbfhealth.org/progressreport2013.

Yudkin, P. L., Burger, E. H., Bradshaw, D., Groenewald, P., Ward, A. M., & Volmink, J. (2009). Deaths caused by HIV disease under-reported in South Africa. *AIDS, 23*, 1600–1602.

From Tragedy to Renaissance: Improving Agricultural Data for Better Policies

CALOGERO CARLETTO, DEAN JOLLIFFE & RAKA BANERJEE

Development Research Group, The World Bank, Washington, DC, USA

ABSTRACT *Agricultural development is an essential engine of growth and poverty reduction, yet agricultural data suffer from poor quality and narrow sectoral focus. There are several reasons for this: (1) difficult-to-measure smallholder agriculture is prevalent in poor countries; (2) agricultural data are collected with little coordination across sectors; and (3) poor analysis undermines the demand for high-quality data. This article argues that initiatives like the Global Strategy to Improve Agricultural and Rural Statistics bode well for the future. Moving from Devarajan's statistical tragedy' to Kiregyera's statistical 'renaissance' will take a continued long-term effort by individual countries and development partners.*

1. Introduction

Agricultural development is an essential engine of poverty reduction in sub-Saharan Africa, where an estimated 75 per cent of the extreme poor reside in rural areas (Livingston, Schonberger, & Delaney, 2011), and are largely engaged in agriculture-related activities. While the exact relationship between poverty reduction and agricultural growth in any country depends on the agricultural and social structure of a given location (DFID, 2004; Prowse & Chimhowu, 2007), development in the agricultural sector tends to result in greater benefits accruing to the poorest segments of the population, with a 1 per cent rise in agricultural GDP resulting in an estimated 6 per cent increase in income growth for the poorest 10 per cent of the population (Chen & Ravallion, 2007; Ligon & Sadoulet, 2008).

The connection between agricultural growth and poverty reduction has been tied to various pathways, such as the creation of wage employment in rural areas. In particular, growth in smallholder agricultural productivity continues to be heralded as a key driver of poverty reduction: for every 10 per cent increase in farm yields, Irz, Lin, Thirtle, and Wiggins (2001) estimate that there has been a 7 per cent reduction in poverty in Africa. Given that the pool of smallholders on the continent is vast, with approximately 33 million farms of less than two hectares in size,[1] policies that increase the productivity of small-scale farmers can serve as important drivers of poverty reduction and improved food security in sub-Saharan Africa.

Despite the key role of smallholder agriculture in the sector and the economy as a whole, serious weaknesses persist in the measurement of agricultural outcomes and in our understanding of the factors hampering agricultural growth among smallholders. While governments and donors alike target agriculture for large-scale investments with ambitious goals of raising agricultural productivity multi-fold, little is done to ensure that accurate statistics are produced to monitor agricultural development. For instance, of the 44 countries in sub-Saharan Africa rated by the Food and Agricultural

Organisation (FAO), only two are considered to have high standards in data collection, while standards in 21 countries remain low (FAO, 2008). Further compounding the problem is the fact that the poorest countries – for which agriculture is a critical source of livelihood – often have the poorest data, being least able to direct their limited resources into improving the quality of their statistics (African Development Bank, 2004).

In spite of the clear need for empirical evidence, these countries lack the financial resources to generate survey or administrative data of sufficient quality and scope to inform policy, let alone to fund these policies. In the 2003 Maputo Declaration on Agriculture and Food Security in Africa, in recognition of the importance of the sector for the 'economic prosperity and welfare of its people', African countries committed to allocating at least 10 per cent of national budgetary resources for the implementation of sound policies for agricultural and rural development (African Union, 2003). However, a 2011 report on financial resource flows to agriculture by the FAO found that although government spending on agriculture has increased for developing countries as a whole, it has decreased as a share of total spending. In particular, one of the key messages of the report was that 'trends in indicators of government spending on, ODA to, and FDI in agriculture are discouraging for sub-Saharan Africa' (FAO, 2011; pg. 37).

Even with sufficient financial resources, countries often lack human resources to collect data in a cost-effective and sustainable manner. External support from donors can provide a short-term patch, but typically has not been successful in leaving in place sufficient capacity to continue the data collection work when the support ends. The low level and inconsistency of budgetary contributions to statistics from own governments, as well as erratic and short-term donor support, directly results in inconsistencies in data collection activities in many countries. This has significant implications for data quality.

As one example, if the implementation of a survey depends on irregular financing by donors, it becomes extremely difficult to plan in advance for multiple years of survey efforts, which in turn has negative repercussions for the collection of time series and panel data. However, as much of the existing agricultural data is cross-sectional, changes across time with regard to specific indicators typically cannot be well captured. The data are unable to track the changes in indicators over time, or to follow important phenomena such as the transition out of agriculture into potentially higher-return activities. In their review of agricultural development, rural non-farm activities and rural poverty, Foster and Rosenzweig (2008; pg. 3055) note that 'very few studies permit direct comparison over time using comparable measures'. Other studies have likewise noted that data quality issues limit analysis (Ngendaumana, 2001; Tiffen, 2003). Past investments and technical assistance efforts in the area of agricultural statistics have failed to produce sustainable systems, while existing statistics continue to suffer from poor quality, lack of relevance, and little use in national policy dialogues (Binswanger, 2008).

The challenge of improving agricultural statistics worldwide is daunting. Recent efforts such as the Global Strategy to Improve Agricultural and Rural Statistics (henceforth referred to as the Global Strategy) and the ensuing regional Action Plans are testament to the renewed commitment of the global community of researchers and practitioners to rejuvenate the sector, following decades of under-investment (World Bank, United Nations and FAO, 2010). The first pillar of the Global Strategy focuses on the identification and establishment of core data with a focus on agricultural productivity and the most important crops to global agriculture production. Due to the enormity of the task at hand, this article sets out to inform the debate in a targeted and selective fashion by addressing a number of specific issues which are the focus of a recent initiative, namely the Living Standards Measurement Study – Integrated Surveys on Agriculture (LSMS–ISA).

Specifically, two claims are made. First, in the advent of new technologies becoming increasingly available at relatively low costs, more rigorous research is needed to create and promote improved, cost-effective standards in agricultural statistics. Improvements in methods for collecting smallholder agricultural statistics have been particularly sluggish over the past three decades and present the typical market failure problem, with clear disincentives for private investments. For instance, the latest guidelines by the FAO on yield measurement date back to the early 1980s, when modern technologies were not available. The lack of up-to-date research on survey methodologies has led to serious gaps in the existing knowledge base, limiting the identification and promotion of effective policies. Second, statistical systems for agriculture lack integration, limiting the utility of the data for examining linkages between agriculture and key issues such as poverty or nutrition, as well as linkages between socio-economic variables and environmental conditions. In order to better inform agricultural policies, approaches based on the enhanced integration of agricultural data and other types of data sources are needed.

This article is not meant to be a comprehensive review of the issues plaguing agricultural statistics but a purposive discussion of selected shortcomings of current systems. Its contribution is meant to focus on a number of well-defined issues which we believe to be both tractable and to offer a high return in terms of data quality and policy relevance. In the ensuing discussion, emphasis is placed on the African continent due to the geographic focus of the LSMS–ISA initiative, as well as the greater potential of smallholder agriculture for poverty reduction and growth, highlighting the importance of overcoming what Devarajan (2013) deems a 'statistical tragedy' towards creating innovative, well-informed agricultural policies.

2. Agricultural Statistics in Africa: An Irreversible Tragedy?

Problems with agricultural statistics are not confined to the African continent, as highlighted by Indian Prime Minister Singh in a speech addressing the state of statistics in India (Singh, 2006). Neither are they new, as reported by Parker Willis (1903) in his exposition of the large discrepancies in US agricultural data. However, in light of the key role played by smallholder agriculture in the economies of African countries, gaining a better understanding of the sector based on sound statistics ranks high in the current continental policy agenda.

A few examples below illustrate existing problems with core agricultural statistics and also highlight some encouraging trends. Figure 1 presents estimates of the annual average maize yields in Tanzania, as reported by FAOStat. The massive two-year decline, dropping by an estimated 2,381 kg/hectare between 2001 and 2003 after a threefold increase since the late 1990s, seems in itself prima facie evidence of a data quality issue. These huge swings are rendered even more concerning by a lack of documentation explaining how reported yield could have first climbed to unusually high levels in the early 2000s and then declined by more than 75 per cent in this short period. While sharp increases observed in input use and cultivated land in the early 2000s may partially explain some of the trends, the magnitude of the changes and the limited information available regarding the data collection processes casts doubt upon the accuracy of the reported estimates. Nonetheless, as seen in Figure 1, the recent trends are more credible, suggesting a possible improvement in the quality of the estimates.

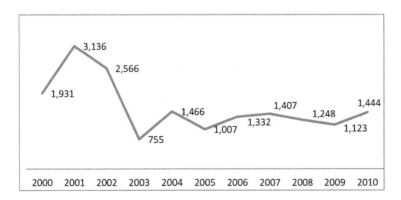

Figure 1. Maize yields in Tanzania, kg of maize per hectare.
Source: FAOStat.

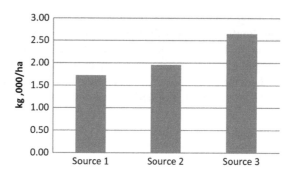

Figure 2. 2006–2007 maize yields from Malawi.
Sources: Source 1: National Census of Agriculture and Livestock; Source 2: Ministry of Agriculture; Source 3: FAO.

Another issue is the occurrence of conflicting estimates for the same indicator in the same country for the same year. In Figure 2, we illustrate this issue by reporting maize yield estimates for Malawi for 2006–2007 from the three available sources, namely the routine data system from the Ministry of Agriculture, the National Census of Agriculture and Livestock (NACAL) conducted by the National Statistical Office, and from the FAO. The differences are significant and have been at the centre of much debate both within the country and among development partners. While some variation in the estimates is to be expected as a result of differences in both survey methodology and sampling, reaching an understanding of what drives these differences has been difficult. The main issue, in Malawi as elsewhere, is a lack of proper benchmarks against which these figures could be compared.

There are also significant differences in the estimates of the total number of farm households between the Malawi Ministry of Agriculture (3.4 million farm households) and the Malawi National Statistical Office (2.47 million rural households), which in turn affects not only total production estimates but also the planning effectiveness for the subsidised input programme (Dorward et al., 2008). On a similar note, Elepu (2006) explores the difficulties inherent in simple quantification of declining agricultural production in Uganda. Without solid benchmarking of yield estimates, it is not possible to assess which estimate is more accurate. Furthermore, due to the general lack of documentation describing the data collection and estimate production processes, no informed conclusions can be drawn as to the accuracy of a given estimate.

In some countries, ambiguity in the institutional mandate for the collection of agricultural statistics complicates even further the establishment of credible, core data for agricultural statistics. For example, until recently, crop production estimates in Ethiopia were produced by both the Ministry of Agriculture and Rural Development (MoARD) and the Central Statistical Agency (CSA). The discrepancy in the estimates has always been striking, with MoARD estimates considerably higher than the already high CSA estimates (Dercon & Hill, 2009). The fact that the two estimates differ significantly should come as little surprise in light of the different methodologies used to estimate both area under cultivation and total production, but this does little to help assess which estimate is closer to the truth.[2]

3. Measuring and Understanding the Role of Agriculture

3.1 Data Sources on Agriculture

Agricultural data often come from different sources, typically resulting in conflicting estimates. Routine data systems based on resident or local extension officers exist in virtually all countries. Extension officers collect different types of data on a frequent basis at a geographically granular level, including information on land usage, crop forecasting and production. One major drawback of current routine data systems is the high degree of arbitrariness and subjectivity in data collection protocols. A second source of agricultural data is the agricultural census, which countries are recommended to implement every 10 years, according to FAO guidelines. However, because of the high costs of full enumeration and the limited amount of information collected, agricultural censuses are increasingly less common.[3]

Sample surveys are the third source of data on agriculture. Farm surveys remain the backbone of agricultural statistics in Africa, with great variation in terms of content, frequency and quality. While in principle indispensable for obtaining a solid depiction of the agricultural sector based on sound statistical foundations, this type of survey suffers from a key drawback: by focusing almost exclusively on the measurement of agriculture, they generally lack sufficient information to understand it as part of a larger context and to thus serve as a useful input for guiding policy-making. Even among the most remote and poorest of rural households, agriculture does not exist in a vacuum, and diversification in terms of income sources at both the household and individual level is the norm, not the exception (Davis et al., 2010). This income source diversification in rural areas may be even greater than the current data suggest; recent research highlights the limitations of existing rural socioeconomic studies, pointing to large numbers of wage workers in rural labour markets in Africa that have not been accurately captured by current survey methodologies (Cramer, Johnston, Mueller, Oya, & Sender, 2014). Furthermore, important policy questions such as understanding the role of agriculture in poverty reduction or the distributional impact of certain sectoral interventions require the collection of agronomic, livelihood and welfare data from the same household, which is beyond the realm of traditional farm surveys.

In many countries, farm surveys are often complemented by other types of household surveys that capture agricultural issues to some extent. These surveys generally use population-based listing as sampling frames and use the household, and not the farming unit, as the unit of selection and analysis. There are obvious advantages and disadvantages to the two approaches; however, based on the need to better integrate agronomic and environmental variables at the farm and locality levels with socio-economic characteristics at the household and individual levels, the utility of such integration is increasingly accepted. This integration, which is one of the pillars of the Global Strategy, can be achieved through improved linkages across different data sources, through integration of different types of information within the same household instrument, or both.

While linkages across different data sources by means of thematic overlap, sampling or geo-referencing should be promoted whenever possible, for certain types of analyses there is no alternative but to collect all information from the same household at the same time through integrated surveys. Relying on multi-purpose surveys to collect data on agriculture also presents its challenges. When integrating different sectoral information into a single instrument, the breadth of the data collected may necessitate compromises in the depth of the instrument in order to prevent the time burden placed on the respondent from becoming too onerous. Additionally, the timing and frequency of the visits must be adjusted to the agricultural season due to the added requirements of collecting information on highly seasonal and volatile processes.

3.2 Policy Relevance of Agricultural Data

Compounding the problem of poor agricultural statistics is the limited policy relevance of the available data. Policy interventions and rural poverty reduction strategies often assume the existence of a strong relationship between increasing smallholder agricultural productivity and poverty reduction; however, even when that is the case, there is no single policy lever that directly increases productivity. Rather, a farmer's productivity is the result of a complex interaction of markets for farm inputs and outputs, credit markets, agronomic and environmental factors, human and social capital, and government policy. In many countries agricultural data are collected with insufficient information on important domains (such as health, labour, education, wealth) to better understand how to inform policy with the goal of increasing agricultural productivity and ultimately improving the wellbeing of the rural poor.

The institutional setting for the collection of agricultural data also engenders poor coordination and inefficient outcomes. Traditionally, agricultural statistics have been collected outside of the National Statistical System (NSS), with little oversight by the National Statistical Office responsible for the enforcement of statistical standards. Oladejo, Chinganya, & Nshimyuremyi (2010) argue that the lack of mainstreaming agricultural statistics into the NSS is one of the underlying causes of the poor state of the numbers. Reinforcing these problems is the compartmentalised set-up and modus operandi of development partners in focusing on agriculture while ignoring the rural space and, more generally, the ecosystem in which it takes place.

The difficulty of collecting reliable and representative agricultural data is only part of the problem. A better measure of crop production or yields in isolation cannot and should not change social policies. The ultimate goal of national policies is to improve the wellbeing of the populace, and the link between agriculture and improved wellbeing can be made through a wide variety of channels. Agriculture comprises only one component of complex household income-generating strategies that involve multiple individuals and activities in different sectors (Davis et al., 2010; Foster and Rosenzweig, 2008; World Bank, 2008). Smallholder diversification into non-farm activities has evolved to be the norm rather than the exception (Bryceson, 2002; Davis et al., 2010; Reardon, 1997). This diversification takes place both at the household and the individual level (Jolliffe, 2004); by taking advantage of different income sources, the rural poor can achieve higher incomes and lower risk exposure.

During the idle months of the agricultural season, for example, farmers that are able to operate a small family business or take on daily wage labour will be better able to provide for themselves, as well as insulate themselves and their families from shocks related to their agricultural output. Given the ubiquity of such diversified income-generating strategies among the rural poor, it is of particular importance to capture a comprehensive set of information on these households in order to better understand the linkages between farm and non-farm activities, as well as between agriculture and different aspects of wellbeing such as nutrition and food security. Income and consumption are the two main ways in which populations are understood along a spectrum of wellbeing; however, this information is not collected in traditional farm surveys. In order to understand how agricultural outcomes result in different impacts for people from diverse socio-economic contexts, it is necessary to be able to understand the basic welfare characteristics of the surveyed population. Understanding these linkages requires an integrated approach to the collection of household survey data, which allows for linking welfare and agricultural information in order to draw conclusions about the distributional effects of agriculture nationwide.

The problems associated with collecting reliable statistics also apply to, and are even magnified in, other aspects of agricultural data, adding further complexity to the task of agricultural data collection. For instance, the role of livestock is important for many agricultural households and is also notoriously difficult to measure. For nomadic, semi-nomadic and transhumant populations, livestock serves as the primary source of welfare; even for those who focus primarily on farming, livestock ownership is often a key to increasing their standard of living. Livestock ownership can signify higher animal protein consumption, a protection or buffer against shocks, as well as a regular complementary source of income for large swathes of the population in certain African countries. A recent analysis of the 2009 Tanzania National Panel Survey found that approximately three out of five rural households reported some income from livestock activities; on average, households earned 22 per cent of total household income from the rearing of livestock[4] (Covarrubias, Nsiima, & Zezza, 2012).

If countries were able to regularly collect reliable, nationally representative agricultural data in a multi-topic, multi-sectoral LSMS-type instrument that accounted for differences across individuals within the households, this would be a tremendous step forward. However, this alone is insufficient to ensure that the data will be used to help shape better policy: creation of the right input does not ensure that it will be properly used if it is not shared or understood. Regrettably, agricultural data are often collected in institutional isolation, with little coordination across sectors and little analytical value-added beyond the sector. In many countries, the data collected by the ministries of agriculture are not linked or utilised in conjunction with data available from the national statistical offices or other line ministries such as labour, education and health. Equally importantly, linking socioeconomic and farm-level variables collected in household surveys with environmental information from remote sensing and other spatial data sources is crucial to gaining a more comprehensive understanding of farm outputs.

In part, this is another consequence of the long-standing failure to recognise the concept that rural economies are diverse and that this diversification is found even within households. This issue was recognised by the Task Team on Food, Agriculture and Rural Statistics (Paris21, 2002), whose key recommendations included rethinking agricultural surveys by broadening their scope to include both agricultural and non-agricultural activities, as well as by improving the coordination of the various agencies responsible for the production of agricultural statistics.

Coordination requires communication, and a key form of communication is the ability to share and exchange data. The most effective way for different data files to speak to each other is to have common identifying traits in each file, allowing data from different agencies and institutions to be easily merged. Without these standardised identifying variables, the data files will remain isolated; with them, the potential value of the data to inform policy is greatly enhanced. Most countries with well-functioning data infrastructures solve this problem via standard identification for geographic regions, or by embedding internationally accepted measures of location such as latitude and longitude degrees. However, in most sub-Saharan African countries, this self-imposed discipline of using standard codes across ministries is not commonplace, and the result is a series of agency-specific data silos rather than effective national data architecture. The systematic geo-referencing of household and plot-level information can partly ameliorate the problems created by missing or inconsistent geographic coding and changing boundaries. In light of the low and ever decreasing costs of GPS units, the routine collection of geo-referenced information is now possible on a large scale.

Another cause of poor data that warrants mention is the lack of analytical capacity in developing countries, which has created a vicious cycle of poor analysis undermining the demand for high-quality data. Poor dissemination of the available data and results has further aggravated the problem. For example, the national and regional reports from the 2003 Agricultural Census Sample Survey (ACSS) in Tanzania were only produced in 2006–2007.[5] Although these problems are common to developing countries around the globe, the problem appears to be more acute in sub-Saharan African countries. The 2002 Paris21 Taskforce stressed the importance of strengthening the statistical and analytical capacities of these data producers.

Finally, the role of politics in data cannot be ignored. These numbers, poor as they may be, are more than just numbers – they have real-life consequences in terms of costs and benefits to various political players, and as a result it is unlikely to be the case that these statistics are finalised without at least some degree of negotiation. Jerven (2013) presents a set of case studies from India, Nigeria and Malawi, and finds that information that does not suit the aims of political leaders is either tampered with, or that choices are made between conflicting information on political grounds. That said, it must be noted that this problem is not confined to developing countries alone, and certainly not only to Africa.

To address some of these weaknesses, the Living Standards Measurement Study (LSMS) team in the Development Research Group of the World Bank, with financial support from several donors, has embarked on an ambitious programme of data production and research, in collaboration with several development partners. The primary objectives of the LSMS–ISA project are to improve our understanding of the inter-relationship between agriculture and poverty reduction, to improve the capacity of national statistics offices to collect and use this data to inform policy, and to foster innovation in the measurement of agricultural data. As such, and by working on a limited number of countries and a well-defined set of statistics, the emphasis of the LSMS–ISA is to support larger initiatives like the Global Strategy in making agricultural statistics more relevant to a larger audience of researchers and policy-makers and raising the profile of the sector within the broader development debate. Table 1 summarises

Table 1. Attributes of LSMS–ISA surveys

	Ethiopia	Malawi	Niger	Nigeria	Tanzania	Uganda
Panel data	✓	✓	✓	✓	✓	✓
Multi-topic information	✓	✓	✓	✓	✓	✓
Nationally representative		✓	✓	✓	✓	✓
Land area measured using GPS	✓	✓	✓	✓	✓	✓
Non-standard conversion factors		✓	✓	✓		✓
Built-in methodological experimentation		✓	✓	✓		✓

various attributes of LSMS–ISA surveys that establish the potential benefits that they offer for research-ers in terms of moving the agenda forward on the analysis of agricultural statistics.

4. Measuring Agricultural Productivity: In Search of the 'Holy Method'

One statistic of particular policy relevance in the poverty debate is the measurement of agricultural productivity, particularly for small farmers. Improvement in the measurement of land productivity has been identified as the highest priority in new research by the Global Strategy, a recent multi-agency initiative endorsed by the United Nations Statistical Commission in February 2010. One of the main goals of the Global Strategy is to develop new protocols and best practices for the estimation of a core set of agricultural indicators, by the promotion of rigorous research and the compilation and dis-semination of key findings.

Productivity can be measured in many ways, whether based on the return to a single factor of production or multiple factors. In this section, we focus on land productivity, or yield, defined as the amount or value of crop harvested (the numerator) over cultivated land (the denominator). To this end, we describe the different methods commonly used to estimate crop production and land area, and summarise findings of recent LSMS research comparing the different methods.

The ease of collecting accurate crop production estimates varies tremendously depending upon the crop in question. For instance, while it is relatively simple for farmers to recall harvested quantities or revenues for high-value, marketed crops like rice, collecting production data for extended-harvest crops like cassava or bananas is a much more arduous task due to the nature of the production process and the length of the harvest period. Root crops such as cassava store better in the ground and the total harvest period spans several months, often through the accumulation of numerous harvest events in small quantities. The same is true for bananas, which are harvested continuously throughout the year, as well as other so-called 'fast commodities' such as onions, tomatoes, peppers and other fruits and vegetables that are produced for the many growing urban markets across Africa. Unlike bananas, however, root crops like cassava are often planted to ward off food insecurity in the case of crop failure. In many cases, therefore, they are only fully harvested when households are faced with hunger, creating further complications with regard to capturing the actual production (which may comprise only a partial harvest of the crop) relative to the potential production (that is, if the plot is harvested in its entirety).

Even for crops such as maize that are generally fully harvested in a single season, problems with quantification may still exist. First, significant portions of the total production may be harvested while still green, particularly in contexts of high food insecurity. Second, many surveys do not collect information on the state of the crop, which may vary even within a single crop for the same household. For instance, maize quantities can refer to maize on the cob, in grain, or flour, and unless information on the physical state of each share of total production and on the correct conversion factors between the different states is collected, large measurement errors may result.

Complicating things further in the case of these and similar crops is the fact that they are almost invariably measured in non-standard units, for example pieces or heaps for cassava, or bunches for bananas. Even assuming that farmers are able to recall the exact number of heaps of cassava or bunches of bananas harvested over a particular reference period, given the enormous variation in weights of different non-standard units, these cannot then be accurately converted into standard units such as kilograms. Figures 3 and 4 illustrate the problem, while Table 2 demonstrates the significant variation in weight for crops reported in terms of a '50 kg sack'.

Thus, with regards to improving quantification, the construction of accurate conversion factors of non-standard units is a crucial first step. As simple as it may sound, this is seldom done in a consistent and systematic manner – and when conversion factors are available they are not easy to find, nor is the methodology on the production of the conversion factors properly documented. The use of new technologies like computer assisted personal interviewing (CAPI) can be instrumental in supporting

Figure 3. Bunches of bananas and pieces of cassava.
Source: Mr. Joachim De Weerdt.

the proper conversion of farmers' responses into standard units by providing a visual interface with the respondents during the interview. Similar types of visual aid in the form of laminated cards with pictures have also been applied in paper surveys (see, for instance, the 2010-11 round (wave 3) of the Malawi Integrated Household Survey). However, the construction of comprehensive libraries for all possible non-standard units in each specific region of a country is often a missing input to fully effective CAPI design.

Even with proper conversion factors in hand, there continue to be challenges in the measurement of crop production quantities and/or values. We have already referenced the difficulties for farmers to recall events over periods of several weeks or months. One major complication is due to the fact that many of the poorest smallholders consume the largest share of their production, which thus never reaches the market. As a result, quantification and valuation of own-production consumed by the household is particularly challenging, in part due to the fact that farm-gate prices are rarely available in these cases. Lacking farm-gate prices, valuation is generally based on either market prices or unit values derived from the survey by computing an average (or median) value over some geographic area of reference. In

Figure 4. '25 kg' sack of cassava.
Source: Mr. Gero Carletto.

Table 2. Weight (kg) of crops in 50 kg sack

Crop	Kg
Maize	50.0
Groundnut	44.2
Ground bean	43.2
Rice	56.2
Finger millet	50.5
Sorghum	49.6
Pearl millet	50.5
Bean	77.6
Soyabean	53.1
Pigeonpea	57.1

Source: Malawi, 2004/2005 Integrated Household Survey.

addition to the fact that these prices do not properly reflect the value of production, other difficulties result from the fact that large variations in prices frequently occur throughout the year.

Another potential source of measurement error in properly valuing unsold own-production results from the fact that when poorer farmers do sell some of their production, they tend to sell low (immediately following the harvest) and buy high (prior to harvest, when stocks have been depleted). Figure 5 below illustrate the issue for Malawi: compared with better off households, larger shares of poor households tend to buy maize, the main staple food in Malawi, during the lean season when prices are highest. Consequently, estimating total value of production using prices only at one time of the year (that is, generally post-harvest, when most product is sold and when prices are lower) is likely to bias the estimations. Thus, the lack of adequate price data continues to be a hindering factor in the proper estimation of values of production, particularly in relation to the valuation of own production used for consumption.

Even for the marketed share of production, smallholders seldom keep records of purchases and sales, which could result in an inability to correctly recall these transactions. Beegle, Carletto, & Himelein (2011), however, demonstrate that in the context of a few African countries and for specific agricultural inputs and crops, farmers' responses do not seem to suffer from large recall biases. Instead, respondents tend to recall information fairly accurately over periods of several months, particularly when questioned about salient, high-value events such as costly fertiliser purchases or the bulk sale of crops, particularly cash crops. Despite these positive findings on the low level of recall error for

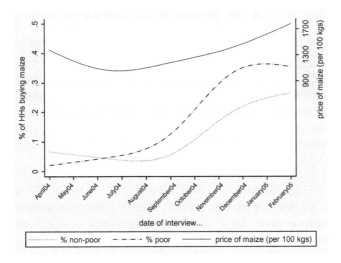

Figure 5. Share of household selling maize, by month and poverty status (Malawi Integrated Household Survey, 2004/2005).

transactions of staple crops such as maize and cash crops like tobacco, it is difficult to imagine how the same findings would apply to root crops such as cassava and/or continuous crops such as banana.

What, then, are the options for better quantification of these types of crops, which represent a significant share of total African agricultural output? Some recent research by Deininger, Carletto, Savastano, & Muwonge (2012) validates the use of harvest diaries vis-à-vis recall methods to estimate crop production. The authors report on the result of a field experiment as part of the 2005/2006 Uganda National Household Survey (UNHS), in which sampled farmers were asked to keep a diary for the entire duration of the agricultural season. Data from the diaries were compared with the recall-based responses given by the same farmers in the course of biannual personal interviews using a structured questionnaire. In almost all cases, farmers' responses based on recall are lower than the diary-based estimates both in terms of number of crops reported and quantities produced. In spite of concerns, respondent fatigue in filling out the diary did not appear to be a major problem. While diaries have some clear potential advantages, the method can be costly and difficult to supervise, which implies concerns about quality. Furthermore, in countries with low literacy and numeracy, keeping diaries may be unfeasible without frequent visits by a local enumerator, thus virtually turning the diary into repeated short recalls. Surprisingly, very little additional empirical evidence beyond the Deininger et al. study exists in this area of agricultural statistics.[6]

In terms of quantification of production, crop cutting is often considered the gold standard, but it is more applicable and easier to conduct for cereal crops than for root and/or continuous crops. Subplots of size ranging from 2 × 2 metres (generally for cereal) to 5 × 5 metres (for root crops) are chosen at random from the randomly selected plots of sample households. The procedure is time-consuming and costly, requiring multiple visits from planting to harvest. Due to the high costs involved, the method is not common in large farm and household surveys, and is practised at other times on a selected basis, as in the case of the 2012–2013 Agricultural Sample Survey in Ethiopia, where estimates for individual crops at the national and subnational level were generated from five crop cuts in each primary sampling unit (PSU).

Another common problem in estimating crop production is intercropping, which complicates the allocation of different crops to the plot area. The preferred method for handling intercropped plots, though challenging, is to apply a notion of seeding rate to estimate the actual area under cultivation for a particular crop. Easier alternatives include asking the farmer's own assessment of the share of the land allocated to a given crop. Needless to say, different methods result in significant differences in terms of average yields, thus resulting in limited comparability in countries' estimates. This is why yields are often reported only for pure stand crops, or estimates are presented separately for the different cultivation practices.

Turning now to the denominator of a yield measure, land area: according to the FAO, traversing (compass and rope, or compass and tape) is considered the gold standard for land area estimation. However, its implementation is time-consuming and costly. For instance, a study as part of the 2003 pilot of the Uganda Agricultural Census compared land measurement by traversing versus GPS units, and found that the average time use per plot measured was over three hours for traversing, more than three times as much as when GPS technology was employed (Schoning, Apuuli, Menyha, & Zake-Muwanga, 2005). Due to the significant time involvement, traversing is seldom feasible in the context of large national household surveys.

Another potentially accurate alternative option for land area measurement is the delineation of parcel boundaries by satellite imagery. However, at present this is largely impractical, particularly in tree-dense areas and areas with regular cloud cover, where the ability to produce accurate and timely measures is limited. Furthermore, the spatial and temporal extent of national household surveys generally makes the acquisition and processing of such high resolution imagery still largely prohibitive from a cost standpoint. Another option widely used in routine data collection is based on the 'eye estimates' of agricultural extension officers, who are often assigned the impossible task of frequently reporting on newly planted areas for each crop over vast areas with little or no transportation facilities.

The two options which are most commonly used for collecting land area measurement are farmers' self-reporting and GPS-based area measurement. While widely used, self-reported land area is believed to be imprecise, particularly in land-abundant contexts. There are a number of reasons why self-reports may be subject to measurement error. First, farmers may knowingly overstate or understate their landholdings for strategic reasons if they believe that the information may be used for a purpose such as property taxes or access to a social programme. Second, the natural tendency to round off numbers and provide approximations of land area leads to heaping of the data around discrete values. Geography, particularly the slope of the parcel, can also change the way farmers interpret the land (Keita & Carfagna, 2009). Slope-related effects on area measurement are rooted in the fact that the actual area should be the horizontal projection of the parcel as opposed to the parcel area itself, since plants and trees grow vertically and not perpendicularly to the slope, thus requiring for their growth a vertical cylinder of soil (Keita, Carfagna, & Mu'Ammar, 2010; Muwanga-Zake, 1985). The difference between actual area and projection appears to be particularly important for slopes greater than 10 degrees (Fermont & Benson, 2011). Finally, as seen in the case of crop production, an additional cause of error is the common use of non-standard units, even across different regions within the same country. Table 3, listing the conversion factors for different regions within the country of Nigeria, exemplifies this problem.

As GPS technology becomes more affordable, accurate and user-friendly, GPS-based area measurement provides a practical alternative to farmer self-reported areas and is increasingly being applied in surveys worldwide. For example, in an assessment of agricultural data collection in sub-Saharan Africa, Kelly, Diagana, Reardon, Gaye, & Crawford (1995) highlight GPS technology as having the potential to

Table 3. Zone-specific conversion factors into hectares

Zone	Conversion factors		
	Heaps	Ridges	Stands
1	0.00012	0.00270	0.00006
2	0.00016	0.00400	0.00016
3	0.00011	0.00494	0.00004
4	0.00019	0.00230	0.00004
5	0.00021	0.00230	0.00013
6	0.00012	0.00001	0.00041

Source: Nigeria, 2010/2011 General Household Survey-Panel.

enable land area measurement to become a much less time-intensive and costly exercise. Using field experiments, Keita and Carfagna (2009) indicate that GPS-based area measurement is a reliable alternative to traversing and that 80 per cent of the sample plots were measured with negligible error.

Recent empirical evidence based on the 2005/2006 Uganda National Household Survey (UNHS) comparing GPS-based and self-reported measurement of parcel areas also suggest the existence of systematic errors in self-reported parcel areas (Carletto, Savastano, & Zezza, 2013). Specifically, smaller-scale farmers consistently over-report the area of their plots, while the opposite appears to be true for larger holdings. It would thus seem obvious and inexpensive to improve on the current productivity estimates by simply training household survey enumerators and extension officers on the use of GPS units.

Unfortunately, even GPS technology has a number of drawbacks which are yet to be fully resolved. For instance, GPS-based coordinates are subject to known types of measurement error rooted in satellite position, signal propagation and receivers. Approximate contributions of these factors to the overall position error range from 0.5 to 4 metres (Hofmann-Wellenhof, Lichtenegger, & Wasle, 2008). On a large plot this may not be substantial, but on a smaller plot the errors may be significant, thus raising potential questions about the validity of using GPS for very small plots (Keita and Carfagna, 2009).[7] Irrespective of this, from a technical standpoint areas measured by GPS would be expected to create land data with classical measurement error.

Another problem associated with GPS measurement derives from the failure to measure all plots of sample households. Kilic, Zezza, Carletto, & Savastano (2013) in Uganda and Tanzania suggests that systematic bias in missing GPS measurements may be a problem, particularly at high level of non-random missingness. They argue that careful use of imputation techniques facilitated by the regular collection of self-reported plot area measurements assists in overcoming this limitation and in rendering GPS a viable alternative.

In summary, productivity measures and other agricultural statistics are highly sensitive to the methods used for their collection. Consequently, the existing lack of consensus on protocols and standards has resulted in agricultural statistics that suffer from uncertain quality, poor comparability and low credibility.

5. Agricultural Statistics in the Twenty-First Century: Reversing the Tragedy

Knowledge gaps in the area of agricultural statistics remain endemic and the challenges ahead are daunting. Given the importance of the agricultural sector in promoting growth and reducing poverty, improving the availability, quality and policy relevance of agricultural data is of paramount importance, particularly for countries in Africa, which lack fundamental information to inform the design of effective policies. This article has attempted to highlight a few of the shortcomings of the current system and to offer ideas on how integrated household surveys can contribute to filling these knowledge gaps, particularly in the areas of methodological validation and policy analysis. We recognise that while integrated surveys are only one of many tools available to researchers and practitioners, with their attendant set of limitations, they are nonetheless an indispensable instrument for gaining an improved understanding of the role of agriculture in poverty reduction and growth.

Due to the neglected state of agricultural statistics today, jumpstarting the renewal process has proven difficult. Reversing this situation will take a concerted effort by individual countries and stakeholders to develop and implement global standards and best practices in agricultural statistics. Initiatives like the Global Strategy, led by the FAO, and its ensuing plans of action, are a step in the right direction. However, given the importance of this work to the design and implementation of key policies for the wellbeing of citizens of countries in Africa and elsewhere, we must make rapid progress. The window of opportunity made possible by recent events may close at any time. The digital revolution can assist in offering more efficient and cost-effective ways to capture the complexity of agriculture; the progress made to date with technologies such as global positioning systems, satellite imagery, computer assisted personal interviewing[8] and mobile phones leaves room for optimism. Nonetheless, embracing the digital revolution by promoting the use of new technologies without paying requisite attention to the 'analogue' experiences of the past will lead to an inefficient allocation of resources and poor results. The validation of these tools and the applicability of these innovations to African realities must precede any full-fledged scaling-up.

It is undeniable that better agricultural data are needed, but moving from Devarajan's (2013) statistical 'tragedy' to Kiregyera's (2014) statistical 'renaissance' will require addressing a number of key issues in a timely manner. Furthermore, reversing the decades of under-investment in agriculture will take an equally protracted effort by individual countries and development partners alike. It is our hope that the combination of a long-term strategy of methodological improvement, capacity building and institutional strengthening with shorter-term goals based on the 'quick-wins' and low-cost solutions highlighted in this article will ultimately lead to better-informed agricultural policies that have the potential to improve the lives of the millions of people involved in the agricultural sector worldwide.

Acknowledgements

The authors are grateful to Morten Jerven and Deborah Johnston for their valuable feedback, as well as to participants at the conference on 'African Economic Development: Measuring Success and Failure', Simon Fraser University, for many useful comments on an earlier draft of this article. The authors gratefully acknowledge financial support from the Bill and Melinda Gates Foundation in support of the Living Standards Measurement Study – Integrated Surveys on Agriculture (LSMS–ISA). The views expressed here are those of the authors and may not be attributed to the World Bank, IZA, or NPC.

Notes

1. Comprising about 80 per cent of all farms in Africa (FAO, 2009).
2. CSA is now in charge of producing and reporting annual estimates of production of the main crops based on the Agricultural Sample Survey.
3. In some cases, sample-based agricultural censuses based on very large samples are deployed as an alternative to full enumeration. This is the case, for instance, in Tanzania, where a sample-based agricultural census is planned every five years.
4. Conditional on having some positive income from livestock activities.
5. Fortunately, there are also some notable exceptions. For instance, results from the latest Census of Agriculture in Mozambique were released within 6 months.
6. For some examples on consumption diaries, see Gieseman (1987), Gibson (2002), Battistin (2003), Ahmed et al. (2006) and Beegle, DeWeerdt, Friedman, & Gibson (2010).
7. Other sources of measurement error resulting from GPS units are linked to topography and canopy cover, as well as to weather conditions at the time of measurement (Keita & Carfagna, 2009).
8. The LSMS is currently supporting the development of a freeware CAPI system by the Computations Tool team in the Development Research Group of the World Bank. The multi-component application, known at 'Survey Solutions', is available at https://solutions.worldbank.org.

References

African Development Bank. (2004, February). The Marrakech action plan for statistics: Better data for better results: An action plan for improving development statistics. 2nd International Roundtable on Managing for Development Results, Marrakech.

African Union. (2003, July). Declaration on agriculture and food security in Africa. Assembly of the African Union, Second Ordinary Session, Maputo.

Ahmed, N., Brzozowski, M., & Crossley, T. F. (2006). Measurement errors in recall food consumption data (No. 06/21). IFS Working Papers. Institute for Fiscal Studies, London.

Battistin, E. (2003). Errors in survey reports of consumption expenditures (No. 03/07). IFS Working Papers. Institute for Fiscal Studies, London.

Beegle, K., Carletto, C., & Himelein, K. (2011). Reliability of recall in agricultural data (Policy Research Working Paper 5671). Washington, DC: World Bank.

Beegle, K., DeWeerdt, J., Friedman, J., & Gibson, J. (2010). Methods of household consumption measurement through surveys: Experimental results from Tanzania (Policy Research Working Paper 5501). Washington, DC: World Bank.

Binswanger, H. (2008, May). Gates Foundation support to African 'agricultural' data. Presentation to the Technical Review Meeting on Household Panel Surveys in Africa, World Bank, Washington, DC.

Bryceson, D. F. (2002). The scramble in Africa: Reorienting rural livelihoods. *World Development, 30*(5), 725–239.

Carletto, C., Savastano, S., & Zezza, A. (2013). Fact or artefact: The impact of measurement errors on the farm size-productivity relationship. *Journal of Development Economics, 103*, 254–261.

Chen, S., & Ravallion, M. (2007). *The changing profile of poverty in the world* (2020 Vision Briefs, BB01 Special Edition). Washington, DC: International Food Policy Research Institute.

Covarrubias, K., Nsiima, L., & Zezza, A. (2012). *Livestock and livelihoods in rural Tanzania: A descriptive analysis of the 2009 National Panel Survey* (Joint paper of the World Bank, FAO, AU-IBAR, ILRI and the Tanzania Ministry of Livestock and Fisheries. LSMS–ISA Project). Washington, DC: The World Bank.

Cramer, C., Johnston, D., Mueller, B., Oya, C., & Sender, J. (2014) How to do (and how not to do) fieldwork on Fair Trade and rural poverty. *Canadian Journal of Development Studies, 35*(1), 170–185.

Davis, B., Winters, P., Carletto, G., Covarrubias, K., Quiñones, E. J., Zezza, A., … DiGiuseppe, S. (2010). A cross-country comparison of rural income generating activities. *World Development, 38*(1), 48–63.

Deininger, K., Carletto, C., Savastano, S., & Muwonge, J. (2012). Can diaries help in improving agricultural production statistics? Evidence from Uganda. *Journal of Development Economics, 98*(1), 42–50.

Dercon, S., & Hill, R. V. (2009). Growth from agriculture in Ethiopia: Identifying key constraints. In IFPRI's ESSP-II policy conference Accelerating Agricultural Development, Economic Growth and Poverty Reduction in Ethiopia, Addis Ababa. Retrieved from: http://users.ox.ac.uk/~econstd/Ethiopia%20paper%203_v5.pdf.

Devarajan, S. (2013). Africa's statistical tragedy. *Review of Income and Wealth*. doi:10.1111/roiw.12013.

DFID. (2004) *Agriculture, growth and poverty reduction* (Working Paper). Retrieved from http://dfid-agriculture-consultation. nri.org/summaries/wp1.pdf.

Dorward, A., Chirwa, E., Kelly, V., Jayne, T., Slater, R., & Boughton, D. (2008). Evaluation of the 2006/7 Agricultural Input Supply Programme, Malawi: Final report. Retrieved from http://www.future-agricultures.org/pdf'%20files/ MalawiAISPFinalReport31March.pdf.

Elepu, G. (2006). *Value chain analysis for the maize sub-sector in Uganda* (Draft report submitted to ASPS Agribusiness Development Component). Uganda: Department of Agricultural Economics & Agribusiness, Makerere University, Kampala.

Ethiopia Central Statistical Agency. (2012–2013). Agricultural sample survey. Retrieved from http://213.55.92.105/nada4/index. php/catalog/323.

Fermont, A., & Benson, T. (2011). *Estimating yield of food crops grown by smallholder farmers: A review in the Ugandan context* (Uganda Strategy Support Program Working Paper No. USSP 05). Washington, DC: IFPRI.

Food and Agricultural Organization (FAO) of the United Nations. (2008). *The agricultural bulletin board on data collection, dissemination and quality of statistics*. Rome: FAO.

Food and Agricultural Organization (FAO) of the United Nations. (2009). *How to feed the world in 2050: High level expert forum – the special challenge for sub-Saharan Africa*. Rome: FAO.

Food and Agricultural Organization (FAO) of the United Nations. (2011). *Financial resource flows to agriculture: A review of data on government spending, official development assistance and foreign direct investment* (ESA Working Paper No. 11-19, December 2011). Rome: FAO.

Food and Agricultural Organization (FAO) of the United Nations. (2014a). *Annual average maize yields in Malawi*. Rome: FAO. Retrieved from http://faostat.fao.org.

Food and Agricultural Organization (FAO) of the United Nations. (2014b). *Annual average maize yields in Tanzania*. Rome: FAO. Retrieved from http://faostat.fao.org.

Foster, A. D., & Rosenzweig, M. R. (2008). Economic development and the decline of agricultural employment. In T. Paul Schultz and John Strauss (Eds.), *Handbook of Development Economics*, (pp. 3051–3083). Oxford: North Holland.

Gibson, J. (2002). Why does the Engel Method work? Food demand, economies of size and household survey methods. *Oxford Bulletin of Economics and Statistics, 64*(4), 341–359.

Gieseman, R. (1987). The consumer expenditure survey: Quality control by comparative analysis. *Monthly Labor Review*, 8–14.

Hofmann-Wellenhof, B., Lichtenegger, H., & Wasle, E. (2008). *GNSS – global navigation satellite systems*. New York: Springer-Verlag.

Irz, X., Lin, L., Thirtle, C., & Wiggins, S. (2001). Agricultural productivity growth and poverty alleviation.' *Development Policy Review, 19*(4), 449–466.

Jerven, M. (2013). The political economy of agricultural statistics and input subsidies: Evidence from India, Nigeria and Malawi. *Journal of Agrarian Change*. doi:10.1111/joac.12025

Jolliffe, D. (2004). The impact of education in rural Ghana: Examining household labor allocation and returns on and off the farm. *Journal of Development Economics, 73*(1), 287–314.

Keita, N., & Carfagna, E. (2009, August). Use of modern geo-positioning devices in agricultural censuses and surveys: Use of GPS for crop area measurement. Bulletin of the International Statistical Institute, the 57th Session, 2009, Proceedings, Special Topics Contributed Paper Meetings (STCPM22), Durban.

Keita, N., Carfagna, E., & Mu'Ammar, G. (2010, October). Issues and guidelines for the emerging use of GPS and PDAs in agricultural statistics in developing countries. The Fifth International Conference on Agricultural Statistics (ICAS V), Kampala, Uganda.

Kelly, V., Diagana, B., Reardon, T., Gaye, M., & Crawford, E. (1995). *Cash crop and foodgrain productivity in Senegal: Historical view, new survey evidence, and policy implications* (MSU Staff Paper No. 95-05). East Lansing: Michigan State University.

Kilic, T., Zezza, A., Carletto, C., & Savastano, S. (2013). *Missing(ness) in action: Selectivity bias in GPS-based land area measurements* (World Bank Policy Research Working Paper 5671). Washington, DC: World Bank.

Kiregyera, Ben. (2014). The dawning of a statistical renaissance in Africa. (mimeo)

Ligon, E. & Sadoulet, E. (2008). Estimating the effects of aggregate agricultural growth on the distribution of expenditures. *World Development Report 2008*. Washington, DC: World Bank.

Livingston, G, Schonberger, S., & Delaney, S. (2011, January). Sub-Saharan Africa: The state of smallholders in agriculture, Paper presented at the IFAD Conference on New Directions for Smallholder Agriculture. Rome: International Fund for Agricultural Development.

Malawi Ministry of Agriculture and Food Security. (2006–2007). *Annual agricultural statistical bulletin*. Lilongwe: Ministry of Agriculture and Food Security.

Malawi National Statistical Office. (2004–2005). Malawi integrated household survey. Retrieved from http://go.worldbank.org/JR84NBDS70.

Malawi National Statistical Office. (2006–2007). National census of agriculture and livestock. Retrieved from http://www.nsomalawi.mw.

Malawi National Statistical Office. (2010–2011). Malawi integrated household survey. Retrieved from http://go.worldbank.org/DLFL1FPEP0.

Muwanga-Zake, E. S. K. (1985). *Sources of possible errors and biases in agricultural statistics in Uganda: A review*. Kampala: Institute of Statistics and Applied Economics, Makerere University.

Ngendakumana, V. (2001, February). Data quality as limiting factor in the measuring and analysis of food supplier: FAO's Africa experience. Paper presented at Joint ECE/Eurostat/FAO/OECD meeting on Food and Agricultural Statistics in Europe, Geneva.

Nigeria National Bureau of Statistics. (2010–2011). General household survey – Panel. Retrieved from http://www.nigerianstat.gov.ng/nada/index.php/catalog/31.

Oladejo, A., Chinganya, O., & Nshimyumuremyi, A. (2010, October). Framework for mainstreaming agricultural statistics into the NSDS process. Paper presented at ICAS V, Kampala.

Paris21. (2002). *Final report: Seminar on a new partnership to strengthen agricultural and rural statistics in Africa for poverty reduction and food security*. Paris: Task Team Food, Agriculture and Rural Statistics. Paris 21.

Prowse, M., & Chimhowu, A. (2007). *Making agriculture work for the poor* (Overseas Development Institute Natural Resource Perspectives 111). London: Overseas Development Institute.

Reardon, T. (1997). Using evidence of household income diversification to inform the study of rural non-farm labor markets in Africa. *World Development, 25*(5), 735–747.

Singh, M. (2006, December). *Platinum jubilee of Indian statistical institute*. Speech presented at Indian Statistical Institute, Kolkata, India.

Schoning, P., Apuuli, J. B. M., Menyha, E., & Zake-Muwanga, E. S. K. (2005). *Handheld GPS equipment for agricultural statistics surveys: Experiments on area-measurement and geo-referencing of holdings done during fieldwork for the Uganda Pilot Census of Agriculture* (Statistics Norway Report 2005/29). Oslo: Statistics Norway.

Tiffen, M. (2003). Transition in sub-Saharan African agriculture, urbanization and income growth. *World Development, 31*(8), 1343–1366.

Willis, H. P. (1903, September). The adjustment of crop statistics: III. *Journal of Political Economy, 11*(4), 540–567.

World Bank. (2008). *World development report 2008: Agriculture for development*. Washington, DC: The World Bank.

World Bank, United Nations, & Food and Agriculture Organization (FAO). (2010). *Global strategy to improve agricultural and rural statistics* (World Bank Other Operational Studies 12402). Washington, DC: The World Bank.

The Invisibility of Wage Employment in Statistics on the Informal Economy in Africa: Causes and Consequences

MATTEO RIZZO, BLANDINA KILAMA & MARC WUYTS

School of Oriental and African Studies, University of London, UK, REPOA, Dar es Salaam, United Republic of Tanzania, Institute of Social Sciences, Erasmus University of Rotterdam, The Netherlands

ABSTRACT *This article challenges the claim, along with the statistics that support it, that self-employment is by far the dominant employment status in the informal economy. The article begins by reviewing key insights from relevant literature on the informal economy to argue that conventional notions of 'wage employment' and 'self-employment', while unfit for capturing the nature and variety of employment relations in developing countries, remain central to the design of surveys on the workforce therein. After putting statistics on Tanzania's informal economy and labour force into context, the analysis reviews the type of wage employment relationships that can be found in one instance of the informal economy in urban Tanzania. The categories and terms used by workers to describe their employment situation are then contrasted with those used by the latest labour force survey in Tanzania. The article scrutinises how key employment categories have been translated from English into Swahili, how the translation biases respondents' answers towards the term 'self-employment', and how this, in turn, leads to the statistical invisibility of wage labour in the informal economy. The article also looks at the consequences of this 'statistical tragedy' and at the dangers of conflating varied forms of employment, including wage labour, that differ markedly in their modes of operation and growth potential. Attention is also paid to the trade-offs faced by policy-makers in designing better labour force surveys.*

Introduction

It is now common to argue that, in Africa, wage employment has become the exception and self-employment the rule, mainly as a result of the growth of the informal economy. For example, Fox and Pimhidzai contrast the situation in OECD countries, where wage employment is the norm, with that in sub-Saharan Africa where, they argue, 'employment takes the form of self and/or household employment, where a task is performed for family profit or gain (including for home food consumption). Most labour force participants never even enter the labour market' (Fox & Pimhidzai, 2013, p. 3). Theirs is a belief widely held by policy-makers. The most recent labour force survey in Tanzania is no exception to this, as it suggests that working in one's own business is by far the most prevalent type of employment relationship in the informal economy.

This article questions this common assumption that self-employment is the dominant mode of employment in the informal economy, and questions the wisdom of statistics on the informal labour force. The article starts by reviewing some key insights obtained from relevant economic theory, but also from the literature on the informal economy in Tanzania. Our aim is to understand how

This article was originally published with errors. This version was corrected. Please see Erratum 10.1080/00220388.2014.992103.

conventional notions of 'wage employment' and 'self-employment' simultaneously fail to capture the nature and variety of employment relations in the informal economy, and yet these notions are central to the design of workforce surveys in developing countries. The article then uses the 2006 Integrated Labour Force Survey (NBS, 2007) to show that the informal economy is seen almost exclusively as the site of self-employment. The analysis then interrogates this claim by looking at the particular type of wage employment relationships that are found in one concrete sector of the informal economy in Tanzania, urban bus transport. The real labour relations at work therein and the categories and terms with which workers describe their employment situation are then contrasted with the categories and terms used to frame the questions in the latest available Integrated Labour Force Survey (ILFS) in Tanzania carried out in 2006. The article scrutinises how key employment concepts and terms have been translated from English into Swahili, how the translation biases respondents' answers towards 'self-employment', and how the translation then leads to the invisibility of wage labour in the collection of statistics on employment in the informal economy, both urban and rural. The article also looks at the consequences of this 'statistical tragedy'. We argue that this assumption conflates varied forms of employment, including wage labour, that differ markedly in their modes of operation. Attention is also paid to the most significant trade-off faced by policy-makers in designing better labour force surveys.

Informal Economy as Self-Employment?

Keith Hart, the inventor of the term 'the informal sector', claims that the 'distinction between formal and informal income opportunities is based essentially on that between wage-earning and self-employment' (Hart, 1973, p. 68), a dichotomy that has been relentlessly adhered to by policy-makers in developing countries. In clarifying this distinction between wage labour and self-employment, Hart argues that 'the key variable is the degree of rationalisation of work – that is to say, whether or not labour is recruited on a permanent and regular basis for fixed rewards' (Hart 1973, Ibidem). Hart's restricted definition of 'wage labour' as permanent and as regular recruitment for fixed awards is indeed plausible when it comes to describing the nature of the employment contracts in the formal sector. This is the conventional or 'formal' definition of wage labour, which generally refers to 'workers on regular wages or salaries in registered firms and with access to the state social security system and its framework of labour law' (Harriss-White & Gooptu, 2000, p. 89). Production based on this type of 'formal' wage labour is only viable, however, under conditions where productivity is reasonably high and stable relative to the fixed wage rate. 'Formal' wage contracting is indeed unlikely to be widespread under conditions where labour productivity is low, volatile or unpredictable, which are precisely the conditions that prevail so widely within the informal economies in developing countries.

Nevertheless, it does not follow from this that all activities within the informal economy are based on self-employment and, hence, that the capital/labour relation ceases to exist or does so only marginally. In fact, interestingly, Hart gives quite a detailed account of the variety of production forms that exist in the informal economy: 'In practice, informal activities encompass a wide-ranging scale, from marginal operations to large enterprises' (Hart, 1973, p. 68). Yet, surprisingly, he does not draw the obvious conclusion that these varied and often highly differentiated forms of production must imply the existence of a variety of labour regimes, including various forms of wage labour. Part of the problem is that Hart explicitly excluded from his analysis 'casual income flows of an occasional nature' (p. 69), yet recognised that 'some may be hired to small enterprises which escape enumeration as establishments'. He, nevertheless, goes on to say that 'the ensuing analysis is restricted to those who, whether working alone or in partnership, are self-employed' (p. 70).

In making this restriction, however, Hart falls prey to the fallacy of 'misplaced aggregation' (a term borrowed from Myrdal [1968, Appendix 3]): that is, conceptually conflating entities that do not belong together and, thus, should not be aggregated into one category. Indeed, the catch-all category of 'self-employed' conveys a connotation of an individual's own business and/or a family business, of asset ownership, however limited, and of entrepreneurship and some degree of economic independence

(Harriss-White and Gooptu 2001, p. 91); yet, as Breman argues, 'what at first sight seems like self-employment and which also presents itself as such, often conceals sundry forms of wage labour' (Breman, 1996, p. 8).

Interestingly, for example, while Fox and Pimhidzai (2013, p. 3), following Hart (1973), assert that, in sub-Saharan Africa, 'most labour force participants never enter the labour market', Fields (2005), in contrast, models the distinction between the formal and the informal 'murky' sectors (p. 4), as labour market segmentation or fragmentation: a dualism that implies that different workers are paid different wages in different sectors for comparable work (p. 6). Fields, however, defines a 'job' for which a wage is paid as a convenient shorthand for 'both self-employment and wage employment', and, hence, blurs the distinction between different forms of employment, (p.19).

This simplifying assumption of labour market dualism allowed Fields to explore distinctive analytical models of the dynamics of labour earnings in the informal sector: more specifically, whether the informal economy is a free-entry sector of last resort or whether it is a desirable sector for employment in its own right, or, as Fields contends, some combination of both, implying internal dualism within this sector (Fields, 2005,. pp. 17–25). Interestingly, these contrastive views on employment in the informal sector – a sector of despair or of potential – featured very prominently in the debates on the informal economy in Tanzania during the 1990s. Maliyamkono and Bagachwa (1990) and Sarris and Van den Brink (1993), for example, clearly viewed the informal economy as a 'desirable sector', while in contrast Jamal and Weeks (1993) took the opposing view of the informal sector as a last resort.[1]

These authors, however, as well as subsequent work by Tripp (1997), all took the assumption of informal economy as self-employment for granted. More recently, along the same lines, in their analysis of labour market dynamics using the Tanzanian urban household panel survey, Quinn and Teal (2008, p. 4) see the dichotomy between formal and informal employment as identical to that between wage earners and self-employment.[2] That labour regimes in informal production vary widely in nature is thus left out of the picture altogether.

In contrast, the analysis of the informal economy in urban Senegal by LeBrun and Gerry (1974) provides some useful handles to tackle this question, since they focus on differences in forms of petty production, ranging from artisans to petty commodity production and to small capitalist production, thus drawing attention not only to the level of labour earnings within the informal economy, but also to the variety of forms of employment. Moreover, these forms do not coexist in isolation, but give rise to a variety of transitional forms, including varied forms of wage labour. Within this spectrum of petty production, some forms lean more towards independent production (which can be best characterised as self-employment, possibly involving the employment of wage labour), while others lean more towards labour contracting. In the former case, it is the product that becomes a commodity; in the latter case, it is labour power that is being (sub-) contracted. For example, the itinerant street vendor buys commodities in small quantities from a supplier and sells them the customers on the streets. Notwithstanding the asymmetric relation that often exists between the vendor and the supplier, this can best be characterised as petty-commodity production through self-employment A similar situation prevails for the producer-vendor of foodstuff – for example, selling meals at the road side or running a catering service, which may also involve the employment of wage labour (which can be characterised as self-employment using paid labour).

But many other informal sector activities mainly involve the contracting of labour, and not the sale of commodities. In Tanzania, as shown in the next section, employment in informal mining is almost exclusively classified as self-employment. But, as Wangwe (1997), Jonssøn and Bryceson (2009) and Jonssøn and Fold (2009) show, the reality on the ground is much more complex. Production relations in informal mining are distinctly hierarchical, involving claim holders (those holding the mining licence), pit owners (those operating the pit, including the recruitment of labour), and varied types of workers. Typically, these workers are not paid a fixed wage but a share in the output produced, net of 'coverage of workers' reproductive costs (food, medicine, basic health services, and pocket money)' (Jonssøn & Fold, 2009, p. 217). A basic wage is paid, therefore, to cover reproductive costs. Of the remainder, the claim holder usually takes 30 per cent of net output, the pit owner 40 per cent, and workers share the remaining 30 per cent (Jonssøn and Fold, 2009).

Similarly, in the construction industry, informal production has taken on an increasingly more prominent role both in output and in employment, in part because of 'an increase in sub-contracting by the formal sector and a new role for the informal sector as supplier of labour', but also because 'an increasing number of building clients are choosing to by-pass the formal sector altogether, and engage directly with enterprises and operators in the informal sector' (Wells, 2001, p. 270). To recruit labour, the client pays for the building materials and engages a 'labour contractor' to supply the necessary labour, but, at times, the client directly recruits labour, in which case the contractor effectively becomes a foreman (Wells, 2001).

These examples illustrate that lumping together these varied forms of labour contracting that exist within informal production into a single category of self-employment hides more than it reveals. But, as we go on to argue, this is precisely what labour force surveys tend to do.

The 2006 ILFS: Definitions and Patterns of Employment

Labour force surveys are among the least frequently carried out surveys in sub-Saharan Africa (SSA). Since the 1980s, in particular, international donors directed their support towards income and expenditure and household surveys (Oya, 2013, p. 257). Against this trend, Tanzanian authorities have done relatively well, as three labour force surveys were completed in 1990/1991, 2000/2001 and 2006, and a fourth one is now in preparation. Although the quantity of available data on labour is higher in Tanzania than elsewhere in SSA, the quality of such data is low.

The 2006 ILFS (NBS, 2007) allow us to explore different ways of looking at informal employment using different sets of classifications of the structure of employment: in particular, by industry; by sector; and by status. A further distinction is made between main and secondary activities of employment, but, for the purpose of aggregation, only main activities are included to avoid double-counting. The definition of informal sector relates to the type of enterprises, while that of self-employment to the status of employment.[3] Following prevailing ILO guidelines, the 2006 ILFS in Tanzania defines the informal sector as 'a subset of household enterprises or unincorporated enterprises owned by households' (NBS, 2007, p. 7). These enterprises 'may or may not employ paid labour and the activities may be carried out inside and outside the owners' home' (*ibid.*). The informal sector comprises both informal own-account enterprises as well as enterprises of informal employers: the former employ workers on a continuous basis, while the latter employ workers on an occasional basis or make use of the employment of unpaid family helpers (*ibid.*). This definition of the informal sector, therefore, does not exclude the employment of wage labour.

Self-employment constitutes one of the four categories of the status of employment, alongside paid employees, family worker and traditional agricultural worker. More specifically, self-employment is defined as 'persons who perform work for profit or family gain in their own non-agricultural enterprise, including small and larger business persons working in their own enterprise'(NBS, 2007, pp. 7–8). This category is sub-divided into those with employees and those without employees (*ibid.*). Table 1 gives a cross-tabulation of employment status against sector of main employment for the 2006 ILFS.

This table shows that 'paid employment' accounts for only 0.7 per cent of informal sector employment (main activity only) and, hence, is deemed to be a very rare type of employment relationship. Self-employed workers without employees constitute the dominant type of employment status, at 83.8 per cent. Together with self-employed workers with employees, at 13.8 per cent, self-employment totals a staggering 97.6 per cent of employment in the informal sector. This also reveals an interesting anomaly in these data: while paid employees constitute only 0.7 per cent of the total, the self-employed with employees account for 13.8 per cent. Assuming that the self-employed with employees employ at least one employee each, these figures appear to hide the importance of paid employment. Conceptually, therefore, the definitions of informal sector and self-employment clearly differ, but as

Table 1. Employment status by sector of main employment: 2006 (main activities only)

Employment status	Central/local government	Parastatal	Agriculture	Informal	Other private	Household economic activities	Totals
Paid employee	439,355	66,307	0	12,274	1,206,395	31,563	1,753,481
	100.0%	100.0%	0.0%	0.7%	84.2%	6.1%	10.5%
Self-employed (non- agr) with employees	0	0	0	232,334	66,552	899	299,786
	0.0%	0.0%	0.0%	13.8%	4.6%	0.2%	1.8%
Self-employed (non- agr) without employees	0	0	0	1,409,698	99,828	3,025	1,512,551
	0.0%	0.0%	0.0%	83.8%	7.0%	0.6%	9.1%
Unpaid family helper (non- agricultural)	0	0	0	29,366	61,035	485,974	575,798
	0.0%	0.0%	0.0%	1.7%	4.3%	93.2%	3.5%
Unpaid family helper (agricultural)	0	0	1,316,724	0	0	0	1,316,724
	0.0%	0.0%	10.5%	0.0%	0.0%	0.0%	7.9%
Work on own farm or shamba	0	0	11,168,792	0	0	0	11,168,792
	0.0%	0.0%	89.5%	0.0%	0.0%	0.0%	67.2%
Total	439,355	66,307	12,485,516	1,682,383	1,432,370	521,202	16,627,133

Source: Constructed by the authors using ILFS 2006 (NBS, 2007, Tables 5.8, B4 and B5, pp. 38, 119).

far as the statistical evidence is concerned informal sector employment essentially equals self-employment.

Table 2 gives a more detailed breakdown of employment figures for selected subsectors of employment for the 2006 survey. The selection of sectors was confined to those sectors with significant employment in the informal sector, but the aggregate totals, however, give the total employment across all sectors of the economy. Table 2 shows that the informal sector is mainly concentrated in trade,

Table 2. Sectoral structure of employment by male and female: 2006 (selected subsectors: main activity only)

Industry	Currently employed population (main activity only)					
	Total			Informal		
	Male	Female	Total	Male	Female	Total
Agriculture/hunting/forestry & fishing	5,880,789	6,832,446	12,713,234	13,296	6,202	19,498
	72.7%	80.0%	76.5%	1.4%	0.8%	1.2%
Mining & quarry	72,862	11,463	84,325	39,987	7,492	47,478
	0.9%	0.1%	0.5%	4.3%	1.0%	2.8%
Manufacturing	272,872	161,335	434,206	133,470	109,533	243,003
	3.4%	1.9%	2.6%	14.4%	14.5%	14.4%
Construction	171,995	6,686	178,681	50,699	412	51,111
	2.1%	0.1%	1.1%	5.5%	0.1%	3.0%
Wholesale & retail trade	750,999	518,357	1,269,356	538,496	428,990	967,487
	9.3%	6.1%	7.6%	58.1%	56.8%	57.5%
Hotels & restaurants	86,882	240,552	327,433	46,746	170,387	217,132
	1.1%	2.8%	2.0%	5.0%	22.6%	12.9%
Transport/storage & communication	231,116	13,111	244,227	25,968	17,081	43,050
	2.9%	0.2%	1.5%	2.8%	2.3%	2.6%
Other community/social & personal service activities	79,336	35,206	114,543	78,789	14,835	93,624
	1.0%	0.4%	0.7%	8.5%	2.0%	5.6%
Totals	8,086,325	8,540,809	16,627,133	927,452	754,932	1,682,383

Source: Constructed by the authors using ILFS 2006 (NBS, 2007, Figure 5.2, p. 35, Table B3, p. 118, Table C2, p. 119).

Table 3. Sectoral structure of employment by male and female: 2006 (selected sectors: secondary activity only)

Industry	Total			Informal		
	Male	Female	Total	Male	Female	Total
Agriculture/hunting/forestry	1,218,842	573,391	1,792,234	120,175	18,538	138,714
	35.9%	12.3%	22.2%	10.7%	1.8%	6.5%
Mining & quarry	256,669	301,134	557,803	209,572	273,729	483,301
	7.6%	6.4%	6.9%	18.7%	27.2%	22.7%
Manufacturing	1,289		1,289	1,289		1,289
	0.0%	0.0%	0.0%	0.1%	0.0%	0.1%
Construction	625,468	496,099	1,121,567	569,892	458,202	1,028,094
	18.4%	10.6%	13.9%	50.8%	45.5%	48.3%
Wholesale & retail trade	76,501	242,783	319,285	69,289	227,784	297,073
	2.3%	5.2%	4.0%	6.2%	22.6%	14.0%
Hotels & restaurants	51,882	3,144	55,026	31,011	899	31,910
	1.5%	0.1%	0.7%	2.8%	0.1%	1.5%
Transport/storage & communication	873		873	16,814	12,026	28,840
	0.0%	0.0%	0.0%	1.5%	1.2%	1.4%
Other community/social & personal service activities	854,801	3,013,198	3,867,999	103,022	16,208	119,230
	25.2%	64.4%	47.9%	9.2%	1.6%	5.6%
Totals	3,397,310	4,677,151	8,074,461	1,121,063	1,007,387	2,128,450

Source: Constructed by the authors using ILFS 2006 (NBS, 2007, Table C2, p. 119, Table D2, p. 120).

followed by manufacturing. However, Tables 1 and 2 feature employment totals by main activity only. But the labour force data also give information, albeit less detailed, on employment in secondary activities. In 2006, 48.6 per cent of employed persons were engaged in secondary activities (NBS, 2007, p. 52). Moreover, participation in secondary activities is most common in rural areas, at 51.8 per cent of employed persons (NBS, 2007). Table 3 gives a more detailed breakdown of employment in secondary activities for selected subsectors of employment for the 2006 survey.

In Table 3, the dominant sector appears to be other community, social and personal activities (with 47.9% of employment), the definition of which is left rather vague in the ILFS 2006. What is perhaps most striking in Table 3, however, is the size of employment in mining and in construction, both of which involve heavy reliance on labour contracting rather than direct commodity production by persons employed in this sector. The implication is that looking at employment by main activity only yields a wrong impression of the size of informal sector employment. Moreover, according to the ILFS 2006, self-employment constituted 97.6 per cent of those employed in secondary activities of the informal sector (NBS, 2007, p. 46). Once more, the statistical evidence suggests that informal sector equals self-employment, in contrast with our earlier discussion on mining and construction. This shows that this supposedly overwhelming dominance of self-employment is by no means as straight-forward as reality on the ground suggests.

One possible reason for the invisibility of paid labour in labour force surveys is that its modules are designed with the realities of advanced economies in mind (Standing, 2006); that is, the tools used for surveys on employment stem from OECD and are not fit to record information about employment statuses. A recent survey experiment by the World Bank in Tanzania aimed to test the extent to which labour statistics are affected by the way in which questions are asked. The experiment included a shorter and longer module to determine employment status. Although its authors claim that there is a 'significant' impact from the way questions on employment status are asked in terms of results obtained (Bardasi, Beegle, Dillon, & Serneels 2010, p. 25), the picture that emerges from both modules, however, suggests that self-employment remains the norm in SSA. The percentage of people in 'paid employment', for example, varies by a maximum of 5.5 per cent, and as little as 0.1 per cent, but never exceeds 20 per cent. Hence, self-employment, with or without employees, and unpaid family work, when combined, still make up the lion's share of employment, at no less than 77 per cent (Bardasi et al., 2010, p. 41).

However, with others (Oya, 2013, pp. 257–259), we argue instead that the main consequence of the OECD origin of labour force surveys is that their definition of paid employment, rooted in the conventional conceptualisation of formal wage employment that can be observed in these countries, is inadequate for capturing informal and precarious forms of wage labour in developing countries.

Informal Labour in Urban Transport: The Case of the *Daladala* Workers

This article has argued that the dividing line between wage employment and self-employment is not as clear-cut as theory and the labour force data suggest, thus leading to considerable underestimation of the importance of wage labour in informal production. In this section, we look in more detail at a fieldwork-based study of the public transport sector in Dar es Salaam and of its informal employment relations. The analysis draws on long-term research on the sector, and, for this article, on fieldwork carried out in 1998, 2001–2002, and in 2009. The results of a questionnaire on labour relations in the sector, administered to over 650 workers in the sector in 1998, have been triangulated with the observation of the dynamics at work therein, as well as with semi-structured interviews with urban bus workers about their employment. We analyse how employment relationships can be categorised, how the dividing line between wage and self-employment becomes blurred, and how workers themselves refer to these employment relations in Swahili. We then contrast workers' wording of and thinking about employment with the words and categories used by ILFS to capture such reality.

Dar es Salaam is Tanzania's largest city, with no less than four million people.[4] Approximately ten thousand privately owned minibuses, known in Swahili as *daladala,* provide the cheapest form of public transport in the city. Results from two different questionnaires administered in the late 1990s and early 2000s to these bus workers (Rizzo, 2002; UWAMADAR, Konrad Adenauer Stiftung, & Development Dynamics International, 2003) found that family or household employment, so central to mainstream conceptualisations of economic informality (De Soto, 1989), are the exception rather than the rule in this sector. Instead, the *daladala* operations are characterised by a clear division between a class of bus owners and a class of transport workers. Over 90 per cent of the *daladala* workforce, whose total number is estimated to be between 20,000 and 30,000, sell their labour to bus owners. The vast majority of these workers (83.9 per cent) are employed without a contract (*kibarua* in Swahili) (Rizzo, 2002, p. 155).

They are casual workers who do not own the buses on which they work. Their actual employment relationship with bus owners does not easily translate into any of the conventional categories of 'paid employment' and 'self-employment'. Workers pay a daily rental fee (*hesabu* in Swahili) to bus owners. The daily return for workers will consist of whatever remains after paying the daily rent to bus owners, petrol costs and any other work-related expenditures (such as the cost of repairing a tyre or bribing oneself out of the hands of traffic police) have been deducted from the gross daily income. These workers do not earn fixed wages, nor are they pieceworkers. Their daily earnings are, in fact, unknown and highly volatile. Working at a loss is a common occurrence. For example, ending the working day without having enough cash to fill the full tank with petrol is not an uncommon outcome, in which case workers would fill part of the tank, implying that daily earnings the day after will be even lower.

The fact that workers are not waged in a conventional sense, nor are they pieceworkers, does not imply, however, that labelling them as self-employed micro-entrepreneurs, as policy-makers and official statistics on the informal economy commonly do, is a better fit. Indeed, these workers do not own the bus they operate, nor any other capital. Depicting them as self-employed conveys a misleading notion of entrepreneurship and economic independence, and conceals the fundamental power relation at play between bus owners and workers. *Daladala* workers sell their relatively unskilled labour to employers in a context of an oversupply of unskilled job seekers. Taking advantage of this, bus owners impose on workers the daily sum expected for a day's work without any real negotiation. Extremely long working hours (the average day lasting 15 hours and the work week lasting more than 6.5 days) and occupational uncertainty (on average, employment on a bus lasts no more than seven months) are the consequences of the very high daily rent that owners expect from bus workers (Rizzo, 2002, p. 155). Workers respond to this financial squeeze by speeding, overloading the buses and denying boarding to passengers entitled to social fares, all actions that aim at maximising returns from work on a given day. Their situation is similar to Breman's description of rickshaw runners in Calcutta, who also pay a daily rental fee to rickshaw owners and face uncertain daily returns from work. These workers, Breman argued, are not 'independently-operating small entrepreneurs ... but dependent proletarians who live on the defensive' (Breman 2003, p. 154).

The modalities of employment and remuneration of the workforce can in fact be best understood as a strategy by bus owners, or de facto employers, to transfer business risks squarely onto the workforce. Bus owners confront labour not as risk-taking entrepreneurs but as rentiers, leaving workers to manage the risks inherent in low and volatile productivity, a condition that is conducive to self-exploitation by the worker rather than to growth in productivity. In these circumstances, therefore, workers act as entrepreneurs only in the sense that they have become managers of two sets of risks under adverse conditions of extreme competition: the daily insecurity that results from an uncertain income, on the one hand, and the ever-present chance of erratic job loss, on the other (Wuyts, 2011).

This is just one example of the employment relations that prevail in informal settings. It illustrates the way in which conventional categories of both 'wage/paid employment' and 'self-employment' do not easily apply to the reality faced by informal workers and the complexity of the employment relationship that link them to employers. At the same time, however, it is important not to lose sight of two key characteristics that ultimately define their employment status. First, these workers do not own any of the capital with which they work. A clear division between capital and labour can be observed here, making the notion of self-employment implausible in this case. Second, it is precisely because of workers' economic vulnerability that they are deprived of a conventional wage employment relation-ship with employers.

Importantly, *daladala* workers see themselves as casual wage workers rather than as self-employed workers, as is evident from the goals of their political organisation since the late 1990s. When these workers established their association, and built an alliance with the Tanzanian transport union, their main objective was to lobby the state and employers to spell out the employment relationship with bus owners. Their agenda was not entrepreneurial agenda, not did it entail a request for micro-credit. Instead, they demanded employment contracts and a fixed wage (Rizzo, 2013).

Such workers are best categorised as people in paid employment in the informal economy. Many other forms of paid employment are to be found in different economic sectors and in different contexts, with the working poor often straddling precarious wage employment with some ownership of equally insecure, very small-scale activities in the informal economy (Bernstein, 2010). Notwithstanding the heterogeneity of such employment relations, however, they do not easily match the conventional conceptualisation of both 'paid employment' and 'self-employment'. Yet, labour force surveys consistently suggest that paid employment is statistically irrelevant in the informal economy, and self-employment the norm. Why this happens requires us to look at how wage-employment and self-employment are defined in questionnaires, and translated into Swahili, to generate statistics on the informal economy.

The 2006 ILFS Questionnaire: Lost in Translation?

The importance of paying attention to the way in which key employment and work concepts are worded by labour force surveys is well understood (Campanelli, Rothgeb, & Martin, 1989; Martin & Polivka, 1995). The way in which concepts are translated from English into other languages in labour force surveys is less often investigated (see Flora and Komatsu [2011] for an exception). This is problematic, as ultimately it is in languages other than English that questions are posed to labour force survey respondents. Translating words and concepts, often ideologically loaded and context specific in their origin, into other languages is not an easy task. A lot can be lost in the process of translating the labour force questionnaire into Swahili. Moreover, questionnaire respondents make sense of employment questions in the light of how they perceive the realities that they confront in their daily working lives.

Putting concerns about the household as a unit of analysis aside for a moment (Guyer & Peters, 1987; Randall & Coast, 2014), consider, for instance, the ILFS introductory question on household economic activities, to be answered by the head of the household on behalf of his/her household members. In English it reads:

Does this household or anyone in this household engage in any of the following activities? a) Wage Employment (yes/no), b) Working on own or family business (excl. Agriculture), c) working on own shamba, fishing or animal keeping d), do you have any paid employees. (NBS, 2009a, p. 3)

What differentiates the four (not mutually exclusive) possible answers, at least in the English version of the questionnaire, are the three possible types of employment status: (1) being a wage employee, as per option (a); (2) being self-employed, as per in options (b) and (c); and (3) being an employer, as per option (d). In Swahili, however, 'working on own or family business' is translated as 'kazi isiyo ya kilimo' (NBS, 2009c, p. 3), which literally means any 'work that is not agriculture'. This means that the reference to self- or family employment in business or agriculture, central to the English wording of the questionnaire, is dropped altogether in the Swahili version.

The section of the questionnaire on the individual respondent's main economic activity (rather than on households at an aggregate level) does better, as it presents an accurate correspondence between English and Swahili survey questions. Respondents are in fact asked whether their work entails self-employment: 'kujiajiri mwenyewe' (NBS, 2009d, p. 3). But what most influences respondents' choice of the category that best describes their employment status is how they understand the main alternative answer they might opt for, namely 'paid employment'.

In the 2006 ILFS, the Swahili translation of the term 'wage employment' is also problematic. The term used in this case is 'ajira ya msharara' (NBS, 2009c, p. 3). While this literally means wage (mshahara) employment (ajira), such terminology clearly connotes registered employment in the formal sector, 'proper jobs' for the lay Swahili mother-tongue speaker, with a formal employer, a contract and a wage. Part of the problem lies in the ambiguity of the term 'ajira' in Swahili. Broadly speaking 'ajira' is used to denote employment of any type. In this sense, one reads and hears that 'Tanzania tatizo ni kwamba *hakuna ajira*' (the problem in Tanzania is that there is *no employment*; interview with bus worker, Dar es Salaam, 16 September 2009). Yet, at the same time, people use the word 'ajira' to mean registered employment, as opposed to employment of precarious and informal nature. Along these lines, a *daladala* worker, commenting on his informal and precarious employment, stated that 'tatizo la kazi ya *daladala* ni kwamba *hakuna ajira*.' (The problem of work in *daladalas* is that *there is no formal employment*; interview with bus worker, Dar es Salaam, 7 July 2009). Failure to appreciate the two possible meanings of the word 'ajira' in Swahili would potentially allow the implausible translation of the sentence above as 'the problem of work in *daladalas* is that there is no employment'! Instead, when workers refer to their work as work without 'ajira', they mean that it is work without contract, rights and security, in other words informal. This suggests that there is therefore a remarkable dissonance between the way in which the concept of 'paid employment' is worded in Swahili by ILFS, and the way in which informal casual workers understand and word it.

The bias against recording informal wage employment is present also in the questionnaire section focusing on working patterns of individual members of the household. The question on 'what was the economic activity in which you spent most of your time?' has 'employee in a wage job' as one of its five possible answers (the other four being self-employed, working on your own or family farm, unpaid work in family business and other). The Swahili wording of 'employee in a wage job' as 'mwajiriwa wa kulipwa' once more points to formal sector employment. And so does the range of subsectors in which an 'employee in a wage job' might be employed: the central government; the local government; a parastatal organisation; a political party; co-operatives; NGOs; international organisations; religious organisations; and the private sector (NBS, 2009b, p. 3). It is very plausible that a respondent answering this question will fail to match his/her informal employer with any of the possible employers from the survey list, and will not opt for declaring himself/herself as an 'employee in a wage job'.

ILFS, therefore, puts forward a stark and questionable dichotomy between paid and self-employment, and a leading one at that. Consider the implications of the translation issues of 'self-employment' and 'paid employment' together. On the one hand, 'self-employment' is translated in extremely loose terms, to the point that any work outside agriculture seemingly fits into it, or that work by people who do not own any capital can be misleadingly identified as 'self-employment'. On the other hand, paid employment is translated in very narrow terms, so that only those in formal and registered paid employment are likely to identify themselves as 'paid employees'. Arguably, it is out of this contrast between an overly expansive notion of self-employment and an extremely narrow notion of paid employment that the official statistics are created, thus suggesting that the informal economy consists of a teaming mass of family entrepreneurs.

A depiction of economic informality as self-employment is then consistently built upon by the 2006 ILFS (NBS, 2007), specifically through its modules on the informal economy, where information on informal business is sought (see NBS 2009b, p. 8, questions 26–32, which are designed for 'business owners only'). The focus is on understanding how businessmen in the informal economy set up their businesses, from where they operate and how often, and their sources of credit and training, but without much consideration of how many of these respondents can really be understood as businessmen in any meaningful way.

Concluding Remarks

This article has argued that in Tanzania, as elsewhere in Africa, self-employment is seen as the almost exclusive type of employment in the informal economy. The result of this, we argued, is that the importance of wage employment has been largely rendered invisible, in part, because wage labour is often overlooked and lumped together with self-employment and, in part, because the significant trend towards the sub-contracting of informal labour services rather than the direct production of commodities is poorly understood. The article showed, for example, that, while the *daladala* workers in urban Dar es Salaam are directly involved in the sale of urban transportation services, it is nevertheless questionable to classify them as self-employed, given the lack of control they have over the capital that they operate and the precarious nature of the terms of their 'employment'.

At the root of the invisibility of informal wage labour lies the fact that conventional categories of 'self-employment' and 'wage employment', on which labour force surveys rest, are inadequate for capturing the heterogeneity of employment relations found in the informal economy and the heterogeneity of relationships between capital and labour that mediate poor people's participation in the (informal) economy. Using the case of Tanzania, the article has highlighted the remarkable distance between the complexity of the employment relationships linking informal wage-workers to employers and the clear-cut categories used to frame questions for the 2006 ILFS (NBS, 2007). As field-based research repeatedly shows, the simple dichotomy between self-employment and wage employment does not work. More attention needs to be paid in survey analysis to the results of field-based qualitative research that does not only focus on differences in earnings, but also on the myriad of labour regimes that prevail in informal production.[5]

The analysis has further argued that the Swahili words chosen for asking workers whether they are in wage employment communicated a very narrow connotation of paid employment in the formal sector. By contrast, 'self-employment' is translated in extremely loose terms, arguably acting as a 'catch-all' category in the Tanzanian context. The ILFS statistical suggestion that only 0.7 per cent of workers in Tanzania's informal economy are wage workers, and the remaining are self-employed in one way or another, therefore, rests on disturbingly shaky grounds.

To address this major shortcoming requires in-depth research to understand the language and categories used by informal workers. Such research would be essential to design better surveys questions aimed at detecting and understanding the nature of informal wage labour, or the work of *kibarua*, a word ubiquitously referred to by informal wage workers in Tanzania to describe their status, yet a status that is strikingly at the margin of the 2006 ILFS. If the picture of informal economies presented by ILFS has indeed no analytical purchase on actual realities on the ground, as we would argue with reference to the Tanzania 2006 ILFS that efforts to identify labour categories that are intelligible to respondents should take priority.[6]

This article, then, sought to emphasise the urgent need to move away from the problem of 'misplaced aggregation' in the classification of labour regimes, which results from conflating into one catch-all category various forms of production and employment that are essentially different, not just as static entities but also in terms of their dynamic potential. It is indeed difficult to see how one can address the issue of the dynamic potential of the informal economy without taking explicit account of these diversities in production and their corresponding labour regimes. Coming to terms with these issues, however, would require a shift in focus towards the analysis of capital accumulation and its relation to the transformation of labour regimes in the so-called informal economy, an issue on which mainstream literature on economic informality is sorely silent and labour force surveys provide insufficient insights.

Acknowledgments

We would like to thank the editors and two anonymous reviewers for their comments on previous drafts of this article. The transcript of the interview quoted in the article and the ILFS 2006 questionnaires will be provided on request by the authors.

Notes

1. See Wuyts (2001, pp. 424–431) for a discussion of the underlying models of informal sector behaviour that underscore these two contrastive views.
2. In their own words: 'the distinction between formal and informal employment is fundamental to understanding the Tanzanian labour market' (Quinn & Teal, 2008, p. 4). In this survey, all income-earners 'were required to assign themselves to one of two mutually exclusive categories: wage-earners and the self-employed' (*ibid.*), to conclude that 'it is clear that informality is a key characteristic of the Tanzanian labour market: approximately two-thirds of interviewed respondents in 2004 reported being self-employed' (*ibid.*).
3. Importantly, more recently, taking into account criticisms of the narrowness of earlier definitions of informality, there has been greater awareness, at least conceptually, that 'employment in the informal sector' and 'informal employment' are concepts which refer to different aspects of the 'informalization' of employment and to different targets for policy-making' (ILO, 2013, p. 33).
4. UDA, Dar es Salaam public transport company, was operating about 20 buses in 2010. Unless otherwise stated, this section draws on Rizzo (2011, pp. 1183–1200).
5. For a discussion of how to overcome the invisibility of rural wage workers in surveys and fieldwork in rural areas, see Cramer, Johnston, Mueller, Oya & Sender (2014).
6. See Jerven (2013, pp. 114–115) for a useful discussion of the possible role for qualitative research in the collection of less 'poor numbers'.

References

Bardasi, E., Beegle, K., Dillon, A., & Serneels, P. (2010). *Do labor statistics depend on how and to whom the questions are asked? Results from a survey experiment in Tanzania* (Policy Research Working Paper no. 5192). Washington, DC: The World Bank.
Bernstein, H. (2010). *Class dynamics of agrarian change*. Toronto: Fernwood.
Breman, J. (1996). *Footloose labour: Working in India's informal economy*. Cambridge: Cambridge University Press.
Breman, J. (2003). *The labouring poor in India*. New Delhi: Oxford University Press.

Campanelli, P. C., Rothgeb, J. M., & Martin, E. A. (1989). The role of respondent comprehension and interviewer knowledge in CPS labor force classification. In *American Statistical Association, Proceedings of the Section on Survey Research Methods*. Alexandria, VA: American Statistical Association.

Cramer, C., Johnston, D., Mueller, B. Oya, C., & Sender, J. (2014). How to do (and how not to do) fieldwork on Fair Trade and rural poverty. *Canadian Journal of Development Studies, 35*(1), 170–185.

De Soto, H. (1989). *The other path*. New York: Harper and Row.

Fields, G. S. (2005). *A guide to multisector labor market models* (Social Protection Discussion Paper 0505). Washington, DC: World Bank.

Flora, M. S., & Komatsu, H. (2011). Gender and work in South Africa: What can time-use data reveal? *Feminist Economics, 17*(4), 33–66.

Fox, L., & Pimhidzai, O. (2013). *Different dreams, same bed: Collecting, using, and interpreting employment statistics in sub-Saharan Africa – the case of Uganda* (World Bank Policy Research Working Paper 6436). Washington, DC: World Bank.

Guyer, J. I., & Peters, P. (1987). Introduction in conceptualizing the household: Issues of theory and policy in Africa. *Development and Change, 18*(2), 197–214.

Harriss-White, B., & Gooptu, N. (2000). Mapping India's world of unorganized labour. In L. Panitch and C. Leys (Eds.), *The Socialist Register 2001* (pp. 89–118). London: Merlin Press.

Hart, K. (1973). Informal income opportunities and urban employment in Ghana. *Journal of Modern African Studies, 11*(1), 61–89.

International Labour Organization (ILO). (2013). *Measuring informality: A statistical manual on the informal sector and informal employment*. Geneva: ILO.

Jamal, V., & Weeks, J. (1993). *Africa misunderstood*. London: Macmillan.

Jerven, M. (2013). *Poor numbers. How we are misled by African development statistics and what to do about it*. Ithaca, NY, and London: Cornell University Press.

Jonssøn, J. B., & Bryceson, D. F. (2009). Rushing for gold: Mobility and small-scale mining in East Africa. *Development and Change, 40*(2), 249–279.

Jonssøn, J. B., & Fold, N. (2009). Handling uncertainty: Policy and organizational practices in Tanzania's small-scale gold mining sector. *Natural Resources Forum, 33*, 211–220.

LeBrun, O., & Gerry, C. (1974). Petty producers and capitalism. *Review of African Political Economy, 1*(2), 20–32.

Maliyamkono, T. L., & Bagachwa, M. S. D. (1990). *The second economy in Tanzania*. London: James Currey.

Martin, E., & Polivka, A. E. (1995). Diagnostics for redesigning survey questionnaires. *Public Opinion Quarterly, 59*, 547–567.

Myrdal, G. (1968). *Asian Drama* (vol. 3). London: Penguin.

NBS, Tanzania. (2007). *Integrated labour force survey (ILFS) 2006, analytical report*. Dar es Salaam: National Bureau of Statistics.

NBS. (2009a). *ILFS 2006, LFS form 1*. Dar es Salaam: National Bureau of Statistics.

NBS. (2009b). *ILFS 2006, LFS form 2*. Dar es Salaam: National Bureau of Statistics.

NBS. (2009c). *ILFS 2006, Dodoso la LFS 1*. Dar es Salaam: National Bureau of Statistics.

NBS. (2009d). *ILFS 2006, Dodoso la LFS 2*. Dar es Salaam: National Bureau of Statistics.

Oya, C. (2013). Rural wage employment in Africa: Methodological issues and emerging evidence. *Review of African Political Economy, 40*(136), 251–273.

Quinn, S., & Teal, F. (2008). *Private sector development and income dynamics: A panel study of the Tanzanian labour market* (CSAE Working Paper Series 2008–2009). Oxford: Centre for the Study of African Economies, University of Oxford.

Randall, S., & Coast, E. (2014). Poverty in African households: The limits of survey representations. *Journal of Development Studies*. doi:10.1080/00220388.2014.968136.

Rizzo, M. (2002). Being taken for a ride: Privatisation of the Dar es Salaam transport system 1983–1998. *Journal of Modern African Studies, 40*(1), 133–157.

Rizzo, M. (2011). 'Life is war': Informal transport workers and neoliberalism in Tanzania 1998–2009. *Development and Change, 42*(5), 1179–1205.

Rizzo. M. (2013). Informalisation and the end of trade unionism as we knew it? Dissenting remarks from a Tanzanian case study. *Review of African Political Economy, 40*(136), 290–308.

Rizzo, M., & Wuyts, M. (2014). *The invisibility of wage employment in statistics on the informal economy in Africa: Causes and consequences* (Working Paper 14/1). Dar es Salaam: REPOA.

Sarris, A. H., & Van den Brink, R. (1993). *Economic policy and household welfare during crisis and adjustment in Tanzania*. New York and London: New York University Press.

Standing, G. (2006). Labour markets. In D. A. Clark (Ed.), *The Elgar companion to development studies* (pp. 323–328). Cheltenham: Edward Elgar.

Tripp, A. M. (1997). *Changing the rules: The politics of liberalization and the urban informal economy in Tanzania*. Berkeley and London: University of California Press.

UWAMADAR, Konrad Adenauer Stiftung, & Development Dynamics International. (2003). *Working environment of Dar es Salaam commuting bus drivers and conductors* (Final report, November). Dar es Salaam: UWAMADAR, Konrad Adenauer Stiftung, & Development Dynamics International.

Wangwe, S. M. (1997). *Small-scale mining and mineral stone/gemstone cross border trade and marketing in Tanzania* (Discussion Paper). Dar es Salaam: Economic and Social Research Foundation.

Wells, J. (2001). Construction and capital formation in less developed economies: Unravelling the informal sector in an African city. *Construction Management and Economics, 19*(3), 267–274.

Wuyts, M. (2001). Informal economy, wage goods and accumulation under structural adjustment: Theoretical reflections based on the Tanzanian experience. *Cambridge Journal of Economics, 25*(3), 417–438.

Wuyts, M. (2011, December). *The working poor: A macro perspective.* Valedictory address as Professor of Applied Quantitative Economics, Institute of Social Studies, The Hague.

Poverty in African Households: the Limits of Survey and Census Representations

SARA RANDALL & ERNESTINA COAST

Department of Anthropology, University College London, UK, Department of Social Policy, London School of Economics, UK

ABSTRACT *African poverty statistics depend on household-level measurements from survey data, making the definition of household of critical importance. Detailed case studies from Tanzania and Burkina Faso explore (1) understandings of household membership and ambiguities, and (2) how well survey definitions capture households as economic units, and the implications for household size and responses to and mitigation of poverty. We develop an analytic framework of 'open' and 'closed' households. 'Open' households cope with poverty using flexibility, movement and extra-household networks, but are poorly represented by survey data. Closed households are likely to be better described by survey data.*

1. Introduction

Measuring poverty in Africa and understanding its determinants and dynamics have become increasingly important with the targets set by the Millennium Development Goals (MDG) and the post-MDG agenda. There are diverse approaches to studying poverty: it can be measured as relative or absolute (Kakwani & Silber, 2008) and conceptualised as multidimensional or fuzzy (Alkire & Roche, 2012; Qizilbash & Clark, 2005). Although analysis may be undertaken at individual, household, district, national or regional level, understanding determinants and outcomes of poverty has largely focused on the household level.

In countries with minimal state support of the poor and vulnerable, the domestic (that is, co-residential and usually familial) group is the primary source of support, socialisation and resources. Although the really poor often live outside households (homeless, street children), few data capture and measure their well-being, because not being attached to households makes them statistically invisible. Many researchers see poverty, particularly persistent poverty, as fundamentally a household-level problem (Barrett, Carter, & Little, 2006). Livelihood approaches construct the household as 'a site in which particularly intense social and economic interdependencies occur between a group of individuals' (Ellis, 2000, p. 18). Thus, data for poverty analyses need to be collected on households. This article focuses on difficulties and dilemmas in doing this where survey and census definitions of 'household' encompass a notion of a bounded, largely impermeable, unit. We examine the limits of the survey approach when such a unit is applied, the implications for variables such as household size, and the ramifications for data analysis and thus understanding poverty and its determinants. We consider what sorts of poverty-related issues may be missed or inaccurately represented because of the ways 'household' is defined in surveys.

Anthropological critiques of economic well-being using the notion of 'household' are well-established. Guyer and Peters demonstrated that an economic concept of household mapped poorly onto African social and economic organisation (Guyer, 1981; Guyer & Peters, 1987). They emphasised three key conceptual principles: (1) African households are not discretely bounded groups and different household members can draw on different personal networks to access resources; (2) households are not fixed forms but constantly evolving; and (3) households are differentiated along lines of gender and generation. These principles continue to apply today, and Guyer and Peters's perceptive analysis is an essential backdrop to this article. Despite these longstanding anthropological insights into the nature of African households, much quantitative data collection and many analyses choose not to take account of them.

2. Household-level poverty

Analyses, measures and understandings of the dynamics and determinants of household-level poverty reveal issues and contradictions about the ways in which the concept of household is used in the poverty literature.

2.1 Measures, Data and Reliability?

Disciplinary background (economics, anthropology, geography, and so forth) plays a key role in shaping data and analytic approaches to poverty (Howe et al., 2012). Studies of poverty outcomes, or those using poverty as an explanatory variable, exploit a wide variety of data sources; nationally representative household surveys – Household Budget Surveys (HBS), Living Standards Measurement Surveys (LSMS), Demographic and Health Surveys (DHS) – purpose-designed representative household surveys for geographic areas; and studies with total or partial coverage of small communities. National surveys use definitions of household developed by the local statistics office with membership based on criteria largely designed to avoid double counting (Randall, Coast, & Leone, 2011), although some surveys (notably HBS) allow absent members of the household and their assets to be included, whereas DHS excludes absentees. Purpose-designed surveys and small-scale studies often develop their own definitions of household, but many publications are unclear about what definition has been used and how they treat categories of people such as absent household heads, migrant men, polygamous unions, students and children at boarding school.

Data availability influences analyses of poverty dynamics over time (Booysen, Van Der Berg, Burger, Maltitz, & Rand, 2008; Owens, Sandefur, & Teal, 2011). Prospective, high-quality data remain rare in sub-Saharan Africa, reflecting the burdensome administrative and financial costs involved, although the production of longitudinal and panel data (Adato, Lund, & Mhlongo, 2007; INDEPTH, 2013; NBS, 2009), and analyses (Barrientos & Mase, 2012; Bigsten, Kebede, Shimeles, & Taddesse, 2003; Dercon & Krishnan, 2000; Emwanu, Hoogeveen, & Okiira Okwi, 2006; Hoddinott, 2006; Little, Stone, Mogues, Castro, & Negatu, 2006) is increasing. Small-scale studies of the mobility of households into and out of poverty have used longitudinal data to retrace households and their transformations through time with qualitative assessments of poverty (Mushongah & Scoones, 2012; Peters, 2006; Whitehead, 2006).

Household-level data collection has the practical advantage of generating data for several people from interviewing one person: this assumes that one person is capable of responding accurately for the whole unit – shown to be incorrect in Malawi (Fisher, Reimer, & Carr, 2010). Comparing data from livelihood portfolios with Participatory Rural Appraisal data, Jagger, Luckert, Banana, and Bahati (2012) concluded that the different methodologies tell very different stories and that relatively few findings are robust across data sets.

2.2 Quantitative, Qualitative or Mixed Methods?

Economic approaches to poverty require quantifiable measures; income, expenditure or an assets-based index (Howe et al., 2012) which largely ignore dimensions of poverty related to [lack of] social support, social networks, aspirations and social participation that are difficult to capture through standard household survey data (Thomas, 2008; White, 2002). Development practitioners working in small-scale rural communities have used relative wealth-ranking techniques (Grandin, 1988) for categorising households into poor and less poor, which integrate detailed preparatory group discussions to reveal local ideas about critical dimensions of poverty. Ranking of households can be compared with data from household surveys. Scoones criticises wealth indicators derived from survey data, both because they are chosen by the analyst and the survey instrument design limits potential analyses (Scoones, 1995). His household-ranking work in Zimbabwe uses local definitions of household which 'relate[s] to a spatially defined unit associated with a particular group of people' (p. 69, fn.3), including potentially absent household members, especially men aged 30–45 who would be excluded from many survey-defined households but are critical household members.

Mixed methods research on household poverty (Ellis & Freeman, 2004, Hargreaves et al., 2007, Mushongah & Scoones, 2012) finds that local perceptions are frequently grounded in social exclusion – those with limited social networks and support systems. Throughout Africa, 'wealth in people' remains important and a key dimension of poverty is an absence of access to extra-household networks. Guyer and Peter's conceptual principle (Guyer and Peters, 1987) that households are not discretely bounded remains valid despite rapid social change.

2.3 Household Size

Most quantitative analyses of survey data on household wealth and poverty include household size as an explanatory variable. White and Masset (2003) challenge such analyses on several grounds: household size over time is not stable; and whilst, in surveys, household size is typically measured cross-sectionally, economic (consumption and production) data tend to use a recall period. African seasonal labour migration, livelihood diversification and child mobility contribute to high levels of household membership mobility. We could find no African studies focussing on the stability of household membership, but in El Salvador only about half the households remained stable over a year, both losing and gaining members (Halliday, 2010).

2.4 Understanding African Household Poverty

Contradictory findings emerge from the many ways of measuring and interpreting African household poverty with attendant problems in pinpointing the nature of poverty and appropriate policy interventions. Analyses rarely explicitly consider the nature of the 'households' they are studying. This is particularly the case with secondary analyses of nationally representative surveys, which tend to find that increasing household size is associated with increasing poverty. The more anthropological and qualitative the research, the more likely it is that the researchers explain what they understand by household and use locally grounded definitions of household; frequently the definition of household membership is more inclusive than definitions used in national household surveys (Randall, Coast, & Dial, 2013; Randall, Coast, & Leone, 2011). Such studies generally find that larger households are less vulnerable (Scoones, 1995; Sharp & Devereux, 2004; Whitehead, 2006).

Whitehead's (2006) longitudinal study in rural Ghana describes: 'a virtuous circle between wealth and household labour supply and a vicious circle between poverty and small household size and poverty traps existed so that those with too little labour and too little wealth engaged in strategies which entrenched them in poverty' (p. 278). Whitehead's anthropological approach, taking emically defined households and demonstrating the wealth and security that people bring, contrasts with definitions used in nationally representative surveys which split large compounds into small constituent nuclear families or husband–wife units, thus losing sight of collective responsibilities and solidarities.

Extra-household social relationships and networks are critical in affecting vulnerability to experiencing poverty and the ability to cope with crises: such issues are missed by measures of household income, expenditure or assets, or by research which focuses on the household as a bounded and discrete unit. 'Wealth in people' emerges repeatedly from anthropological studies, and from discussions of the nature of wealth and poverty in wealth ranking exercises, alongside the critical importance of extra-household social networks and relations for not being categorised amongst the poor (Barrett et al., 2006; Little et al., 2006; Whitehead, 2006). People who have had social connections excised through death or migration are regularly highlighted as being poor: widows; the divorced; orphans; and elderly people whose families live elsewhere (Ellis & Freeman, 2004)

3. Aims

This article investigates what sorts of poverty-related issues may be either missed or inaccurately measured because of the ways 'household' is defined in nationally representative household surveys. Household definitions usually preclude individuals belonging to two or more households. They are critical in constructing 'household size' and may limit analyses of flexible household membership. We examine potential relationships between household size, flexible household membership and poverty and how these differ between local understanding of the basic domestic and economic unit and that generated by a nationally representative survey.

3.1 Data and Methods

This article uses two sources of data collected within a multi-country, mixed methods research project. A review of the definitions used in African surveys and censuses since independence examines changing constructions of the survey household over time and countries (Randall et al, 2013), and informs our analyses of in-depth interviews with purposively selected 'households' in Tanzania and Burkina Faso. In each country around 50 in-depth interviews[1] focused on emic perceptions of their household membership. We did not impose a definition of household but used local words for residential or domestic group along with the words or phrases used to translate 'household' in national surveys to explore who were considered to be members of the residential group and how this mapped onto economic solidarity or independence. Because many census and survey definitions emphasise eating from the same pot, we also investigated cooking and eating arrangements. Our discussions collected data on relationships between different members, and thus identified absent husbands/wives/ sons/daughters and so forth. In doing so, we explored why absent people might be included or excluded from the group, the support links within and outside the household, evidence for membership of several households or transitory status and ambiguous household membership. In Burkina Faso we interviewed 12 households in each of an unplanned poor settlement and a well-established district within the capital city, a small town and a rural area.[2] Tanzanian households were selected from two rural areas and a planned and unplanned district in Dar Es Salaam. Our case study areas in each country were selected because prior knowledge suggested they might include situations which were poorly represented by household surveys and to capture some linguistic and social organisation diversity. They are not statistically representative – they provide indications of the limitations for understanding poverty and responses to poverty through household survey data, and point to directions for further research.

In order to examine the parameters of standardised surveys we post-hoc applied the DHS definition[3] (identical in both countries) to our self-defined case study households. We chose to apply the standard, and relatively simplistic, DHS definition because internationally recognised DHS data are widely used by secondary analysts, in part because of their easy availability and their comparability and DHS data are one data source for indicators for the Millennium Development Goals.

3.2 Analytic Framework

We develop the analytic concept of 'closed' and 'open' households. We assume that in all societies the majority of people feel obliged to provide support for their own children. In much of Africa there is a strong obligation to contribute also to the family of origin – elderly parents and adult siblings – despite evidence that, faced with increasing demands, monetisation, costs of schooling and demands for material goods, the pressures to invest in the younger generation nuclear family are increasing (Aboderin, 2004; Roth, 2010). We describe as 'closed' a household whose members invest resources and support those in their nuclear families of descent and origin and receive or ask for help only from these same people; such households generally have fairly stable membership without a constant flux of people with different rights, expectations and obligations. Households who offer, give, receive or ask for help or support from a wider range of kin or others we classify as 'open'. It is often difficult to establish membership of these open households in a survey because of frequent movements and reconfigurations as different individuals exploit different social networks and obligations to try to generate some security in stressful economic contexts.

4. Results

Using case study households, we illustrate the concepts of openness and closedness, the reasons behind and ways in which closedness/openness are rationalised and explained, and then consider the ways in which these interact with household definitions and the implications for household size and resources in surveys and practice.

4.1 Open Households

Many case-study households had very flexible membership, with multiple support links (both providing and receiving support); deciding who should be counted as a household member and where household boundaries lay was problematic. The openness of Tanzanian rural households was partly a consequence of the villagisation process which, in our study sites, separated residential areas from key production areas (whether fields, water bodies or pastures), thus enforcing mobility.

4.1.1 Flexible urban households. A key asset of urban households was provision of accommodation for incomers. In both Dar Es Salaam and Ouagadougou there were large heterogeneous households in compounds, with flows of individuals in and out, often circulating from rural areas, bringing rural produce, working in the city and then returning.

4.1.1.1 Case study 1: Ouagadougou planned district. Around 20 related (children, grandchildren, nephews/nieces) people (aged 11–60) lived in seven rooms around the compound inherited by Aicha and Fadi, the two widows of the former owner. No one had full-time employment – many did petty commerce or worked as servants when they could. Two cooking pots belonged to Aicha and Fadi, but they hadn't cooked and eaten together for two weeks because they lacked resources. Those with money each day would go and buy street food and might share with those who didn't. The compound provided free accommodation for new arrivals from the village – residents would borrow (and repay) from other residents if they needed money. There were no identifiable 'households', and yet the 20 people did not form a single economic unit. In a survey this compound would be treated as many single- or two-person households – yet there was far more kinship-based solidarity between the individuals than this implies. Although Aicha, Fadi and their sons were always present, other residents changed frequently.

4.1.1.2 Case study 2: Dar Es Salaam planned district. An impoverished widow, Grace, lived in squalor with her four adolescent children on a valuable plot of land. Two of her husband's nephews had lived with her for many years – she fed them when she had food and money, they contributed when they had money. Three other nephews lived, rent-free, in a separate house on the plot. They rarely ate with Grace's family and occasionally gave money, but their presence contributed to her strength in fighting a family battle over ownership of the plot. These nephews provided legitimacy and signified support for her greatest asset – yet they were not members of her household in terms of rights and obligations in the way that her children or the long resident nephews were.

In both cases plot ownership meant that economically insecure people offered free accommodation to others. The group benefitted from the increased probability that someone would have resources for food or other needs. All were very poor and frequently went hungry, although for both 'households' the plot was an asset which allowed the 'household' to be open to flows of members and the benefits this brought.

4.1.2 Schooling and open urban households. Schooling is a key pathway of developing human capital and moving out of poverty for policy-makers and African families alike. Managing access to education has complex interactions with household level measurements of poverty.

In all urban contexts, schooling is a constant source of mobility and often depends on 'open' households. To access good schools or schools with places, children move between households on a weekly or longer-term basis. Sometimes the family of origin pays for support, others depend on (or exploit) richer relatives to support their children. Resources and children flow in all directions; these movements may develop and consolidate networks or exploit relationships in order to improve future prospects through education. The students' economic relationship with the household where they stay may differ from those of more permanent resident children. Students usually come accompanied by some resources and their absence from their household of origin does not necessarily signify that they are no longer an economic drain. In small-town Burkina numerous education related strategies were observed: households received rural kin to attend secondary school, some paid for and maintained, others supported by their host families; primary school children were sent to live with kin in villages where there was less competition for school places; older children were sent to Ouagadougou to live with poor but well-placed relatives and received (often ill-afforded) resources from their households of origin; others were strategically placed with better-off relatives who supported their rural cousins.

4.1.2.1   Case study 3: education mobility in Dar Es Salaam.   A nuclear family with two daughters live in one rented room without electricity. The clever older daughter, Mabel, spends weekdays at her aunt's, a teacher, who lives in a house with electricity where Mabel can do her homework. This strategic placement countered some of the effects of poverty. This family was not participating in the 'people are wealth' reciprocal networks: they were closed to resources and people going in and out with the exception of this one, highly strategic link. Her parents saw Mabel as part of their household, but she spent most of her time at her aunt's.

In such, frequently encountered, cases, household membership and, thus, size is difficult to determine. It would be hard to identify a single household where such children belong and where they would be declared in a survey, although clearer in a de facto census. Parents bear some costs and relatives bear others. Such movements of children both alleviate poverty and develop networks of obligation.

This leads us to reflect on what the household size captured by a survey actually means. Individuals who might be recorded as being household members have some rights and obligations in that domestic unit, but many have rights and obligations (often rather different ones) in a number of other households too.

In both capital cities plot-owning households were often forced into openness because of their accommodation resource, whereas those who rented rooms in the same areas were more likely to be closed because of space constraints. The latter were often attached to another rural household, undermining the idea of the urban household as a self-contained economic unit.

4.2 Closed Households

African traditional responses to uncertainty have developed around openness and flexibility of domestic unit organisation (Guyer, 1981, 2004), strategies that continue to be used to resolve short-term problems and develop long-term securities. But is household flexibility a ubiquitous response to poverty or potential poverty? Is there evidence that households are closed because they are poor, poor because they are closed, or are closed households very heterogeneous?

4.2.1 Closed because 'poor in people'. A number of households, mainly in informal districts in the capital cities, epitomised the idea that lack of networks engenders closedness and is a major dimension of poverty.

4.2.1.1 Case study 4: Dar Es Salaam. Mariame works as a night guard and lives in a rented hovel with her four daughters and a granddaughter. They all live off her guard's wages, and one clever daughter couldn't continue her education because they couldn't afford it. When asked why they didn't request relatives to help out, she replied that they had none who were in a better position.

4.2.1.2 Case study 5: informal district, Ouagadougou. Widowed Aichatou lives in a tiny house with her daughter Balkiss (20) who stopped lycée because of poverty. They came here when her husband's brothers sold her husband's plot when he died. Mamadou (aged 22) eats, washes and does his laundry in his mother Aichatou's house, but sleeps nearby with a friend – it is inappropriate for a man of his age to share a room with his mother and sister. Mamadou gets occasional work mending motorbikes and Aichatou sells firewood. They have few material goods, no one they can ask for help in an emergency and no one to whom they offer help. Aichatou cried during the interview; her dead husband's brothers never help.

Many closed and impoverished case study households are female-headed, although not all are devoid of potential male labour. Often there are kin who, in theory, could provide support, but either those kin are equally destitute or the links cannot be mobilised. Once a household has inadequate resources for food, they are then unable to participate in the networks of exchange and openness that could provide a safety net.

4.2.2 Deciding to be closed despite poverty.
4.2.2.1 Case study 6: planned area Ouagadougou. Maurice is an unsuccessful mechanic who lives with his wife and four children (aged 8–22) in a small house on a large bare plot which they own. Another house on the plot is let out and provides some income, but the plot has no water or electricity. Maurice struggles to send his younger three children to school, even with the assistance of a European sponsor, and although he has rich relatives he is too ashamed to ask for help.

Whereas others might exploit their large plot by receiving relatives, this household is very self-contained, neither receiving nor participating in kin networks.

4.2.3 Strategically closed households. Our study included some wealthier households. Although they were generous in terms of helping others, they did not do this through receiving large numbers of people, nor through household members moving around. There was a sense of control over movements in and out of the household which contributed to financial security. These households were not forced to be closed – and in fact they were only closed with respect to movement of people: they all contributed resources to poorer relatives and two were notable for general local good works. We can hypothesise that such strategically closed households are attempting to develop a virtuous spiral of poverty-prevention. By controlling movements in and out of the household, they were avoiding the potential negative consequences of unwanted additional household members and their needs.

Having established our analytic categories of open and closed households, present in both countries and in all contexts, we next consider the implications of household survey data for household size calculations, and potential associations between household size and poverty.

4.3 Household Size and Resources in Surveys and Practice

Household size is important, both as an explanatory variable but also, through income, expenditure or assets indices (Johnston & Abreu, 2013), because of the assumption that household members share access to resources and have comparable poverty or wealth.

In household survey data collection, large co-resident extended families are usually separated into smaller nuclei because household definitions depend on eating together. Yet, in both urban and rural Burkina and Tanzania, patterns of cooking and eating are often a matter of tradition – wives have always cooked separately – or practical convenience with little to do with access to household resources.

Particularly in rural areas, the self-defined households we studied were substantially bigger than those which would have been recorded in the DHS and most nationally representative surveys. This was very marked amongst the rural Maasai population in Tanzania where, for example, a 25-person polygamous household (a man, four wives and many children) would become four DHS households of which three would be female-headed. Ironically, such an approach means that bigger households may appear poorer because, by disaggregating down to a woman and her children, household size is largely determined by numbers of children; the largest households would have many dependent children, little adult labour and few assets. Furthermore self-defined units usually included a number of absent individuals: often young men away on labour migration who would be excluded from DHS surveys, yet who provided important remittances into the household. There were many examples, in both Tanzania and Burkina Faso, where the survey definition of household misrepresented household size and the group who were mutually supportive and pooled both resources and strains.

In south-west Burkina Faso, polygamously married wives often have separate cooking pots and, according to a DHS definition, should be treated as separate households with at least one being female-headed. However, all wives work the same fields and the harvest is stored in the same granary from which each wife gets her grain allocation; when the grain runs out it runs out for all. Resources or assets (rarely more than a radio or a bicycle) usually belong to the man, and thus the wife and children associated with him would appear to be a more asset-rich household. Women manage their own income from brewing beer, which husbands know about, but not how much, nor can they access this money (except through borrowing and repayment). To some extent these women-centred units are economically independent, but to a greater extent they are interdependent, because the man controls the household fields which provide the staple food, everyone works in the fields and the father pays children's school fees. Furthermore there is considerable co-wife collaboration over brewing and cooking. In terms of mutual support and solidarity, the larger emically defined household which contains several cooking pots and much cooperation and sharing of both resources and poverty is the key economic unit which generates wealth or experiences poverty.

Most 'open' domestic units included nieces, nephews, grandchildren, as well as dependent aunts or uncles. Accepting responsibility for these relatives adds more dependents and more mouths to feed; if the household is split in surveys according to women's cooking pots, it is not always clear where such dependents should or would be allocated. In both countries dependents from outside the nuclear family usually had some access to wider household resources and not just those from the woman with whom they ate. When these nieces/nephews/grandchildren grow up, the investment in them may be repaid through the wider network of obligations, thus exemplifying wealth in people, likely to be missed or misrepresented in cross-sectional household surveys.

4.3.1 Case study 7: cooking arrangements and household boundaries. One large (21-person) compound in a small Burkinabe town contained an old couple with married and unmarried children and grandchildren. People ate from three different cooking pots, and the old man, as household head, was given food from all three pots every night – as a symbolic gesture that they were one unit. They had one granary and all worked together on the household fields. Each son had occasional income from casual labour which was used for his wife and children. All the women occasionally brewed beer and the daughters-in-law sent part of their brewing income to their own mothers elsewhere. Thus, in some ways each small nuclear family was an economic unit, but in more important ways this was one large interdependent unit.

Despite its size, this was a closed unit. Apart from help sent by daughters-in-law to their mothers, household members asked no one outside the household for financial help or support, but neither did they give it: their solidarity and security (they were poor but not destitute) came from within the compound. Such support would be lost in a survey, where three different households would be recorded: one, which would look extremely vulnerable with an old couple in their late 60s; and two unmarried daughters (one disabled), each with a young daughter. However, this apparently vulnerable unit received security from co-resident sons, their wives and older children.

4.3.2 Rural household size and poverty. Sometimes the openness of households combined with social responsibility of the household head generates economic stress.

4.3.2.1 Case study 8: accumulating dependents. Martin is 38 and lives in a small Burkinabe town. He is the household head and responsible for 28 people. His wife cooks for everyone. Martin describes himself as unlucky – his grandparents and his father all died young, and as the oldest son he inherited their obligations: he supports his mother (58); his father's unmarried brother (70); a grand-father's wife (75); and his father's divorced sister (45). He inherited responsibility for two unmarried female cousins with two and three children respectively. He has four younger brothers and three sisters, one of whom is widowed with two young children. Two of his brothers are married, one with two young children, the other with a pregnant wife, but their only source of income is the family fields, so they too depend on Martin. He has two children with his current wife. Household members work on the family fields, and some of the women brew beer. Martin works part-time as a butcher and had recently installed electricity into his personal house.

Martin's large household and numerous dependents are stressful but manageable. Without all these dependents his small nuclear family would be well-off, but many of his current dependents would be destitute. By maintaining this open household, not only is he reducing the net poverty in the community, he is also building up considerable moral credit. By investing in 'wealth in people' it is likely that, as his siblings and children become more productive and older people die, he could become very economically secure. Urban open households often included more dependents than they could really cope with, but by doing so kept large numbers of people out of extreme poverty.

Large (emically defined) households can reduce poverty because they permit diversification – as in Maasailand, where some adults cultivate, others herd cattle or work as migrant labourers. The security provided by such large domestic units allows them to be more open to absorbing the less fortunate. Despite an extremely strong patrilineal Maasai ideology, for whom the best translation of household, *olmarei,* is a patrilineal descent group, in three out of eight case study households, a married daughter was living in her father's *olmarei,* either with her husband or whilst her husband was away on migration. One such household head said 'they aren't really our *olmarei* but he is too poor to support her properly'. Another specifically noted that this was a temporary measure until her husband had enough resources to go it alone. The value of 'wealth in people' here is symbolised by breaking the residential rules. The impoverished woman and her husband become less poor because they are absorbed into the larger household.

Dividing social groups into the smallest constituent parts (as with many survey households) under-mines understanding the ways poverty is managed through temporal dynamism of household econom-ics and extra-household support provided by kin.

4.3.2.2 Case study 9: in the throes of accumulating dependents. Komo is a fairly poor newly married Maasai man. His mother (60) and four younger brothers (aged 13–30) live with him, although two brothers are currently working in Kenya. Komo encourages them to invest their earnings in livestock. Komo's drunkard older brother is in a separate household, but Komo is already taking care of him and his family: 'my oxen work his field; his small children get milk from my cows; his older children get grain from my granary; his wife milks my goats'. He gave his brother a field and the village gave his brother's wife a field. Komo anticipates that 'I will have to take care of them completely when my brother deserts.'

In this transitional phase whereby two smaller households are merging, one is already almost totally dependent on the other, with poverty being managed by absorption and openness. Even when they merge, the married women will continue to have their own house and cooking pot; most surveys would treat them as separate households.

Applying any concept of household in rural Rufiji, Tanzania, is difficult (Lockwood, 1998). Diverse economic activities include fishing and farming which take place several miles from the village. Some household members (often an elderly couple) live by the fields all year round and others live in the village, with much movement between the two, sharing labour and harvest. Any survey would split such households because people are residentially separate. Within each emic household most married women had their own cooking pot and house, which would lead to further fragmentation of survey households. The 17 households interviewed in Rufiji would be at least 31 households using a DHS definition. Discussions around relationships between households demonstrated the role of openness in addressing crises. Hunger or acute poverty leads to temporary merging of households. One said 'we each have our own *kaya* [household]. Maybe when we are hungry we eat together: this can go on for months – one *kaya* will cook one day and one the next.' Rufiji adults had well-developed under-standings about relatives they would cook and share food with regularly, sometimes, or very rarely. Children circulated much more freely; children in a poor, food-deficient household were usually fed by other households.

In rural areas and small towns two key issues need to be disentangled in order to understand the relationships between poverty and household size. Firstly, a major way of resolving poverty is for the poor to be either temporarily or permanently absorbed into a larger, wealthier unit, or to temporarily pool resources with another household. This makes wealthy households appear both bigger and poorer, whereas their very wealth and security enabled them to absorb dependents in the first place: the strategy for coping with poverty (pooling resources and problems) becomes an indicator of that poverty. Secondly, such strategies will rarely become apparent in survey data because survey house-hold definitions split households into minimal cooking and sleeping units, which actually break ups the real units of social solidarity so that they cannot be observed.

4.3.3 Urban household size and poverty. In urban areas it is harder to say whether big households contribute to resolving poverty, because, since living space is both a key resource and constraint, the peopling of this space differs from rural areas. In both Dar Es Salaam and Ouagadougou most emic households were similar in size to DHS-defined households, with the exception that several also included absent household members. In many open urban households those who were received into apparently well-off households would have been poor or destitute otherwise; often, but not exclu-sively, unmarried daughters and their offspring, and orphaned or migrant nieces and nephews.

5. Discussion

Our detailed analyses of these case study households show the ways in which African households are (mis)represented in survey data. We extend the ways of thinking about collecting data from, and about, households, by developing complementary analytic categories: openness and closedness. These analyses have implications for understanding what household-level poverty statistics derived from surveys might be saying.

Survey definitions of a household often refer to those who eat together (Randall et al., 2013) assuming that this indicates an economic unit of consumption. However, eating together frequently does not constitute the key economic unit but is more a consequence of practicality or cooking traditions. Furthermore, it is often practically difficult to identify who does eat together, and urban poverty often entails street food rather than cooking.

Most nationally representative surveys require individuals to be members of one household only, but many people contribute to and/or take resources from two or more households, with temporally varied movements between households an integral part of poverty alleviation or poverty avoidance strategies. Temporary migrants are often excluded from surveys either as household members or contributors through remittances (Cramer, Johnston, Mueller, Oya, & Sender, 2014). Education is a major contribution to spatial mobility, manipulation of living arrangements and obtaining resources from multiple sources. Survey instruments and definitions that split households into geographical co-resident parts will make many look poorer and smaller than they actually are. Whereas such structural influences are geographically variable, national survey data may also mask local specificities.

Household 'openness' is a key dimension of short-term poverty avoidance and a long-term strategy for insuring against poverty by building and consolidating networks of obligation. 'Wealth in people' remains critically important in both urban and rural settings. Successful people attract others; coping, would-be medium-sized, households may become large households with many dependents because of their (relative) economic success. Yet, by becoming larger and absorbing impoverished kin, any relationship between household size/structure and economic security becomes difficult to disentangle. Contemporary investment in 'wealth in people' may cause temporary hardship, but has potential long-term benefits because of reciprocal obligations generated.

The idea of 'open households' should not be seen as a new definition and a burdensome tool to add to the complexities of data collection in African surveys. It is an interpretative category encompassing households for whom poverty indicators may be less reliable or restricted in the dimensions they capture. The challenge is therefore to find simple additional questions which could be added to surveys which would allow openness (or some dimensions of it) to be identified and explored in flexible ways, whilst retaining comparability. Our data collection experience suggests this should not be too challenging: most respondents clearly distinguished between occasional movements of resources to individuals who were not seen as members of their household (inter-household transfers) and people who were household members – albeit sometimes on rather different terms or at different times and who were often also part of another household. Openness thus does not constitute 'anyone' who contributes or benefits, but is about individuals who are generally perceived to have some claim to membership.

Much of African life remains inherently unpredictable (Johnson-Hanks, 2005): the AIDS epidemic has transformed many previously wealthy lineages; structural adjustment, civil service cuts and high graduate unemployment mean that education is no longer a guaranteed pathway to social success and security. In this context, strategies focusing on building networks of obligations and support remain valuable counteractions to poverty but are difficult to capture using household surveys.

6. Study Limitations

Our research design, with a limited number of purposively selected households, uses a small number of cases drawn from poor communities, and excludes wealthier urban households, who may have very different strategies where being closed may be the pathway to economic success. However, the educated middle classes remain a small minority in most African countries, and our analysis is strengthened by its comparative approach and the diversity of contexts which reinforce the generalisability of our findings.

We limited our post-hoc application of survey definitions to the DHS because the data are open access, widely used and frequently include household-level poverty indicators through quintiles and assets indices, either as explanatory variables or as the dependent variable (Booysen et al., 2008; Ickowitz, 2012; Masset & White, 2004; Sahn & Stifel, 2000).

7. Conclusions

The implications of household definition for analyses of household survey data as they relate to poverty are poorly understood and rarely studied (Beaman & Dillon, 2010; Guyer, 2004; Hosegood &

Timaeus, 2006; White & Masset, 2003), despite long-established anthropological challenges to the notion of bounded, stable economic units. This lacuna persists despite a large volume of social science research that includes household-related indicators in its analyses. Our approach develops an interpretively grounded understanding of the ways in which households and individuals try to reduce, confront or avoid poverty, highlighting implications for the ways in which household survey data are analysed and interpreted.

For reasons of comparability, the definition of the household in many national surveys follows census operationalisation even though the rationales for the two exercises differ (Randall et al., 2011) with the census about complete enumeration and avoiding double counting. Surveys aim to provide micro-level information about individuals, their relationships with others and the determinants of outcomes, and our evidence shows that many adults and children mitigate and prevent poverty through membership or rights in resources of two or more households and therefore probably should be double (or multiple) counted in a survey. This approach has been successfully implemented in limited South African longitudinal data collection and analyses (Hosegood & Timaeus, 2006).

There are two related but different issues raised by our analyses: first, whether a minimalist survey household definition represents living arrangements well, and is an appropriate unit for measuring poverty; and second, that of closed and open households. Although survey household definitions represent closed households quite well, with the exception of those who are polygamous or with multiple cooking pots, these definitions will rarely be an adequate unit for analysing poverty levels and determinants for open households. This is because open households have fluid membership and ground their approaches to mitigating poverty through a combination of immediate and longer-term strategies which often involve developing and maintaining a 'wealth in people' approach which builds on and consolidates wide networks of obligations and support. They draw and receive not only monetary support but also social and political capabilities from beyond the survey household.

Both these issues have implications for household size as both a dependent and independent variable in analyses. Survey household definitions can underestimate household size if a household is understood to be the local economic production and support unit. Cross-sectional survey household definitions also make assumptions about the fixed nature of household size that are untenable in the case of open households, or from the perspective of individuals with both obligations to and benefits from two or more households. Contradictory findings in poverty research may be a consequence of how the survey household is defined and thus how data are collected and configured. We suggest that some analytic findings might be implausible – for example, that larger households are poorer – and emerge simply as a function of the bounded approach to household definitions.

Cross-sectional data collection remains the most practical and cost-efficient way of trying to understand the nature and determinants of poverty, yet the household in such surveys is a snapshot of the stock of people, their attributes and resources, with flows in and out of this stock at various temporal and spatial scales inevitably only partially captured and also subject to respondents' interpretations of questions (Guyer, 2004). Using a minimalist definition of household where individuals can be attributed to one and one only contributes to further analytical misrepresentations.

Closed households seem to take three forms which (excepting those with multiple hearths) are all likely to be well represented in cross-sectional surveys, both in terms of members and the delimitation of assets upon which they depend. Closed households, with no kin to call upon through bad luck or previous poor management of developing links and obligations, have been observed to struggle to emerge from poverty because of their limited social networks (Ellis & Freeman, 2004; Hargreaves et al., 2007; Hulme, 2004; Little et al., 2006; Peters, 2006; Whitehead, 2006). Others may not seek help because of pride or shame, conflict or tension. Equally, there may be successful households who do not support less fortunate kin because they want to invest their resources into their own children in order to maximise further success; these may also be more likely to control fertility.

Open households are poorly represented by survey data and, because their openness is integrally related to poverty and poverty avoidance, household poverty statistics are based on data which do not and cannot represent the nature and extent of poverty and the creative ways in which people address it. For open households 'wealth in people' remains a powerful social value; supporting vulnerable kin is an obligation which may bring potential future benefits; strong social networks with multiple ties of obligation and support offer good insurance against unknown future perils and the predictable problems of old age and potential incapacity. Open and closed households were found in all contexts in both countries.

How can data be collected about these extra-household links and flows in a cross-sectional household survey whilst retaining coherent and manageable data collection tools? A first step requires a rethinking about who is ex/included in the household and types of household membership. Any such questions will themselves bring potentially arbitrary decisions about, for example, a timeframe within which to ask questions about co-residence/dual-residence and receipt/sending of resources to people beyond the co-residential household. One relatively straightforward way to improve survey household data is through improved relationship data collection. Most large-scale surveys record relationships to the household head, thus assuming that individuals are part of that household through their relationship with the head – shown by many of our case studies to be incorrect. By replacing this relatively arbitrary description of household structure with a household relationship grid (where the relationship – whether kin or not – of each person to every other household member is recorded), data collection is likely to improve who is recorded. This may be unfeasible in contexts with very large households, in which case an approach which focuses on identifying smaller family nuclei within large households, prioritising relationships between married couples and parents and children is practically easy, as done in the 1976 Senegal census (BNR, 1976). This approach allows a much better understanding of small subgroups within large households, and does not relate everyone to a household head but to their closest support and facilitates more detailed probes about potentially omitted persons. In the fieldwork reported here, it identified a number of 'forgotten' household members.

A further advance would be to record the type of household membership and evidence of membership of other households. Such suggestions, whilst straightforward, would require a fundamental shift in the design and execution of internationally standardised household surveys, including the training and support of survey interviewers (Randall, Coast, Compaore, & Antoine, 2013). Designing longitudinal data collection of multiple household membership in South Africa (Hosegood & Timaeus, 2006) was achieved through discussion by the fieldworker with the respondents in order to identify whether an individual was a *full member* (considered by the household and themselves to be a member) or an *affiliated member* (not considered to be a member of the household but to reside with it and be involved intimately with it). Such types of questions could be included in survey instruments in order to identify meaningful categories of household membership. Data collected as outlined above would allow different configurations and degrees of openness to be analysed, ranging from households with a single person with multiple household membership to those with many. Further sophistications (recording patterns of residence) could be added, but would add significantly to costs and complexity.

Much of the debate about how to study and measure poverty, its influences and its outcomes is located in contrasting epistemological and disciplinary traditions that, on the surface, have little in common (for example, economics vs anthropology [Guyer, 2004]). Such contrasting disciplinary perspectives, and languages, can make it difficult to open up conversations about the ways in which survey data can (and should) contribute to understanding poverty and its trajectories. We suggest that it is better to explicitly acknowledge the consequences of methodological assumptions, rather than to ignore the issue that people and the links between them are an integral part of coping with poverty, uncertainty and insecurity in modern rural and urban Africa.

There are two ways forward from this research. It is probably unrealistic to expect large international surveys like the DHS to change their definitions and ways of recording households. However, it is perfectly reasonable to expect analysts of such data to articulate much more clearly in their analyses and publications the limitations of the definitions used in data collection and to reflect on the implications of these limitations – and in particular the validity of their analyses for different parts of the population. More triangulation with work produced by other disciplines on study populations would be a step forward, as would a frank reflection on the limitations and biases of specific approaches.

Surveys that are not constrained by being part of international comparative series could experiment with different approaches to recording household membership and wider definitions of household, as outlined above. This would allow a differentiation of closed and open households and an exploration of the implications of different degrees of openness via the economic measures being used. It is unfortunate that the very heterogeneity of openness and difficulties in identifying and collecting data on the myriad manifestations, time frames and transactions mean that quantitative data that truly reflect these diverse strategies for confronting and managing poverty are probably unachievable – and we may have to accept that some things are real and important but ultimately unmeasurable.

Acknowledgements

The research in Tanzania was funded by the ESRC (UK) (RES-175-25-0012) under the Survey Design and Measurement Initiative. The research in Burkina Faso was financed by ESRC (UK) under the collaborative ESRC-ANR research programme (RES 062-33-0007). We would like to thank the entire ANR-ESRC research team, Philippe Antoine, Eva Lelièvre, Fatou-Binetou Dial, Sadio Ba Gning, Stephen Wandera, Valerie Golaz, Alex Fanghanel, Natacha Compaore and Bilampoa Gnoumou, for ideas and inputs during the project workshops. Most of the interviews in Burkina Faso were conducted jointly with Natacha or Bilampoa. We would also like to thank Beth Bishop, Ernest Ndakaru, Marie-Annick Moreau, Deograsias Mushi, George Mkude, Eugenia Mpayo, Anthony Kija and, Musa Magafuli for their assistance in data collection in Tanzania.

Notes

1. Anonymised transcripts of the household grids have been deposited in the ESRC data archive and can be found at http://reshare.ukdataservice.ac.uk/ Tanzanian data: record id: 850668 and Burkinabe data: record id: 850730.
2. See http://www.householdsurvey.info for details of methodology.
3. As described in http://www.measuredhs.com/pubs/pdf/DHSM1/DHS6_Interviewer_Manual_29May2012.doc.

References

Aboderin, I. (2004). Decline in material family support for older people in urban Ghana, Africa: Understanding processes and causes of change. *The Journals of Gerontology Series B: Psychological Sciences and Social Sciences, 59*(3), S128–S137. doi:10.1093/geronb/59.3.S128

Adato, M., Lund, F., & Mhlongo, P. (2007). Methodological innovations in research on the dynamics of poverty: A Longitudinal study in KwaZulu-Natal, South Africa. *World Development, 35*(2), 247–263.

Alkire, S., & Roche, J. M. (2012). Beyond headcount: The Alkire–Foster approach to multidimensional child poverty measurement. In I. Ortiz, L. M. Daniels, & S. Engilbertsdottir (Eds.), *Child poverty and inequality: New perspectives* (pp. 18–22). New York: UNICEF.

Barrett, C. B., Carter, M. R., & Little, P. D. (2006). Understanding and reducing persistent poverty in Africa: Introduction to a special issue. *The Journal of Development Studies, 42*(2), 167–177. doi:10.1080/00220380500404587

Barrientos, A., & Mase, J. (2012). Poverty transitions among older households in Brazil and South Africa. *Eur J Dev Res, 24*(4), 570–588.

Beaman, L., & Dillon, A. (2010). *Do household definitions matter in survey design? Results from a randomized survey experiment in Mali* (IFPRI Discussion Paper, 01009, 32). Washington, D.C.: International Food Policy Research Institute.

Bigsten, A., Kebede, B., Shimeles, A., & Taddesse, M. (2003). Growth and poverty reduction in Ethiopa: Evidence from household panel surveys. *World Development, 31*(1), 87–106.

BNR. (1976). *Instructions aux agents recenseurs*. Dakar: Bureau National du Resensement, République du Sénégal.

Booysen, F., Van Der Berg, S., Burger, R., van Maltitz, M, & de Rand, G. (2008). Using an asset index to assess trends in poverty in seven sub-Saharan African countries. *World Development, 36*(6), 1113–1130.

Cramer, C., Johnston, D., Mueller, B., Oya, C., & Sender, J. (2014). How to do (and how not to do) fieldwork on Fair Trade and rural poverty. *Canadian Journal of Development Studies/Revue canadienne d'études du développement, 35*(1), 170–185.

Dercon, S., & Krishnan, P. (2000). Vulnerability, seasonality and poverty in Ethiopia. *The Journal of Development Studies, 36*(6), 25–53. doi:10.1080/00220380008422653

Ellis, F. (2000). *Rural livelihoods and diversity in developing countries*. Oxford: Oxford University Press.

Ellis, F., & Freeman, H. A. (2004). Rural livelihoods and poverty reduction strategies in four African countries. *The Journal of Development Studies, 40*(4), 1–30. doi:10.1080/00220380410001673175

Emwanu, T., Hoogeveen, J. G., & Okiira Okwi, P. (2006). Updating poverty maps with panel data. *World Development, 34*(12), 2076–2088.

Fisher, M., Reimer, J. J., & Carr, E. R. (2010). Who should be interviewed in surveys of household income? *World Development, 38*(7), 966–973.

Grandin, B. E. (1988). *Wealth ranking in smallholder communities: A field manual.* London: Intermediate Technology Publications.

Guyer, J. I. (1981). Household and community in African studies. *African Studies Review, 24*(2/3), 87–137.

Guyer, J. I. (2004). Balances: Household budgets in a Ghanaian study. In *Marginal Gains: Monetary Transactions in Atlantic Africa*, Vol. 1997 (pp. 131–151). Chicago: University of Chicago Press.

Guyer, J. I., & Peters, P. E. (1987). Introduction. *Development and Change, 18*(2), 197–214. doi:10.1111/j.1467-7660.1987.tb00269.x

Halliday, T. J. (2010). Mismeasured household size and its implications for the identification of economies of scale. *Oxford Bulletin of Economics and Statistics, 72*(2), 246–262. doi:10.1111/j.1468-0084.2009.00570.x

Hargreaves, J. R., Morison, L. A., Gear, J. S. S., Kim, J. C., Makhubele, M. B., Porter, J. D. H., Watts, C., Pronyk, P. M. (2007). Assessing household wealth in health studies in developing countries: A comparison of participatory wealth ranking and survey techniques from rural South Africa. *Emerging Themes in Epidemiology, 4.*

Hoddinott, J. (2006). Shocks and their consequences across and within households in rural Zimbabwe. *The Journal of Development Studies, 42*(2), 301–321. doi:10.1080/00220380500405501

Hosegood, V., & Timaeus, I. (2006). Household composition and dynamics in KwaZulu Natal, South Africa: Mirroring social reality in longitudinal data collection. In E. van de Walle (Ed.), *African Household: Censuses and Surveys* (pp. 58–77). New York: Sharpe.

Howe, L. D., Galobardes, B., Matijasevich, A., Gordon, D., Johnston, D., Onwujekwe, O., .. Hargreaves, J. R. (2012). Measuring socio-economic position for epidemiological studies in low- and middle-income countries: A methods of measurement in epidemiology paper. *International Journal of Epidemiology, 41*(3), 871–886. doi:10.1093/ije/dys037

Hulme, D. (2004). Thinking 'Small' and the understanding of poverty: Maymana and Mofizul's story. *Journal of Human Development, 5*(2), 161–176. doi:10.1080/1464988042000225104

Ickowitz, A. (2012). Wealthiest is not always healthiest: What explains differences in child mortality in West Africa? *Journal of African Economies, 21*(2), 192–227.

INDEPTH. (2013). INDEPTH network: Better health information for better health policy. Retrieved from http://www.indepth-network.org/

Jagger, P., Luckert, M. K., Banana, A., & Bahati, J. (2012). Asking questions to understand rural livelihoods: Comparing disaggregated vs aggregated approaches to household livelihood questionnaires. *World Development, 40*(9), 1810–1823.

Johnson-Hanks, J. (2005). When the future decides. *Current Anthropology, 46*(3), 363–385.

Johnston, D., & Abreu, A. (2013). *Asset indices as a proxy for poverty measurement in African countries: A reassessment.* Paper presented at the African Economic Development: Measuring Success and Failure, Simon Fraser University, Vancouver, Canada. Retrieved from http://mortenjerven.com/conference-program-2013/

Kakwani, N., & Silber, J. (2008). Introduction: Multidimensional poverty analysis: Conceptual issues, empirical illustrations and policy implications. *World Development, 36*(6), 987–991.

Little, P. D., Stone, M. P., Mogues, T., Castro, A. P., & Negatu, W. (2006). 'Moving in place': Drought and poverty dynamics in South Wollo, Ethiopia. *The Journal of Development Studies, 42*(2), 200–225. doi:10.1080/00220380500405287

Lockwood, M. (1998). *Fertility and household labour in Tanzania: Demography, economy, and society in Rufiji District, c. 1870–1986.* Oxford: Oxford University Press.

Masset, E., & White, H. (2004). Are chronically poor people being left out of progress towards the millennium development goals? A quantitative analysis of older people, disabled people and orphans. *Journal of Human Development, 5*(2), 279–297.

Mushongah, J., & Scoones, I. (2012). Livelihood change in rural Zimbabwe over 20 years. *Journal of Development Studies, 48*(9), 1241–1257.

NBS. (2009). *Tanzania national panel survey report: Round 1, 2008–2009.* Dar Es Salaam: National Bureau of Statistics.

Owens, T., Sandefur, J., & Teal, F. (2011). *Poverty outcomes and incomes in Ghana and Tanzania: 1987–2007. Are macro economists necessary after all?* Paper presented at the CSAE 25th Anniversary ConferenceRetrieved from http://www.csae.ox.ac.uk/conferences/2011-EDiA/papers/490-Teal.pdf.

Peters, P. E. (2006). Rural income and poverty in a time of radical change in Malawi. *The Journal of Development Studies, 42*(2), 322–345.

Qizilbash, M., & Clark, D. A. (2005). The capability approach and fuzzy poverty measures: An application to the South African context. Social Indicators Research, 74, 103–139.

Randall, S., Coast, E., Compaore, N., & Antoine, P. (2013). The power of the interviewer: A qualitative perspective on African survey data. *Demographic Research, 28*(27), 763–792.

Randall, S., Coast, E., & Dial, F.-B. (2013). *UN 'households' and local interpretations in Burkina Faso, Senegal, Uganda and Tanzania.* Paper presented at the 5th European Conference in African Studies., Lisbon, Portugal. Retrieved from http://cea.iscte.pt/ecas2013/index.shtml

Randall, S., Coast, E., & Leone, T. (2011). Cultural constructions of the concept of household in sample surveys. *Population Studies, 65*(2), 217–229.

Roth, C. (2010). Les relations intergénérationnelles sous pression au Burkina Faso. *Autrepart*1, 95–110.

Sahn, D. E., & Stifel, D. C. (2000). Poverty comparisons over time and across countries in Africa. *World Development, 28*(12), 2123–2155.

Scoones, I. (1995). Investigating difference: Applications of wealth ranking and household survey approaches among farming households in southern Zimbabwe. *Development and Change, 26*(1), 67–88.

Sharp, K., & Devereux, S. (2004). Destitution in Wollo (Ethiopia): Chronic poverty as a crisis of household and community livelihoods. *Journal of Human Development, 5*(2), 227–247.

Thomas, B. (2008). Methodological debate in poverty studies: towards 'participatory qual–quant'? *Development in practice, 18*(2), 280–288.

White, H. (2002). Combining Quantitative and Qualitative Approaches in Poverty Analysis. *World Development, 30*(3), 511–522.

White, H., & Masset, E. (2003). The importance of household size and composition in constructing poverty profiles: An illustration from Vietnam. *Development and Change, 34*(1), 105–126.

Whitehead, A. (2006). Persistent poverty in north east Ghana. *The Journal of Development Studies, 42*(2), 278–300.

The Making of the Middle-Class in Africa: Evidence from DHS Data

ABEBE SHIMELES & MTHULI NCUBE
African Development Bank

ABSTRACT   *This article examines the size and profile of the middle class in Africa using alternative definitions based on pooled unit record data from the Demographic and Health Survey for 37 African countries covering the period 1990–2011. Results suggest that size of the middle class has grown modestly in many countries in the 2000 decade as compared with the 1990s. The article approached the making of the middle class in Africa from institutional and policy perspectives. Quality of institutions, ethnic fractionalisation and education play a significant role in determining the rise of the middle class.*

1. Introduction

Recent interest in understanding the evolution of the middle class in the context of developing countries is inspired partly by economic successes in Asia and Latin America, where the emerging middle class has played a major role in driving growth (Chun, 2010; Desgoigts & Jaramillo, 2009; Easterly, 2001). Studies also highlighted the role of the middle class as an agent of change reforming institutions (Loyza, Rigolini, & Llorente, 2012), a catalyst for the realisation of inclusive growth (Birdsall, 2010; Ravallion, 2012), and innovation and entrepreneurial drive (Banerjee & Duflo, 2008). Despite these positive contributions of the middle class to development, very little is known about its size and attributes in Africa until recently (African Development Bank [AfDB], 2011; McKensie Global Institute, 2010).

   This study builds on recent work to provide evidence on the making of the middle class in Africa, noting the challenges African statistics face in terms of reliability, comparability and consistency. Recent studies highlighted severe faults in the national accounts of African statistics that pervade cross-country comparisons both spatially and temporally (Jerven, 2013a, 2013b). Statistics on household welfare are even murkier where such basic concepts as 'wealth', 'poverty', 'middle class' or units of analysis such as a 'household' vary considerably across livelihood systems and data collection methods (for example, Randall & Coast [2013]).

   Available evidence on the making of middle class so far is based on per capita consumption expenditure collected through large budget surveys. Such data are collected infrequently and in irregular time intervals in many countries in Africa, making contemporaneous comparisons difficult (Deverajan, 2013). It is not also unusual for survey methods and procedures to change between surveys without due regard to comparability issues. Furthermore, systematic measurement errors in the

An Online Appendix is available for this article which can be accessed via the online version of this journal available at http://dx. doi.org/10.1080/00220388.2014.968137 construction of consumption expenditure abound due to complex livelihood systems. In rural areas, subsistence farming means non-marketable goods dominate the consumption basket, making valuation an intricate and complex task, while in urban areas consumption data have to rely on reliability of respondents' memory (Deaton, 1997). For example, recently Beegle, De Weerdt, Friedman, & Gibson (2012) reported that the measurement error arising from different methods of collecting consumption data has significant bias on per capita consumption expenditure aggregates in Tanzania. In addition, consumption surveys in rural areas are complicated by the existence of large spatial and temporal price differences and diverse measurement units across villages (Howe et al., 2012).

This article proposes to use asset or wealth status reported in the Demographic and Health Surveys (DHS) instead of income or consumption expenditure as a key indicator to identify the population of the middle class. This approach has several advantages. First, it provides an opportunity to compare existing estimates of the size of the middle class based on consumption expenditure or income. Second, asset or wealth status reported in DHS is not only better measured than consumption (Moser & Felton, 2007), but also designed carefully to be comparable over time and across countries. Comparatively, it is also available for many countries in multiple waves. In addition, most of the countries covered in this study do not have well-developed financial systems or borrowing against future earnings are available to smooth consumption. Assets are built often by drawing down cash savings. Household assets are accumulated in part as a buffer against shocks and also as a way of improving the standard of living (tap water, better roofs, floors, bedrooms, and so forth). Given the predominance of food in total expenditure in a number of African countries, many of the factors commonly believed to constitute a middle class status are easily missed. Furthermore, the data on asset ownership are based on a wide range of indicators offering an opportunity to capture a broader meaning of the middle class.

While ownership of assets in the DHS data set provides a reasonable source of information to measure the size and trend of the middle class, it is not without caveats. The most serious refers to the arbitrariness in the treatment of ownership of a variety of durable goods and the inherent difficulty in using the asset index to make inter-temporal comparisons (Johnston & Abreu, 2013). However, to redress some of the deficiencies, our measure of a middle class based on the asset index was compared with other approaches such as consumption-based measures, multi-dimensional measure using assets and subjective measures of social class.

This study goes further in examining the factors driving cross-country differences, as well as in providing household and individual characteristics correlated with the middle-class characteristics using unit record data covering 37 African countries with multiple data points. The total sample size used for such analysis consisted of the history of over 790,000 households. It also utilises carefully constructed synthetic or pseudo panel from this sample to examine the dynamics of the middle class across cohorts. Institutional and policy aspects are presented as correlates of the size of the middle class. In particular, the role of ethnic fractionalisation and level of trust among citizens in assisting social mobility is examined. With respect to policy, we focus on governance, education and health as the main pathways into nurturing the middle class using unit record data and a synthetic panel constructed from the country surveys.

Our result is informative and revealing. The trend in the size of the middle class in the last decade depends mainly on how the middle class is defined. We present four definitions of the middle class that reflect the different approaches in the recent literature, but also allows comparisons across countries and surveys (see Section 2 for details). Based on our preferred definition, the size of the middle class has been growing in several African countries, though very slowly compared with the rapid economic growth witnessed, particularly in the last decade. The factors that led to the changes could be broadly classified into those of asset shrinking (average asset index declined), or rising asset inequality, or rapid asset accumulation. Country cases are provided to illustrate these patterns.

The cross-country variation in the size of the middle class is explained largely by differences in initial level of development, social structure (mainly ethnic fractionalisation and the degree of mutual trust among citizens), and most of all the degree of asset inequality. Generally, countries that have homogenous ethnic groups, stronger social capital as captured by mutual trust, and high initial level of development tend to have higher size of the middle class. These results very much echo previous studies for other regions (Easterly, 2001; Knack & Keffer, 1997) for developing world. We also recognise the debate on the use of ethnic fractionalisation as a proxy to capture fragility in institutions and other political economy dynamics (Jerven, 2011).

Findings from analysis of multiple country-level household surveys indicate that individuals in the middle class tend to be well educated and the 'returns' to education in terms of higher asset accumulation are consistently higher for all level of education than no education at all. What would be the implications of expanding education opportunities as a policy to promote the middle class? This has to be seen cautiously, since our results indicate that the 'returns' to additional level of education declines with stock of educated people at secondary and tertiary levels, while it remains unchanged for primary education. But it should also be welcome, as it could lead to a decline in overall inequality by narrowing relative differences across the education spectrum. The rest of the article is organised as follows. Section 2 describes data and methodology, Section 3 presents the key results and Section 4 concludes the article.

2. Data and Methods

2.1 Definition of Middle-Class using Asset Index from DHS Data

The evidence reported in the literature on the size of the middle class in Africa has so far relied mainly on consumption expenditure aggregates drawn from household surveys. The most common source is World Bank's *povcalnet*. It makes available grouped distributional data along with mean consumption expenditure. For African countries the data covers the period 1981-2008. The database starts initially with data from one country in 1981, but across the period it covers 44 countries. Distributional information in early years is/was based on imputations drawn from few available surveys.

By contrast, in this study we report results based on unit record data from the Demographic Health Survey. This database covers 37 countries compiled over the period 1987–2011, where 27 countries had at least two waves and 12 countries four or five waves (see the Online Appendix, Table A1). The drawback of the DHS is that there are very few countries covered in the same year. In our analysis we combined periods in blocks of five years (pre-1995, 1995–2000, 2000–2005 and 2005–2011] to capture the size of the middle class. Admittedly, it is a brave assumption, but one that may not be avoided given the paucity of such data in Africa, and similarly analysis based on the *povcalnet* data rely on projections.[1]

The strength of the DHS data set is that it provides a wide range of information on household and individual wellbeing, including basic social and demographic characteristics. In defining the middle class we have used responses to 10 questions on the following: sources of water for the household (such as pipe water, tap water, water kiosk and well, and so forth); condition of housing (number of rooms, floor material – perke, cement, ceramic, earth – roof material – bricks, tin, grass, earth, and so forth); access to electricity; and ownership of durable assets (radio, television, refrigerator and car). The challenge is to generate a single asset index with appropriate weighting to measure the size of the middle class for each country. The following construct clarifies the assignment. Let W_j is a welfare measure for an individual j defined over a set of variables c_i with a property that:

$$W_j = \sum_{i=1}^{k} a_i c_{ij} \tag{1}$$

where the i represents the k assets that individual j possesses to achieve a welfare level W_j, which could be cardinal or unit free (ordinal) depending on how the components enter the welfare measure. The linearity in Equation (1) assumes that the welfare is additive over the constituents (in our case, the individual assets) allowing a possibility for a perfect substitution across the individual assets. The marginal rate of substitution is given by the ratios of the a_i parameters that would keep a constant welfare level. It measures how much of unit of c_i be given up in relation to c_k to keep the welfare level unchanged. It is also the weight by which each of the assets contributes to the overall welfare.[2] To get the intuition, let us take a case where W is total consumption expenditure over c_i commodities. Then, the a_is will represent prices. The most expensive commodity contributes the highest per unit welfare and vice versa. In the case of assets, respondents provide information on assets via discrete responses such as whether or not they own a particular asset; or from a list provided, they pick the one that appropriately fits the type of asset they own. The data thus generated are categorical and a_is remain unidentified from surveys, unlike market prices.

One simple possibility is to assume all assets bear equal weight.[3] Such an assumption, although simplifies immensely the computational requirements, comes at a great cost. For instance, in the case of asset ownership, valuing owning a car in the same manner as owning a radio would simply imply that an individual is as well-off owning a radio as a car. As a result of this assumption, it becomes also analytically difficult for data to discriminate adequately across welfare tiers defined over a set of assets. Researchers often rely on a statistical method to derive the weights from the data using what is commonly known as factor analysis or principal components analysis. Both of these approaches are data reduction methods that allow the researcher to pick the factor that most likely contributes to the overall variance of the ownership of assets across individuals. An intuitive argument in this context would be, for instance, a person who owns a car is very likely to own radio, perhaps TV, lives in a house provided with electricity and running water. Thus, among the list of assets, car ownership could play the pivotal role in discriminating across households into a set of distinct groups (such as poor, middle class and upper-middle class). We apply this framework in this article to generate the weights given in Equation (1).

We specifically use multiple correspondence analysis (MCA) which is closely related with factor analysis or principal components analysis. The only difference is that the MCA is suitable for categorical variables (for example, Booyseen, van der Berg, Burger, Maltitz, & Rand, 2008).[4] Formally, if we denote a_j the weight of category j and R_{ij} the answer of household i to category j, then the asset index score of household i is:

$$MCA_i = \sum_{j=1}^{J} a_j R_{ij} \tag{2}$$

This index can then be normalised between 0 and 1 to allow for inter-temporal and cross-country comparisons by the following formula:

$$normalized\_MCA_i = \frac{MCA_i - \min(MCA)}{\max(MCA) - \min(MCA)} \tag{3}$$

It is important to bear in mind that the asset index constructed in a manner described in Equation (2) is based on a strong assumption that there is a unique correspondence between a middle-class status and the individual 'asset' or 'wealth' components or indicators that make up the asset index. It is possible that some assest may be acquired through different means that may not necessarily reflect the wealth status of the household, such as through community or government intervention, or where prices have changed dramatically, so that the relative prices of assets is much lower than before and so forth (Johnston & Abreu, 2013). When it comes to inter-temporal comparisons, a problem one is likely to encounter is that assets owned by households represent 'stocks' for which no allowance can be made for obsoleteness or depreciation or other processes that affect the real value of the asset over time, which frequentlytend to overestimate real wealth acquisition.[5] For the purpose of this article, there is no clear method to correct for such possible biases except to compare our measure of middle class based on the asset index with other alternative measures such as consumption expenditure and subjective measures to see how cross-country comparisons perform under different approaches.

Once the asset index is generated for each country from unit record data, the next step is to identify the middle class. There is a growing literature on the definition of the middle class in the context of developing countries. Some focus on relative definition where the upper and lower bounds are a certain percentage of either the median or mean income (for example, Birdsall, Graham, & Pettinato, 2000). Others define a middle class in absolute terms as those individuals living on between $2 and $10 per day (AfDB, 2011; Banerjee & Duflo, 2008; Birdsall, Lustig & Meyer, 2014; Milanovic & Yitzhaki, 2002).[6] While each definition has some grounding, arbitrariness cannot be avoided.

For the purpose of this study, the size of the middle class per country and survey was constructed in a manner that would allow comparisons across countries and surveys. This would require, first, the asset index to be constructed from the pooled data and, second, the lower and upper bounds of the asset index that define the middle class need to be fixed across countries and surveys. This would give an 'absolute' measure of the middle class where the status of households would be compared easily across countries and surveys. A total of about 790,000 households were pooled and the MCA was applied over the 10 asset-variables, using sample and country level population as weights.[7] Four definitions of the middle class that resonate with the empirical literature were constructed from the pooled data. The first two measures relied on the mean (median) values of the asset index for the pooled data. Households that fell within the bounds of 75 per cent to 125 per cent of the median (mean) asset index were classified as belonging to the middle class.[8] The third measure of a middle class was defined in similar spirit, but the bounds were based on one and two standard deviations above the mean of the asset index for the pooled data. The mean asset index of the pooled data was 0.27, with a standard deviation of 0.23. A fixed bound of 0.5 and 0.7 was then applied on the pooled data to construct the size of the middle class for each country and survey. For the sake of robustness, the size of the middle class based on the concept of multi-dimensional measure of the asset index in line with Akilire and Foster (2011) was constructed, where a household is classified as a middle class if it owns a particular asset. Then the number of times a household is middle class is counted to give a score for each household. Table A2 in the Online Appendix provides the threshold used for each asset for all countries in classifying a household into a middle class.

2.2 Framework to Understand the Drivers of Middle Class

A profile of the middle class based on observed individual and community/country characteristics is presented to enrich the discussion on the evolution of the middle class. Three approaches are presented in this article to undertake the exercise. The first is a comparison of the size of the middle class at a country level with a set of variables that have some resonance to the political economy literature, such as governance, ethnic diversity and mutual trust among citizens as drivers of the middle class.

The second is the use of synthetic or pseudo-panels to analyse mobility in and out of the middle class as well as examine, with some degree of robustness by controlling for unobserved time invariant factor, an important aspect of promoting the middle class, which is education and health of citizens.[9] The pseudo-panel (unbalanced) was set up from over 790,000 observations covering 37 countries with multiple waves. We used time-invariant characteristics such as age and sex of the individual to define a cohort and obtained 1,385 individual–country–period matched data. The unit of analysis is therefore the cohort belonging to a particular age–sex group in a given period.

The third approach we followed is to use unit record data for the 37 countries in multiple waves to estimate the correlates or determinants of the middle class by focusing mainly on individual characteristics (household size, age, sex and education level attained) and spatial factors (region of residence) in a consistent way to obtain comparable estimates across countries.

Additional data needed for the study were obtained from the following sources: ethnic fractionalisation from Easterly and Levine (1997), trust and confidence; subjective measure of wellbeing; life satisfaction from the World Values Survey for 2007,[10] the Moi-Ibrahim governance index series provided by the Moi-Ibrahim Foundation, and macro indicators from AfDB data portal.

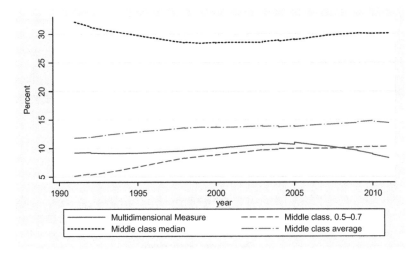

Figure 1. Lowess estimate of the trend of middle class in Africa under different definitions.

3. Results

3.1 Evolution of the Middle Class in Africa

The trend in the size of the middle class in Africa depends on the definition adopted (Figure 1). There has been an increase over time for a middle class defined either as those households with a value of a normalised index in the interval between 0.5 and 0.7, or those between 75 per cent and 125 per cent of the average normalised index for the pooled data.[11] The former definition encompasses households that lie within the 65 to 75 percentile of the distribution of the normalised asset index. On the other hand, the size of the middle class remained constant or showed a slight decline respectively for middle class defined between 75 per cent and 125 per cent of the median of the normalised asset index, or the multidimensional measure of the middle class.

Table 1 summarises the size of the middle class for Africa for the four periods – pre-1995, 1995–1999, 2000–2004 and 2005–2011 – using the four definitions adopted. The trend fits into the pattern documented in Figure 1. The trend in the size of the middle class reported in Table 1 remains unaffected by changes in the sample of countries with multiple waves, or manner of aggregation at a continental level.

A full picture of the pattern of the middle class could be obtained by examining the kernel density of the normalised asset index for the pooled data covering the four periods (see Figure 2). It is possible to infer that for the definition of the middle class over which the cut-off was based on mean or median of the normalised index, there is a lot of overlap so that the size of the middle class may have remained unchanged in these periods. On the other hand, the middle class defined between 0.5 and 0.7 of the

Table 1. The size of the middle class under alternative definitions in Africa (%)

Period	No of countries	Middle-class size (Definition 1)	Middle-class size (Definition 2)	Middle-class size (Definition 3)	Middle-class size (Definition 4)
Pre-1995	20	16	10	24	11
1995–1999	18	11	10	28	17
2000–2004	20	18	14	20	12
2005–2011	37	15	12	25	13

Note: Definition 1: Multidimensional measure of middle class; Definition 2: Middle class with 0.5 and 0.7 lower and upper bounds; Definition 3: Middle class 75 per cent and 125 per cent of the median for the pooled data; Definition 4: Middle class 75 per cent and 125 per cent of the mean for the pooled data.

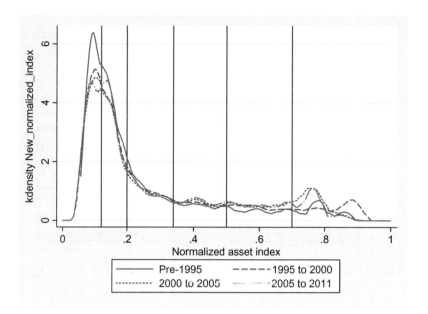

Figure 2. Kernel density of the asset index for Africa (N=795 305).

normalised asset index showed an increase in the 2000 decade against the 1990s. The kernel density even suggested a bi-modal distribution for the latter periods.

To clarify elements embedded in the concept of the middle class, Table A3 in the Online Appendix compared four definitions of the middle class with each other and self-reported social status obtained from the World Value Survey Association in 2007. The table reports pair-wise correlation coefficients across a wide range of middle class definitions and social class obtained from the World Value Survey.[12] There is a strong and positive correlation (0.85) between a definition of middle class based on multidimensional measures of the asset index and that based on the normalised asset index where the bounds were set between 0.5 and 0.7. In addition, these estimates correlate strongly with the subjective measure of wellbeing mainly with households that considered themselves as belonging to the upper ($p < 0.01$) or lower middle class status ($p < 0.001$). More importantly, the correlation with those households who regarded themselves as poor was negative and strong. The converse applied to the middle class status defined over 75 per cent and 125per cent of either the median or the mean. It is therefore tempting to classify the first group as middle class in a strict sense and the others as struggling middle class/poor or floating middle class, a definition which is gaining popularity in recent literature (for example, AfDB [2011]; Birdsall, Lustig & Meyer [2014]).

In support of the case for such a useful classification, we found a strong and positive correlation between a 'strictly middle class' based on consumption expenditure (the population with income between $5 and $10 in PPP per day per person) and the conservative definition of middle class based on the asset index at 0.5 and 0.7 band (see Figure 3).

The size of the middle class defined conservatively has shown an increase in several African countries when compared with the pre-1995 period (Figure 4). In particular, the decade 2000 showed a substantial improvement in the size of the middle class in about 21 African countries, some showing dramatic increases over time. Most of the countries that have shown a growing middle class in recent years are also those that recorded sustained growth in the last decade, such as Senegal, Kenya, Ghana and Nigeria.

A decline in the size of the middle class does not necessary follow from a rise in income inequality or an increase in the size of the poor population. We provide interesting comparisons on the evaluation of the middle class using unit record data for Egypt, Ghana and Madagascar based on DHS where each underwent different paths.

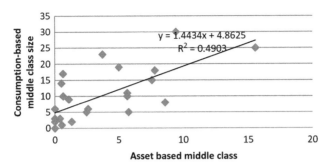

Figure 3. Correlation between asset-based and consumption-based middle class for selected African countries.

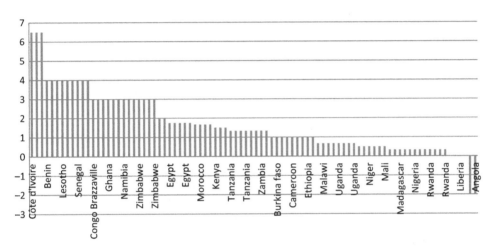

Figure 4. Change in the size of middle class since the pre-1995 period: percentage points.

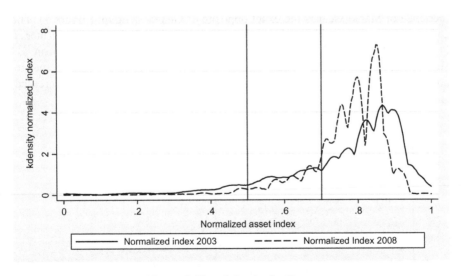

Figure 5. Kernel density for Egypt.

Figure 5 depicts a kernel density on the evolution of the distribution of the asset index for Egypt between 2003 and 2008. It can be seen that the share of the middle class (those with an asset index lying between 0.5 and 0.7) has declined considerably, even though asset poverty has declined as well

75

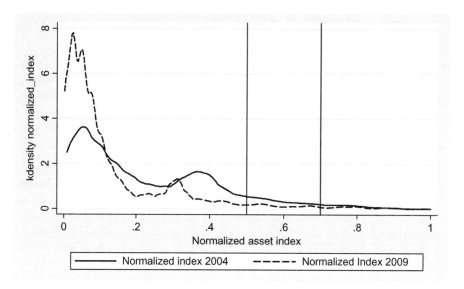

Figure 6. Kernel density for Madagascar.

as asset inequality (the Gini coefficient for 2003 was 11%, while for 2008 it was 8%). The experience of Egypt suggests that the middle class in 2003 moved upwards, perhaps into what would be classified as 'upper-middle class', and many who have been asset poor escaped poverty, echoing a situation documented in the United States during the 1980s (Daly, 1997). In this context, a shrinking middle class may be interpreted differently.

The experience of Ghana is a typical case, as shown in Figure 6, where the size of the middle class expanded significantly, asset poverty declined and the Gini coefficient for asset also declined dramatically from 43 per cent in 2003 to 36 per cent in 2008. This is a pattern we would expect to see in a situation where previously poor people join the ranks of the middle class in the process of development.

The experience of Madagascar is the exact opposite of Ghana or Egypt (Figure 7). The country experienced a rise in asset poverty and also inequality (Gini coefficient for asset increased from 42% in 2004 to 54% in 2009). There was a general deprivation where the mean asset index declined from 0.21 to 0.13. This trend is consistent with the estimate of extreme poverty (at poverty line of 1.25 dollars per person a day) provided in *povcalnet*, where it increased from 68

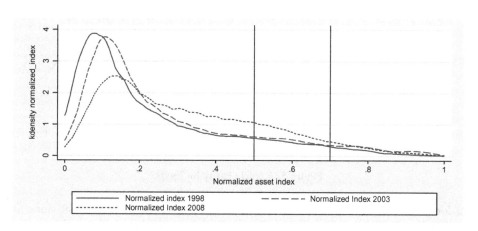

Figure 7. Kernel density for Ghana.

Table 2. Transition matrix for middle class status using alternative definitions: synthetic panel

Before 1995	2005–2011			
	Poor	Middle class	Rich	Total
Middle class defined between 0.5 and 0.7 value of normalised asset index from pooled sample				
Poor	97.19	2.81	0	100
Middle class	3.03	89.39	7.58	100
Rich	0	7.14	92.86	100
Total	84.43	11.14	4.43	100
Middle class defined over 75% and 125% of the mean of the Asset index from pooled sample				
Poor	91.88	7.87	0.25	100
Middle class	3.81	76.43	19.75	100
Rich	0	6.71	93.29	100
Total	52.57	23	24.43	100
Middle class defined over 75% and 125% of the median of the Asset index from pooled sample				
Poor	63.95	33.72	2.33	100
Middle class	6.03	82.89	11.07	100
Rich	0	3.8	96.2	100
Total	10.43	41.14	48.43	100

per cent to 81 per cent. The decline in the size of the middle class, however, was not large compared to the size of the poor population, mainly because a rise in inequality prevented the fall in the size of the middle class. In summary, the interaction between asset poverty and inequality with regard to the size of the middle class is non-linear, and several scenarios are possible as illustrated by these three cases.

3.2 Mobility into and out of Middle Class

The trend in the size of the middle class is indicative of temporal change. It does not, however, tell how 'persistent' a middle-class status would be once attained, and nor what are the chances of climbing back in an unfortunate situation if lost due to factors such as temporary shocks. Often, accurate representation of social mobility is captured from real panel data. In Africa such data are sparse. The only country for which the authors have access to such a data is Ethiopia, where close to 1,500 households in urban areas were followed for over 10 years during 1994–2004, for which information on middle-class status (self-reported) is available to complement our analysis (Bigsten

Table 3. Regression-based decomposition of variation in the size of middle class in Africa

Correlates of size of middle class	Contribution to variance (%)
Initial per capita GDP (1980)	24
Gini coefficient for the asset index	27
Ethnic fractionalisation	21
Governance	2
Residuals	26.
Total	100
Number of observations	75

Note: *** significant at 1 per cent, ** significant at 5 per cent and * significant at 10 per cent.
Source: Authors' computations based on country-level data.

& Shimeles, 2011). In this article a synthetic panel fully described in the data section was constructed for all countries for which DHS data were available.

One result that emerges from the transition matrix reported in Table 3 is that on average the probability that an individual would be asset poor in 2005–2011, regardless of his/her background in the early 1990s, was around 84 perc ent; a middle class, using a conservative definition, around 11 per cent; and an upper class around 4 per cent. For the struggling or floating middle class the picture is somehow cosier. Regardless of which definition is adopted, fortune shifts with initial conditions dramatically. Those that started a middle class in early 1990s would have more than 75 per cent chance of staying that way, while the bulk of them would move to the upper class. Very few (about 6%) slip back into poverty. This result certainly is based on highly aggregated panel data and is likely influenced by dynamics across rather than within countries. The upper class and the poor remained entrenched in their relative positions as in the early 1990s. The middle class status is the one that exhibited more churning than the other two extreme classes.

The dimension of mobility takes a different twist when education and sex of the head of the household are taken into account. For household heads with no education, persistence of initial class status was evident with very little mobility across classes. For those household heads with primary education, a significant proportion slipped back from the upper (rich) class to the middle-class status in the last two decades. Among those with secondary education, there was upward as well as downward mobility across classes. For the tertiary educated, mobility was upwards during the period (see Online Appendix Tables A4a and A4b).

Table A5 in the Online Appendix provides a similar type of transition matrix for real panel for Ethiopian urban households based on self-reported class status. Interestingly, there was 70 per cent chance for a household that started middle class to keep their status over a 10-year period. However, more people slipped into the poor category than those that escaped into the upper income class. In addition, more people who started out in the upper class fell into poverty, signifying important churning during the last decade. That may not be surprising; Ethiopia has undergone rapid economic, social and political changes during the period covered in the study, and illustrates what could happen in societies in transition.

3.3 Correlates of Cross-Country Variations in the Size of Middle Class

What factors drive cross-country variations in the size of the middle class in Africa? It can be argued that the middle class thrive in the course of development. Given the absolute definition of the middle class that we adopted, it is plausible to assume that initial conditions play a major role in explaining cross-country variations. These include level of development (which is proxied here by the average per capita GDP measured in PPP in 1980), ethnic fractionalisation,[13] which is an important element that could affect economic and social mobility (Robinson, 2002) for several reasons, either due to inherited differences in educational attainment or difficulty of redistribution (Glaeser, 2005). A recent study reported that, controlling for a number of policy and economic factors, ethnicity explained with a fair degree of robustness what is called 'the African dummy' in the incidence of income inequality in a cross-country regression set-up (Milanovic, 2003). It is important, however, to recognise that the frequent use of ethnic fractionalisation as a proxy for institutional dysfunctions, such as rent-seeking behaviour of political elites, is based on weak theoretical construct, or the presumption that it explains political instability is undermined by the crude formulation used to define it (for example, Jerven [2011]; Kenny and Williams [2001]). In this regard, we limit the use of ethnic fractionalisation as a proxy for capturing time-invariant structural heterogeneity across African countries that potentially pick up important unobserved factors that impede social mobility and the delivery of basic social services to the larger population.

Results reported in Table 3 provide some empirical support to the role of initial per capita GDP and ethnic fractionalisation in affecting the size of the middle class, which account for over 45 per cent of the variation in the size of the middle class across countries.

Table 4. Correlates of the asset index based on synthetic panel: estimates based on random-effects regression model

	Coefficients	p-values
Female headed households	0.000071	(0.997)
Primary completed	0.238***	(0.000)
Secondary completed	0.745***	(0.000)
Tertiary completed	1.141***	(0.000)
Rohrer health index	0.0000344	(0.132)
Log initial per capita GDP (1980)	0.102***	(0.000)
Log of Gini coefficient	−0.0849**	(0.036)
Moi Ibrahim governance index	0.0078***	(0.000)
Ethnic fractionalisation	−0.374***	(0.000)
Mutual trust	7.637***	(0.000)
Constant	−3.745***	(0.000)
Period dummy	Yes	Yes
Number of groups	384	
N	649	
Adj. R^2	0.82	

Note: *** $p < 0.001$, ** $p < 0.01$, * $p < 0.05$.

The results obtained from a random-effects regression model based on the synthetic panel given in Table 4 suggest that ethnicity, trust, governance captured by the Moi-Ibrahim Index[14] play a very important role in affecting the asset index. The catalysing institutions that promote greater integration and trust among citizens remain to be important. In their seminal paper, Zak and Knack (2001) showed the critical role trust plays in promoting growth through its effect on savings and investment.

As much as good governance promotes the emergence of middle class in a society, it is also possible that a large middle class promotes governance or institutions. This reverse causality was investigated in Loayza et al. (2012), where they reported that large a middle class could play an important role in reforming institutions. Our attempt to investigate the role of middle class for the African data set did not lead to any significant result. A simultaneous equation in a three-stage least square framework relating governance indicator with the middle class and other covariate returned a result with a positive (right) sign but not statistically significant. Instead, the effect of good governance on the size of asset index remained robust,[15] albeit with a much reduced coefficient, after we controlled for cohort and country-specific effects. We also note that the coefficients for ethnic fractionalisation and mutual trust in this context remained significant with the right sign.

The other interesting and commonly accepted view is that education can play an important part in the making of the middle class. We undertook a regression decomposition analysis of the asset index for 98 country-years using similar variables as correlates to allow us to make comparisons across countries. This has reduced our choice of variables. However, in all cases we regressed log of asset index on the set of individual characteristics (age, family size, sex and educational attainment), and spatial variations to examine how education featured in the accumulation of assets. It was possible to infer that in at least 30 per cent of cases the share of education in explaining the variation in asset index was more than 20 per cent, which is quite significant and large.[16] Age, family size and sex explained a small part of the variation in the asset index, while differences in region of residence in general contributed a substantial portion, specifically in large countries. The coefficients associated with primary, secondary and higher educations were invariably higher than the reference group (no education) for all countries (see Figure 8).

Furthermore, the coefficients for each of the education levels showed a tendency of declining with the proportion of educated people as measured by mean years of schooling[17] or proportion of population with corresponding level of education.[18] The downward trend in the 'returns' to education for secondary and higher education is suggestive of what could be interpreted as the decline in relative

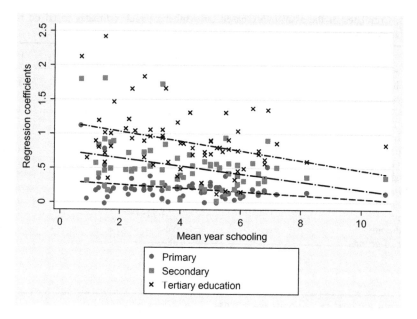

Figure 8. Regression coefficients of education and mean years of education for African countries.

'wages' as the stock of skilled labour increases. Ideally, relative inequality across the education spectrum tends to decline with development. At least from our result it can be inferred that countries with a low stock of educated people could get a rapid gain in fostering the middle class by investing in education, particularly secondary and higher education. Even in countries where the proportion of educated people is large, still the roles of education in acquiring assets remain important. Thus, for both types of countries, focus on education is helpful, but also care should be taken on its limitations. Increasing the size of skilled labour alone is not sufficient and needs to be matched with measures to expand demand for their services.

4. Conclusion

This study provided evidence on the size and profile of middle class in Africa using unit record data from 37 African countries spanning almost two decades. Using 10 different dimensions of asset formation, which are the foundations of class differences, the article constructed a composite asset index for the pooled data. The cross-country correlation between asset, consumption and subjective-based measures of middle class is also strikingly strong, providing some level of comfort on results reported using different approaches. Still, results of the asset-based index on the size of the middle class need to be read carefully, noting the inherent limitations of the approaches used to aggregate a variety of asset owned by households into a single index.

Overall, most countries covered in our survey experienced a rise in the size of the middle class over the last decade. There were, however, cases of shrinking of the middle class. Some of it, such as in Egypt, did decline due to a rapid expansion in asset ownership, which put a large percentage of previously middle-class people into the upper class. In other cases it was because of a decline in the stock of asset, as in the case of Madagascar. The experience of Ghana fitted the ideal pattern. The size of the middle class increased because of an increase in asset ownership as well as a decline in asset inequality.

The main contribution of our article comes from the use of synthetic panel merged from close to 790,000 individual observations to analyse the dynamics of middle-class status for four distinct periods starting from early 1990s, mid-1990s, early 2000 and mid-2000. The results more or less confirmed what was observed in the trends. The probability of retaining a middle-class status for those that started out as such was around 75 per cenr, which is quite significant. The probability of becoming asset-poor during the entire period was around 84 per cent, while that of becoming middle class was 7 per cent. Being in the upper class or rich was 3 per cent. This suggests a continent that is still struggling with widespread poverty and deprivation.

Cross-country variations in the size of the middle class are a result mainly of differences in initial level of per capita GDP, inequality in the asset index, ethnic fractionalisation and lack of trust among citizens. The role of governance and education feature prominently in promoting the middle class in our discussion. Education is found to be a very important factor in driving asset ownership. In more than 30 per cent of the cases investigated, the variation in the asset index due to education exceeded 20 per cent. In addition, the premium for education was evident across countries for primary, secondary and higher education levels. However, such premium or 'high return' exhibited a decline for secondary and to a certain extent for higher education as the proportion of educated people increased. This is intuitive, and also suggests that relatively skill scarce countries can accelerate the making of the middle class through investment in education. The fact that 'returns' to education declines with a growing population of educated people mainly at secondary and tertiary level cautions from excessive investment in the sector and draws attention to issue of generating sufficient demand for labour from the economy to keep benefits of education constant.

Acknowledgements

The authors thank Yaovi Gassesse Silidin, Department of Economics, Montreal University and Tiguene Nabassaga, African Development Bank for excellent research assistance. We thank Morten Jerven and conference participants on African Development: Measuring Successes and Failures in April 2013, Vancouver, Canada, for extensive and helpful comments; Linguere Mbaye, Bereket Kebede and Daniel Zerfu, and we thank participants of the 88th Conference of Western Economic Association International, Seatle, Center for the Study of African Economies Conference in 2013, Oxford University, and African Economic Conference, October 2012, Rwanda, for their insightful comments. All remaining errors are ours. The views expressed in this study are that of the authors and not the African Development Bank Group and its board of directors, nor the countries they represent. Raw and processed data, as well as STATA codes used for this study, are available from the authors on request, or from the journal's website.

Notes

1. See the use of DHS data in Alden Young, African Growth Miracle, and critique of the DHS data in the Klasen et al in this special issue: http://onlinelibrary.wiley.com/doi/10.1111/roiw.2013.59.issue-s1/issuetoc and references in Jerven 2013, http://www1.wider.unu.edu/inclusivegrowth/sites/default/files/IGA/Jerven.pdf.

2.
$$\frac{a_i}{a_k} = -\frac{dc_i}{dc_k}$$

3. This approach is close to the multidimensional measure of welfare that relies on the counting of number of dimensions in which a household or individual is classified into a certain social or economic group (middle class, poor, rich, and so forth) by offering the same weight to each dimension (for example, for poverty see Alkire and Foster [2011]).

4. See Sahn and Stifel (2000) for application of factor analysis to asset poverty in selected African countries.

5. See a discussion of the limitations of asset index as a measure of poverty or middle class in Johnston and Abreu (2013).

6. See Ravallion (2010) for further discussion.

7. The new weight was constructed using the following:

$$\text{New Weight}_{h,t} = \frac{sample\ weight_{c,h,t}}{\sum_h sample\ weight_{c,h,t}} * population_{c,t}$$

8. The 75 per cent and 125 per cent deviations from the mean/median were close to a one standard deviation from the mean/median.

9. See Verbeek (2007) for an excellent review of the properties of synthetic or pseudo-panels.

10. See http://www.worldvaluessurvey.org/.
11. The median and mean for the pooled data are respectively 0.16 and 0.27.
12. The World Value Survey collects data on social status by asking respondents to identify themselves into the following groups: upper class; upper-middle class; lower-middle class; working class; and lower class.
13. The ethnic fractionalisation data used in this study are from Easterly and Levine (1997), which is based on the Atlas Nadorov Mira compiled in early 1960s in the Soviet Union. The formula to construct the index offers the probability that two individuals from the same country could belong to different ethnic groups. There has been serious criticism leveled against this measure; but the alternatives suggested in the literature were not also so different, having a correlation coefficient of over 80 per cent (see, for example, Montalvo and Reynal-Querol [2005]). For the sake of robustness, we used alternative measure of ethnic fractionalisation from Fearon and Laitin (2003) with no conceivable effect on our results.
14. The Moi-Ibrahim Governance Index is produced by the Moi-Ibrahim Foundation, which was established in 2007. The governance index ranges between 0 and 100 and is based on four dimensions: safety and rule of law; participation and human rights; sustainable economic opportunity; and human development. Details of the data sources and methodology are given at: http://www.moibrahimfoundation.org/ie/.
15. Size of middle class is highly correlated with higher asset index.
16. The tables for the regression are available from the authors on request.
17. The data for mean years of schooling was obtained from AfDB data portal. http://www.afdb.org/en/knowledge/statistics/data-portal/.
18. The proportion of individuals who completed primary, secondary and tertiary education was computed from unit record data in the DHS.

References

AfDB. (2011). *The middle of the pyramid: Dynamics of middle class in Africa*. Mimeo. AfDB. Tunis.
Alkire, S., & Foster, J. (2011). Counting and multidimensional poverty measurement. *Journal of Public Economics, 95*(7–8), 476–487.
Banerjee, A. V., & Duflo, E. (2008). What is middle class about the middle classes around the world? *Journal of Economic Perspectives, 22*(2), 3–28.
Beegle, K., De Weerdt, J., Friedman, J., & Gibson, J. (2012). Methods of household consumption measurement through surveys: Experimental results from Tanzania. *Journal of Development Economics, 98*(1), 3–18.
Bigsten, A., & Shimeles, A. (2011). The persistence of urban poverty in Ethiopia: A tale of two measurements. *Applied Economics Letters, 18*(9), 835–839.
Birdsall, N. (2010). *The (indispensable) middle class in developing countries; or the rich and the rest, not the poor and the rest* (Working Paper 207). Washington, DC: Center for Global Development.
Birdsall, N., Graham, C., & Pettinato, S. (2000). *Stuck in the tunnel: Is globalization muddling the middle class?* (Working Paper 14). Washington, DC: Center on Social and Economic Dynamics.
Birdsall, N., Lustig, N., & Meyer, C. J. (2014). The strugglers: The new poor in Latin America? *World Development, 60*(0), 132–146.
Booysen, F., van der Berg, S., Burger, R., Maltitz, M. v., & Rand, G. d. (2008). Using an asset index to assess trends in poverty in seven sub-Saharan African countries. *World Development, 36*(6), 1113–1130.
Chun, N. (2010). *Middle class size in the past, present, and future: A description of trends in Asia* (Working Paper Series 217). Manila: ADB Economics.
Daly, M. (1997). *The 'shrinking' middle class?* (Economic Letter [1997–07]). San Francisco: FRBSF.
Deaton, A. (1997). *The analysis of household surveys: A micro-econometric approach*. World Bank Publisher.
Desdoigts, A., & Jaramillo, F. (2009). Trade, demand spillovers, and industrialization: The emerging global middle class in perspective. *Journal of International Economics, 79*(2), 248–258.
Devarajan, S. (2013). Africa's statistical tragedy. *Review of Income and Wealth, 59*, S9–S15.
Easterly, W. (2001). The middle class consensus and economic development. *Journal of Economic Growth, 6*(4), 317–335.
Easterly, W., & Levine, R. (1997). Africa's growth tragedy: Policies and ethnic divisions. *The Quarterly Journal of Economics, 112*(4), 1203–1250.
Fearon, J. D., & Laitin, D. D. (2003). Ethnicity, insurgency, and civil war. *American Political Science Review, 97*(01), 75–90.
Glaeser, E. L. (2005). *Inequality* (Working Paper Series No. 11511). Cambridge, MA: NBER.
Howe, L. D., Galobardes, B., Matijasevich, A., Gordon, D., Johnston, D., Onwujekwe, O., … and Hargreaves, J. R. (2012). Measuring socio-economic position for epidemiological studies in low- and middle-income countries: A methods of measurement in epidemiology paper. *International Journal of Epidemiology, 41*(3): 871–886.
Jerven, M. (2011). The quest for the African dummy: Explaining African post-colonial economic performance revisited. *Journal of International Development, 23*: 288–307.
Jerven, M. (2013a). Comparability of GDP estimates in sub-Saharan Africa: The effect of revisions in sources and methods since structural adjustment. *Review of Income and Wealth, 59*, S16–S36.
Jerven, M. (2013b). *Poor numbers: How we are misled by African development statistics and what to do about it*. Ithaca, NY: Cornell University Press.

Johnston, D., & Abreu, A. (2013). *Asset indices as a proxy for poverty measurement in African countries: A reassessment*. Paper presented at the African Development: Measuring Success and Failures, Vancouver, Canada.

Kenny, C., & Williams, D. (2001). What do we know about economic growth? Or, why don't we know very much? *World Development, 29*(1): 1–22.

Knack, S., & Keefer, P. (1997). Does social capital have an economic payoff? A cross-country investigation. *The Quarterly Journal of Economics, 112*(4), 1251–1288.

Loayza, N., Rigolini, J., & Llorente, G. (2012). *Do middle classes bring institutional reforms?* (Discussion Paper 6430). Bonn: IZA.

McKinsey Institute, M. G. (2010). *Lion's on the move: The progress and potential of African economies*. Seoul, San Francisco, CA, London, Washington, DC: McKinsey Institute.

Milanovic, B., & Yitzhaki, S. (2002). Decomposing world income distribution: Does the world have a middle class? *Review of income and wealth, international association for research in income and wealth, 48*(2).

Milanovic, B. (2003). *Is inequality in Africa really different?* (Policy Research Working Paper Series 3169). The World Bank.

Montalvo, J. G., & Reynal-Querol, M. (2005). Ethnic polarization, potential conflict, and civil wars. *American Economic Review, 95*(3), 796–816.

Randall, S., & Coast, E. (2013). *Poverty in African households: The limits of survey representations*. Paper presented at the African Development: Measuring Success and Failures, Vancouver, Canada.

Ravallion, M. (2010). The developing world's bulging (but vulnerable) middle class. *World Development, 38*(4), 445–454.

Robinson, B. (2002). *Income inequality and ethnicity: An international view*. Paper presented at the 27th General Conference of the International Association for Research in Income and Wealth, Stockholm, Sweden.

Sahn, D. E., & Stifel, D. C. (2000). Poverty comparisons over time and across countries in Africa. *World Development, 28*(12), 2123–2155.

Verbeek, M. (2008). Pseudo-panels and repeated cross-sections. In L. Mátyás & P. Sevestre (Eds.), *The Econometrics of Panel Data* (Vol. 46) (pp. 369–383). Berlin, Heidelberg: Springer.

World Value Surveys Association. (2007). Retrieved from www.worldvaluessurvey.org

Young, A. (2012). The African growth miracle. *Journal of political economy, 120*(4), 696–739. ISSN 0022-3808.

World Values Survey Association (2005). World values survey wave 5. Retrieved from http://www.worldvaluessurvey.org/.

Zak, P. J., & Knack, S. (2001). Trust and growth. *The Economic Journal, 111*(470), 295–321.

Random Growth in Africa? Lessons from an Evaluation of the Growth Evidence on Botswana, Kenya, Tanzania and Zambia, 1965–1995

MORTEN JERVEN

Simon Fraser University, Vancouver, Canada

ABSTRACT   *Given shortcomings in basic data collection and insufficient resources in preparing official statistics African growth data are unlikely to be very reliable. Estimates of an annual growth rate of 3 per cent may be consistent with a reality between 0 and 6 per cent growth. Although data from international databases are widely used in an expanding literature on African growth there has been no research into how serious these data inaccuracies are. This paper addresses the reliability of the available growth evidence for a selection of countries and offers concrete measures of inaccuracies. It examines the reasons for discrepancies and shows that they can be quite large.*

I. Introduction

A handbook on African statistics states that national accounting practices in African countries 'focus their attention heavily on the main tables, especially the gross domestic product (GDP), and the international agencies reinforce this bias by requesting national statistics offices to provide data for the aggregates long before the preparation is defensible, resulting in figures that are little better than *random numbers*' (Kpedekpo and Arya, 1981: 208, authors' emphasis). Three decades earlier one of the pioneers of development studies warned about the potential pitfalls of producing statistics on developing countries claiming that 'in the hands of authorities, such international comparisons may yield correlations which throw light on the circumstances of economic progress, and they tell us something about the relative inefficiencies and standard of living, but they are widely abused. Do they

An Online Appendix is available for this article which can be accessed via the online version of this journal available at www.informaworld.com/fjds

not on the whole mislead more than they instruct, causing a net reduction in human knowledge?' (Seers, 1952: 160).

Despite these concerns very little research has been undertaken on the reliability of official African statistics. Limited work was carried out under the auspices of OECD on the measurement of the non-monetary economy (Blades, 1975) and on GDP level estimates (Blades, 1980). However:

> the GDP per capita growth rates published by developing countries have never been examined for their reliability [and] it seems unlikely that in developing countries GDP real growth rates have errors of less than 3 per cent attached to them. An estimated year-to-year increase of 3 per cent may mean anything from no growth at all to an increase of 6 per cent. (Blades, 1980: 72)

The issue of data quality is best approached by examining whether the data are valid and/or reliable (Ariyo, 1996). The first question is whether national income is correctly measured. There is generally an element of under coverage in all national accounts, but in African countries this is a problem of larger importance, especially given the magnitude of non-monetary transactions and own-production in the large and important rural sector (van Arkadie, 1971/1972). Furthermore, both in urban and rural areas all types of economic transactions are often not recorded because of the combined effect of the state's lack of capacity of record keeping and the small scale and informality of these transactions (MacGaffey, 1991). The question is whether this element of mismeasurement of national income is consistent through time and space, that is, whether the measure is reliable. This is not likely to be the case. There have been important changes in national accounting practices, and most importantly the resources available to national statistical offices. Initial estimates after independence did not generally include, or included only very modest estimates for, the unrecorded or non-monetary economy. These were improved when series were rebased in the 1970s. Structural adjustment, the growth of the importance of the urban informal sector and a general shortage of resources in the state administration created problems in the 1980s and 1990s. Moreover there was significant variation across countries with regards to the relative strength of the state administrations and the extent of collapse and decline in the 1980s. Some countries have now implemented informal sector surveys, others have not. In some countries state and parastatal activity was very important. Some economies rely on a diverse mix of small scale farmers, whilst elsewhere national income is drawn largely from one natural resource for which the price is determined in world markets.

In conclusion, one has both validity and reliability issues with official African data. This might cause serious problems for cross-country and inter-temporal growth comparisons. To gauge exactly the seriousness of this problem is complicated by the fact that there is no direct way of knowing the extent and variation of the 'unrecorded' element through time and space. This paper first (Section II) examines how these data problems are manifested in official statistics to get a measure of the timing, size and cause of data inconsistencies. Section III then considers why this matters for the interpretation of African growth. The conclusion offers guidance to scholars using historical data to interpret economic change in Africa.

II. Accuracy in Growth Reporting

In this paper the sample of Botswana, Kenya, Tanzania and Zambia is chosen because they form an interesting set of countries to compare. The countries are clearly associated with certain 'negative' and 'positive' features of African countries identified in the literature. Botswana is one of the few African growth successes, cited as support for 'growth promoting policies' (Samatar, 1999; Acemoglu et al., 2003; Maipose and Matsheka, 2008) , while the dismal experience of Zambia is a standard example of African failure attributed to 'economic mismanagement' (Bates and Collier, 1995; Anderson and Morrissey, 2006; Mwanawina and Mulungushi, 2008). Botswana is heavily dependent on revenue from diamond mining and Zambia is similarly dependent on copper earnings. Kenya's relatively good growth performance is widely thought to be underpinned by its commitment to 'capitalist' development (Barkan, 1994; Bigsten and Durevall, 2008; Mwega and Ndung'u, 2008), whilst its counterpart Tanzania is seen as suffering the results of a failed 'socialist' development experiment (Barkan, 1994; Mwase and Ndulu, 2008). Yet both are peasant economies producing a variety of cash crops for the world market and food for the domestic market. Thus, this small group of countries represents a wide range of factors perceived to be important for African economic growth in the post-colonial period (Ndulu et al., 2008a, 2008b).

This paper considers four sources of evidence: the official data as published by the national statistical agencies; the World Development Indicators published by the World Bank (WDI, 2003); the Penn World Tables (Heston et al., 2006, henceforth PWT); and the OECD data (Maddison, 2003). The latter three are the most widely used sources for empirical growth studies. The recently published two-volume study on African growth (Ndulu et al., 2008a, 2008b) uses estimates from PWT, WDI (2003) and Maddison (2003) interchangeably (see for instance Ndulu et al., 2008a: Figure 1.1 and Table 1.4). The reporting of data sources by the international organisations leaves a lot wanting. These series are all loosely based on national account data files, but on which series and how these series are assembled in continuous constant growth time series is not clear. The international database series bridges years when no official data were published and over different base years. The only satisfactory way to deal with inconsistencies in the data and to gauge the effects of revisions is to consult the primary source: the official national accounts data. The advantage of using the national accounts is that they come with guidelines and commentaries. When the underlying methods or basic data for the assembly of the accounts are changed, these changes are usually reported. The inconvenience of the national accounts evidence is that it is not readily downloadable. The publications have to be manually collected, and then the process of data entry and interpretation follows. This study is based on a research visit to the statistical offices of the four countries. In each country reports and handbooks on methodology were collected. This information was supplemented by consultation with representatives of the respective central statistical offices.

The WDI (2003) data are GDP estimates in constant 1995 US dollars. The PWT data used here are real GDP expressed in international 2000 prices (using the chain method) from the International Comparison Programme. The data from Maddison (2003) are annual GDP estimates in international dollars based on

Table 1. Correlation matrix for Botswana

	Botswana	WDI	PWT	Maddison
Botswana	1.00	0.72	0.26	0.38
WDI	0.72	1.00	0.48	0.75
PWT	0.26	0.48	1.00	0.79
Maddison	0.38	0.75	0.79	1.00

Note: Simple correlations between reported annual growth rates (see Online Appendix) for the four series.

Table 2. Correlation matrix for Kenya

	Kenya	WDI	PWT	Maddison
Kenya	1.00	0.50	0.27	0.78
WDI	0.50	1.00	0.90	0.54
PWT	0.27	0.90	1.00	0.32
Maddison	0.78	0.54	0.32	1.00

Note: As for Table 1.

Table 3. Correlation matrix for Tanzania

	Tanzania	PWT	Maddison
Tanzania	1.00	0.13	0.77
PWT	0.13	1.00	0.15
Maddison	0.77	0.15	1.00

Note: As for Table 1; WDI excluded because it only starts in 1988 for Tanzania.

Table 4. Correlation matrix for Zambia

	Zambia	WDI	PWT	Maddison
Zambia	1.00	0.83	0.48	0.90
WDI	0.83	1.00	0.61	0.92
PWT	0.48	0.61	1.00	0.52
Maddison	0.90	0.92	0.52	1.00

Note: As for Table 1.

1990 prices. To obtain internationally comparable estimates the PWT and Maddison (2003) data have been adjusted for purchasing power parity (PPP) prices using the Geary-Khamis method, while the WDI data are adjusted using the Atlas method. The Online Appendix provides details and references to technical discussions of the differences between these methods and sources. The metric that will be compared here is percentage annual growth. While the international databases publish series from the 1960s onwards, the national statistical agencies do not publish estimates before independence. This means that comparative growth evidence analysis based on published national accounts can be made from 1965 onwards. 1995 was chosen as an end year because that was the latest year data were available for all series for all four countries when this field research was conducted.

There are issues that complicate the comparison between the national accounts data and the other series. These are important findings in themselves. There are gaps in the official national accounts of Zambia and Botswana, and for Tanzania WDI does not report any data before 1988. Thus, when the international database compilers are faced with these gaps in the data, different methods are applied to fill the gaps:

> For many countries, the constant series are in different base years, and there are gaps in the series. Where possible, we apply the growth rates from previous national accounts series to the missing data. In other cases, the current price series that existed for a country in 1985 is very different from the current price series today for the same years, resulting in significantly different deflators between PWT versions. We use the latest available series, and users can check for themselves if there are major differences that arise from the underlying countries' national accounts data. (PWT6.2: Technical Documentation)

We are comparing four different sources of evidence. Three of them are expressed in international prices; we can thus compare growth estimates derived from two different types of PPP adjustment. All three international sources are based on national account files, produced by the national statistical agencies. These data have been collected from national statistical agencies, but disseminated and altered by the OECD, the World Bank and others in an essentially non-transparent process (for the end user). The three international databases have in common that they provide national income estimates expressed in one comparable series (i.e. at constant prices) back to 1960 (or 1950 in the case of Maddison (2003)). The official series are not continuous; they are spliced from different base years, with three or four different series covering the period back to independence. We are comparing derived growth rates from these level estimates, and the discrepancies in growth reporting derive from differences in methods of expressing the levels in international prices, filling in gap years, harmonising the original data series across different base years or simply from random errors. A review of the different methods of creating international comparable data issued the following warning:

> Perhaps the overriding message is to exercise caution, particularly with comparisons between countries whose economies are very different, and particularly with the national accounts data provided by countries whose statistical capacity is weak. On the former, there are deep conceptual difficulties that cannot be resolved by collecting better data. On the latter, it must always be remembered that the international accounts are no better than the national accounts of the participating countries. (Deaton and Heston, 2008: 43–44)

At face value we have no criteria for choosing which of the sources is the most correct. The correlations between the growth series presented in Tables 1–4 get us closer to such a judgement. When one of the four series is very different from the other three, this suggests that there is something wrong with that specific series. The extent of mismatch between these sources of growth is a powerful indicator of how accurate any given source of evidence is, and as such it tells us the extent to which an annual growth rate conveys correct or meaningful economic information. Remember that each one of these sources of evidence is supposed to give us a truthful picture of the rate and timing of economic change in the given country. The lack of correlation between four types of evidence that are supposed to relate to exactly the same process using the same indicator is striking.

The discrepancy between the Penn World tables and the official data appears to be large, while the data provided by the OECD (Maddison, 2003) and the World Bank correlate better with the official data (Tables 1–4). In terms of the overall coherence between the national data and the other sources the Zambian data have higher correlations (Table 4). As shown in the Online Appendix, the estimated growth rates in any given year vary between data sources. The highest correlation observed is between the OECD data and WDI on Zambia, with 0.92. The highest correlations in the growth data on Kenya (0.75) and Tanzania (0.53) are lower. The WDI and PWT agree to a considerable extent on Kenya (0.9), but not for Botswana (0.47) and Zambia (0.61). The OECD and the PWT data are seemingly unrelated in the case of Kenya (0.31) and Tanzania (0.15), while the data show a higher level of agreement, though not a satisfactory one, on Zambia (0.51) and Botswana (0.78). The agreement on growth rates for Tanzania is poor, for Botswana and Kenya it is moderate, while for Zambia it is better. In general, based on these four case studies, one source of data cannot be said to better than another. The correlations indicate that if one is interested in growth in any given year for one of these countries what one finds will vary depending on which source one has chosen.

Another way to measure the degree of disagreement on economic growth in these four countries is to investigate the actual discrepancies in the data (the differences between alternative estimates) and the timing of them. Figures 1–4 display the maximum and minimum value of GDP growth from the alternative data sources for each country in each year over 1966–1995. The differences between the two lines represent the annual potential 'error' in the data. Tables 5–8 report two measures of data discrepancies averaged over sub-periods for each country. The 'error range' is the difference between the highest and lowest estimates of average annual growth in each period (this smoothes out some discrepancies in the annual data), while the 'mean error' is the period average of the annual errors.

In all four countries there is a considerable element of error. The difference between the highest and the lowest estimates of period average growth, or the error range, is highest in Botswana, at 4.4 percentage points over 1966–1975 and 1.7 points over the entire period (Table 5). Not in a single year do the four sources agree (see Online Appendix Table A3) and annual discrepancies are marked (Figure 1). This is striking, but does not establish to what extent the difference is unacceptable or statistically important. Small random discrepancies are not the issue, but systematic differences are of concern, as are large random errors that inadvertently bias the results. Between 1966 and 1970 the error range was almost 10 percentage points in Botswana, and the mean error for these early periods was even higher. This is probably explained by gaps in the official data in this period; the errors reflect how

Table 5. Accuracy in growth reporting: Botswana 1965–1995

	WDI	Botswana	PWT	Maddison	Min	Max	Error range	Mean error
1966–1970	11.0	16.8	7.0	10.0	7.0	16.8	9.8	14.2
1971–1975	18.2	16.2	17.2	18.6	16.2	18.6	2.4	12.2
1976–1980	12.2	9.0	13.2	13.2	9.0	13.2	4.2	8.6
1981–1985	10.0	11.2	7.6	10.0	7.6	11.2	3.6	7.3
1986–1990	11.8	12.2	9.2	10.4	9.2	12.2	3.0	7.2
1991–1995	4.0	3.4	4.6	3.4	3.4	4.6	1.2	2.6
1966–1975	14.6	16.5	12.1	14.3	12.1	16.5	4.4	13.2
1976–1995	9.5	9.0	8.7	9.3	8.7	9.5	0.9	6.2
1966–1995	11.2	11.5	9.8	10.9	9.8	11.5	1.7	8.5

Note: The first four rows are averages of annual estimates from the four sources. The error range is calculated as the difference between the highest and the lowest average annual growth rates in each period. Mean error is the average annual error for the period. Averages derived from annual data (see Online Appendix).

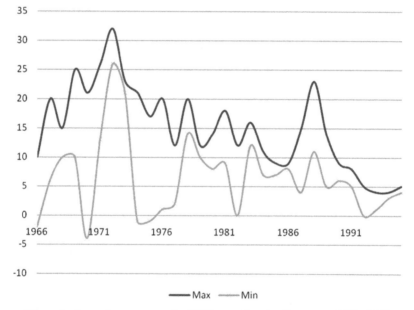

Figure 1. Annual error range in GDP growth rate, Botswana 1965–1995.

different sources 'guesstimate' or interpolate growth differently over this period. Between 1974 and 1977 there were economic shocks both domestically and externally (drought and petroleum prices) and the way the data have picked this up seems to differ. The official data report no or negative growth in 1974 and 1977, while the other sources indicate rapid growth. In the other two periods of large discrepancy 1981–1982 and 1987–1988, it is driven by relatively low PWT estimates of growth, while the other sources report high growth. The disagreement is higher at the beginning of the period and narrows in the latter half of the period. Between 1978

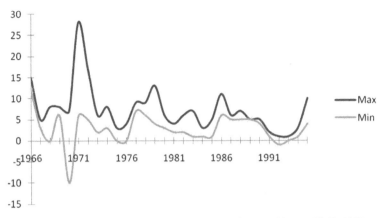

Figure 2. Annual error range in GDP growth rate, Kenya 1965–1995.

Table 6. Accuracy in growth reporting: Kenya 1965–1995

	WDI	Kenya	PWT	Maddison	Min	Max	Error range	Mean error
1966–1970	5.8	8.2	2.6	7.6	2.6	8.2	5.6	6.4
1971–1975	10.0	5.0	11.4	4.2	4.2	11.4	7.2	9.2
1976–1980	6.4	5.6	5.8	6.4	5.6	6.4	0.8	4.2
1981–1985	2.6	4.2	2.2	3.0	2.2	4.2	2.0	3.5
1986–1990	5.6	5.2	6.6	5.6	5.2	6.6	1.4	1.8
1991–1995	1.4	3.2	1.6	1.4	1.4	3.2	1.8	2.4
1966–1975	7.9	6.6	7.0	5.9	5.9	7.9	2.0	7.8
1976–1995	4.0	4.6	4.1	4.1	4.0	4.6	0.6	3.0
1966–1995	5.3	5.2	5.0	4.7	4.7	5.3	0.6	4.6

Note: As for Table 5.

and 1995 annual error range reaches double digits 'only' three times (1982, 1987 and 1988). From 1990 onwards the series all use the same base year, and the error range falls to 1.2 points. In general, PWT provides the minimum estimates of average period growth rates while national or Maddison have the highest estimates.

In Kenya (Figure 2) the mean error is lower, but still considerable at 4.6 percentage points (Table 6) between 1966 and 1995. This high average is driven by a very large discrepancy in the reported annual growth rates between 1970 and 1972 (seen here for 1971–1975). For these two years there are two competing versions of growth (Online Appendix Table A4). If one trusts WDI or PWT, the economy shrank in 1970 (by 5 or 10% respectively) and then grew very fast through 1971 and 1972 (22 and 17% and 28 and 17% respectively). However, if one is more inclined to trust the official or the OECD data instead, the annual rate of growth was stable between 5 and 7 per cent during those three years. There seems to be an error common to both WDI and PWT which explains the spike in the error range those years. A second spike in 1979 is caused by PWT, when growth is reported as 13 per cent, while the official and OECD data agree on 4 per cent growth. The pattern of higher disagreement in the early period in Botswana is repeated in the case of Kenya. The latest official series was based in 1982 which may explain why the error in the series narrows earlier. There is no evident consistency in which sources provide the lowest or the highest estimates.

For Tanzania the mean error for the whole period is lower at 3.6 percentage points (Table 7). The error is not evenly distributed, and in contrast with the other countries except Zambia, the discrepancies in the data are higher towards the end of the period (Figure 3). The WDI does not report growth data for Tanzania before 1988. In 1987 PWT recorded a GDP growth of 20 per cent followed by a negative growth of 33 per cent in 1988. This is due to a mistake in the data, and is also the reason why WDI does not report data before 1988 as reported in a study on Tanzania published by the World Bank (Ndulu and Mutalemwa, 2002: 51). The annual growth rate recorded in 1987 was due to an inclusion of the informal sector while the negative growth rate recorded in 1988 was a change in the statistical method when a World Bank mission judged that existing estimates for agricultural and manufacturing sectors were too

Figure 3. Annual error range in GDP growth rate, Tanzania 1965–1995.

Table 7. Accuracy in growth reporting: Tanzania 1965–1995

	WDI	Tanzania	PWT	Maddison	Min	Max	Error range	Mean error
1966–1970	–	6.0	5.8	6.0	5.8	6.0	0.2	4.2
1971–1975	–	4.6	3.8	4.2	3.8	4.6	0.8	2.4
1976–1980	–	3.2	4.4	3.0	3.0	4.4	1.4	3.4
1981–1985	–	0.8	4.2	0.4	0.4	4.2	3.8	1.0
1986–1990	–	5.6	0.2	3.8	0.2	5.6	5.4	3.2
1991–1995	1.8	2.2	2.2	2.0	1.8	2.2	0.4	7.6
1966–1975	–	5.3	4.8	5.1	4.8	5.3	0.5	3.3
1976–1995	–	3.0	2.8	2.3	2.3	3.0	0.7	3.8
1966–1995	–	3.7	3.4	3.2	3.2	3.7	0.5	3.6

Note: As for Table 5.

high. As for Kenya, there is no evident consistency in which sources provide the lowest or the highest estimates.

For Zambia the average annual error range over the whole period is 3.6 percentage points, the lowest in our sample (Table 8). The gap in the series increases at the end of the period (Figure 4). Accounting practices changed in the late 1990s as a delayed response to a structural change similar to that experienced in Tanzania, and the discrepancies in the data arising from this are clearly visible. The other years when the discrepancy was particularly large, 10 and 9 per cent in 1970 and 1976, coincides with the change of base year in the official data. The PWT most often provides the maximum estimates of average period growth rates, but otherwise there is no clear pattern.

Note that the error ranges reported in tables and referred to above are percentage points. This tends to overstate the proportional error in high growth countries like Botswana, while it understates the error in a low growth country like Zambia. Table 9 represents proportional error as the mean error expressed as a ratio of the average of annual growth estimates reported from the four sources for the relevant

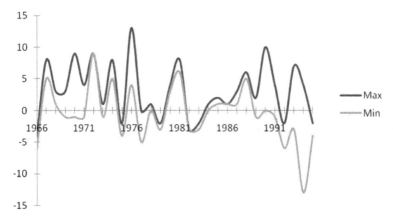

Figure 4. Annual error range in GDP growth rate, Zambia 1965–1995.

Table 8. Accuracy in growth reporting: Zambia 1965–1995

	WDI	Zambia	PWT	Maddison	Min	Max	Error range	Mean error
1966–1970	1.6	3.2	1.2	1.6	1.2	3.2	2.0	4.2
1971–1975	2.4	2.4	3.4	2.4	2.4	3.4	1.0	2.4
1976–1980	0.4	0.8	2.4	0.4	0.4	2.4	2.0	3.4
1981–1985	0.6	0.6	0.8	0.6	0.6	0.8	0.2	1.0
1986–1990	1.8	3.6	2.0	4.0	1.8	4.0	2.2	3.2
1991–1995	−1.2	−2.4	−0.2	−2.2	−2.4	−0.2	2.2	7.6
1966–1975	2.0	2.8	2.3	2.0	2.0	2.8	0.8	3.3
1976–1995	0.4	0.7	1.3	0.7	0.4	1.3	0.9	3.8
1966–1995	0.9	1.4	1.6	1.1	0.9	1.6	0.7	3.6

Note: As for Table 5.

Table 9. Accuracy in growth reporting: Botswana, Kenya, Tanzania and Zambia

	Botswana	Kenya	Tanzania	Zambia
1966–1970	1.27	1.06	0.44	2.21
1961–1975	0.70	1.20	0.95	0.91
1976–1980	0.72	0.69	1.47	3.40
1981–1985	0.75	1.17	3.33	1.54
1986–1990	0.66	0.31	3.88	1.12
1991–1995	0.68	1.26	2.53	5.07
1966–1975	0.92	1.14	0.65	1.45
1976–1995	0.68	0.72	2.77	5.07
1966–1995	0.78	0.91	1.74	2.89

Note: The 'Accuracy' is calculated as the Mean Error (the average annual discrepancy between sources) divided by the average of the growth rates reported in all sources for the relevant period. Table A7 (Online Appendix) reports accuracy using the Error Range and gives a similar picture.

period. When the discrepancy is expressed in this way it becomes clear that while percentage point errors were large in Botswana that was in part due to its high growth rates and that while the percentage point error range in Zambia seemed small that is partly due to its low average growth. In fact, relative to growth rates averaged across sources, errors in Botswana are relatively low (typically the error is less than period average growth) whereas errors are relatively high, often considerably so, in Tanzania and Botswana. Table 9 confirms the observation made earlier that for Kenya and Botswana the accuracy of reporting is poor in the beginning of the period, while in Tanzania and Zambia the accuracy is poor at the end of the period. The extreme is Zambia in 1991–1995 and 1976–1995, where the mean error is five times the average annual growth across sources. For the period 1976–1995 this is driven by a very low average growth rate at only 0.8 per cent, while in the latter period 1991–1995 the error range reached double digits twice and this high error compared to a low growth rate drives the accuracy ratio here.

III. Does Data Quality Matter? Implications for African Growth Analysis

What are the implications for the debate on African growth? A common way to counter this problem is to note that data errors only relate to singular (annual) observations, and one observation alone does not normally inform an economic performance evaluation. In the long run errors can be hoped to be less important. It is true, in mathematical terms, that one mistake in reporting in one year has less impact on the average growth rate if the average is calculated over many years. The effect of an error further depends on how growth in a period is calculated and whether the error is in the starting or end year for the period. A second source of consolation derives from the hope that an error in one direction is evened out over time by an error in the other direction. It may perhaps appear naïve to hope that the average of a sequence of errors will in the end give an accurate result or at least an estimate with a satisfactory accuracy, but in the absence of better methods this is common practice. In this sample, using three decade averages the conventional ranking of Botswana as a star performer and Zambia as a dismal performer is not put in any doubt, and while the relative status of Kenya and Tanzania across shorter time periods would depend on which dataset is used for the comparison across the three decades there is still a growth advantage for Kenya in all three sources.

While the empirical growth literature methodology relies on averaged growth rates over the whole post-colonial period or sub-periods in panel studies it is explicitly based on a correlation between certain policy regimes and economic performance over shorter periods. A recent comprehensive study on African growth is provided by the 'Growth Project' of the African Economic Research Consortium (AERC) that combines both cross-section analysis and 26 country cases to explain the African growth record since 1960 (Ndulu et al., 2008a, 2008b). Here periods of sound and unsound economic policies are picked out based on the growth evidence. This type of analysis is extremely vulnerable to measurement problems (as illustrated in Tables 5–8). The study used different sources of growth data interchangeably, and the soundness of the analysis relies on the cross-country and temporal validity and reliability of the data.

According to PWT Botswana had an average growth of 7 per cent in the first five years after independence compared to 5.8 per cent in Tanzania. Thus the difference between Tanzania and Botswana for this period is surprisingly small. In contrast, Maddison (2003) and the official national evidence report a marked difference between the two countries for the same period. In Kenya during the first five years PWT reports growth as low as 2.8 per cent compared to 8.2 per cent in the official Kenyan data. Using national data for Kenya and Tanzania, and comparing it with scholarship applying PWT data on Botswana, one would find that Kenya outperformed Botswana in the early years and that Tanzania grew slightly slower. A comparison of Zambia and Kenya alone, using official data in Zambia and PWT in Kenya, would have Zambia growing quicker. Academic scholarship often relies on different data in different studies, so there is room for miscommunication given the many different permutations in the ranking of these four countries in the period immediately following independence.

Zambia performed comparatively well at 3.4 per cent average growth in the period 1971–1975 according to PWT, keeping pace with Tanzania's 3.8 per cent according to the same source. The relative performance of countries differs dramatically in the early 1970s if you compare using different sources for each country. For instance, it might come as a surprise to some that Zambia was not lagging significantly behind Kenya, which in the same period was growing at 4.2 per cent according to Maddison (2003) (but averaging 10% growth according to WDI and 11% for PWT). Comparing Tanzania using national data to Kenya according to Maddison's (2003) series, Tanzania outperforms Kenya during this period. It is usually noted in the literature that it was Tanzania's inability to reform quickly enough after the external shocks of the late 1970s that led to its dismal performance in the early 1980s, as compared to Kenya that handled the adjustment fairly well. On this important historical period, PWT takes the opposite view: reporting growth in Tanzania at 4.2 per cent through 1981–1985 compared to 2.2 per cent in Kenya.

The case studies in Ndulu et al. (2008b) divide the four different countries according to periods of economic performance. For Botswana, Maipose and

Matsheka (2008: 512–513) suggest three periods: 1960 to 1975 for 'initial base-creating' followed by 1975 to 1989 referred to as 'consolidation' and the third period, characterised as a move towards private sector-led development, from 1990 to the present. In Kenya four growth episodes are identified: rapid growth 1960–1974, poor performance 1975–1984, a slight recovery 1985–1989 and a slow-down in growth in the 1990s (Mwega and Ndung'u, 2008: 327). Tanzania is treated by Mwase and Ndulu (2008) under the heading of four decades of episodic growth. There is an element of confusion regarding the identification of the relative periods of growth and performance. At times, the early growth period is referred to as covering 1961–1967 and at other times 1960–1970. The 'strong control regime' lasted from 1970 to 1985 when speaking of growth, but started in 1967 when describing policy change. A move towards a market-based economy in 1985, then a period of weakened commitment to reform followed from 1990, before commitment to reforms again strengthened from 1995 onwards. Mwanawina and Mulungushi (2008: 275) propose that Zambia was characterised by a free-market economy between 1960 and 1968, economic nationalisation in 1969 to 1990 and then the familiar u-turn to market-led development in 1991 and onwards. In a similar fashion episodes of growth and policy are identified in other African countries in order to establish a causal link between the different syndromes (state controls, adverse redistribution, inter-temporal unsustainable spending, state breakdown and syndrome free) and GDP growth rates. The robustness of these causal links can seriously be drawn in doubt when one considers the data inconsistencies reported above.

The PWT data for Tanzania have large statistical errors for the late 1980s. These could easily be misinterpreted. Durlauf et al. (2005: 574) argued that a typical phenomenon among low income countries is negative output shocks; being unaware of the statistical error, Tanzania (1987–1990) is included the 'top 10 list' of output shocks in that paper based on the PWT data (national and Maddison estimates are much higher for that period). A recent paper which used PPP growth rates from the World Bank found that high volatility was a defining characteristic of African economies (Arbache and Page, 2007: 9). Table 9 shows the standard deviation in annual growth rates for each data source and there is considerable variation. One should be careful about drawing any conclusions on any systematic bias deriving from four case studies, but it is quite clear that PWT and WDI seem to have a higher volatility than Maddison and the official data for Kenya and Tanzania. This might suggest that volatility, as suggested in the Tanzania example above, is in part explained by statistical errors.

Arbache and Page (2007: 21) study growth over 15-year periods in order 'to get rid of short-run noises'. This will certainly help; the tables above show that the 'error

Table 10. Growth volatility: standard deviation of annual growth rates 1965–1995

	WDI	Official	PWT	Maddison
Botswana	6	7.6	7.5	7.2
Kenya	5.4	2.9	6.6	3
Tanzania		3	9	2
Zambia	4.3	4.5	4.3	5

range' does decrease as the periods of comparison get longer. In their aggregate study they order countries if they are below or above the median per capita growth (0.71 per cent per annum). The findings here using total GDP growth rates show that over the periods 1966–1975 and 1976–1995 the error ranges in percentage points are between 4.4 and 0.7. This indicates that while there are clearly some countries that performed better than others, a number of countries could probably switch from above to below median performance depending on which dataset is used. In a related paper, Arbache and Page (2008) study growth accelerations or decelerations based on four-year moving averages. This type of analysis would be very vulnerable to data problems as the five-year averages reported above show; in particular, what they define as 'turning points' might for some countries be due to the inclusion of an informal sector survey in the 1990s.

The discrepancies between data on the same variable from different sources confound inferences on comparative growth performance, and the problem is likely to be greater when relatively short periods are compared. This has a general implication for studies comparing growth performance before and after structural adjustment, as illustrated above when studies identify 'policy periods' for comparison. The problems are likely to be most severe for the poorest and most unstable countries, but an important question remains regarding the direction of measurement bias: 'Is this dismal performance just an artefact of the data? I think that, on the contrary, the genuine problems that afflict gathering of economic data in the poorest countries are likely overall to have caused an underestimate of their decline. For the countries that have really fallen apart there are no usable data' (Collier, 2007: 9).

A careful reading of descriptions of data collection methods and an examination of the growth evidence presented in this paper would suggest a different interpretation. Data collected by state agencies in the late 1970s and early 1980s, reflecting the declining performance and capacity of parastatals, captured a falling proportion of agricultural output, largely because less of the crop output was marketed through official channels. This resulted in a growing underestimation of GDP because there was inadequate allowance for subsistence production and consumption and/or unrecorded trade and transport, in African countries where these were a major share of economic activity. The change in economic structure with liberalisation temporarily worsened the accounting and record-keeping problem as comprehensive data were no longer available from state agencies. It was not until new GDP series were constructed in the 1990s that new allowances for informal trading based on informal market surveys were introduced. For example, in the case of Tanzania the series connecting the 1980s with the 1990s are not continuous, and incorporating informal sector estimates in the 1990s gives a sudden upward growth effect. Thus decline in the 1980s is likely to have been overestimated, and the (post structural adjustment) growth in 1990 may be similarly overestimated. In studying economic growth throughout this period it is indeed problematic that no source of growth data can be accepted at face value as being inherently accurate. The structural changes in the economy and the subsequent changes in the definition and method of measuring GDP were so radical that the series should be regarded as disconnected.

Regarding Tanzania it is noted is that in the PWT series '1988 is treated as a missing observation because the series shows an erroneous massive downward adjustment in that year' (Ndulu et al., 2008a: 7). The resulting evidence is misleading. The high growth observation (+20% in 1987) was kept, while the misleading low growth (–33% in 1988) was treated as void. In the original series the growth between 1985 and 1995 was measured as averaging almost 2 per cent, but by treating the year 1988 as void the average is 5.4 per cent, thus the resulting data create a fictional rapid post structural adjustment growth recovery.

In Zambia the estimate of total GDP was similarly revised in 1994. According to the new estimates GDP was 13 per cent higher as informal sector activity was incorporated. The Central Statistical Office gave the following warning 'We wish to caution that including the informal sector activity in the Zambia National Accounts may tend to exaggerate the GDP of the nation, relative to other countries or even the previous estimates which mostly excluded it. It must also be recognised that it will be difficult to up-date the sector relation based on indicators in the absence of surveys to monitor the activity in the future' (Republic of Zambia, Central Statistical Office, 1994: 9). Thus while the definition of GDP has increased resulting in a short term adjustment of incomes and bias in growth rate time series, the long term effect is a downward bias. The statistical offices will not be able to recalibrate the estimates of the informal sector annually (estimated at 48% in Zambia in 1994) and will have to rely on rough growth estimates like assuming growth to be proportional to population growth.

An important theme is the concerns voiced in the national accounting method descriptions regarding the difficulty of estimating the size of the informal and subsistence sectors in these economies. The national statistical agencies only get reliable annual information on certain operations. Large-scale manufacturing, state-owned enterprises, large-scale commercial farming, exports and imports and the state's own activities are reasonably well recorded. There are weaknesses related to these data deriving mainly from underreporting to avoid taxation, but there is at least basic statistical data informing the statistical agencies. The remainder of the economy is estimated on various bases. The Zambian Central Statistical Office had two levels of denoting when an estimate is questionable: one asterix denotes 'guesstimate' and two denotes 'guesstimate on a weak basis' (Consolidated National Accounts 1973–1978: Appendix 1). These estimation issues can however be dealt with in more sophisticated analysis.

Based on the reading of national accounting methods in Botswana, Kenya, Tanzania and Zambia (see the Online Appendix for a full list of the documents consulted) some distinct methods of making guesses can be identified. The main differentiation is whether the baseline estimate is grounded in basic data or not. In some cases a sector of the economy is known to consist of one large operator and many small ones and a qualified guess can be made as to how much of the sector is dominated by the large operators for which basic statistical data are available. The statistical office can then assume that the data represent say 60 per cent of the activity in the sector, gross the sector up accordingly, and assume that the rest of the sector grows proportionally. Similar assumptions are made regularly where the sectors are covered by an annual industrial census to adjust for underreporting and non-responding. Here the reported activity would be adjusted upwards on an annual basis assuming proportionality. These methods are not optimal because it is in fact based on guessing, though the guesses might be more or less educated or informed and thus satisfactory. The assumption of proportional growth does preclude any intra-sector structural shifts. A reduction in activity among the large operators in a sector might very well be a result of increased competition from the smaller operators. This would in particular apply to manufacturing, construction, retail trade, transport and other services, and is particularly relevant when one is interested in the relative importance of formal and informal actors in these sectors.

In other cases the national accountants rely on only sporadic censuses for whole sectors or only one baseline estimate. In these cases the means available to the accountants are projections. If there are two points of observations over time, growth will be assumed to have been smooth through these two points, and it will further be assumed that this growth will continue in similar fashion beyond the last observation point. This is the typical method used for estimating population where one usually relies on one census every decade. The main objection to this method is that there is no way of detecting the point of acceleration or deceleration in growth. One further runs the considerable risk of reporting statistical growth. This problem is accentuated by the fact that one census will differ in quality, reliability and coverage from another. Retrospectively there is little chance of determining to what extent the growth is the result of increased statistical efficiency or whether the change relates to the economy itself. The statistical agency is then left with making a guess as to whether the detected growth between the two observations is reasonable, or whether it is a result of a relative under- or over-estimation at one of the points. The statistical office can accept a break in the time series, or extrapolate backwards to change the initial baseline estimate, or simply smooth the growth between the two points of observation. Figure 5 illustrates the different choices available to the national accountants.

Here the value of a sector of the economy was measured or assumed to be 100 in year 1. The sector was assumed to have been growing at 3 per cent per annum. In year 10 a census was undertaken and the sector measured to be 150. 'Measured' represents how the growth pattern would appear if no action to correct backwards

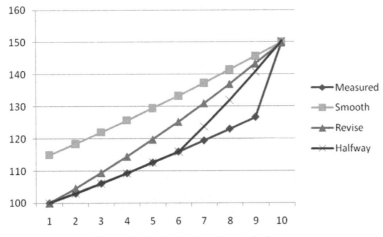

Figure 5. Stylised estimation techniques.

would be taken. 'Revise' is the option taken if the statistical agency chooses to believe that the year 1 baseline estimate was wrong, and that their three per cent growth assumption was correct. 'Smooth' is the choice of changing the annual growth measure when faced with the new year 10 estimate. All these choices have been used at various points in national accounting in the countries studied. The data a scholar uses for evidence for analysis depends on the statistical choice of the accountants, and the evidence obtained in year 9 will be different from the evidence obtainable after year 10. The 'halfway' measure is often opted for, as the agencies are hesitant to revise the series a long way back. This measure was particularly often used in Botswana and Kenya, while in Zambia and Tanzania the offices were willing to accept a break in the series, or wait to include the data when a new constant price series was compiled. The inclusion of new basic data or new estimates, whether they are from 'subsistence', 'informal' or from any other previous 'unrecorded' economic activity does result in random growth effects if a break in the series is not accepted. The case is most radically illustrated in Tanzania and Zambia in the 1990s.

The example of estimation methodology above illustrates the case of a statistical agency having to harmonise two conflicting pieces of evidence. There are also many cases where no such conflict arises as there is no basic statistical evidence at all. This can relate to whole sectors of the economy. Typically this concerns what is called the 'subsistence economy', but it is also done with regard to other sectors or the small-scale operations within a sector. For these sectors a baseline estimate or guess are complemented by assumptions of growth. Food production, water collection, rural construction and real estate growth are assumed to take a certain value per rural household, and then assumed to grow in accordance with rural population growth. Rural population growth was in all African countries slower than total population growth, and so by definition the rural 'subsistence' sector grew slower than the total population. This represents an in-built bias towards a decreasing GDP per capita. This can be quite serious in countries where this sector is particularly large, as in Tanzania. One of the most important conclusions of World Bank (1981: 3) research on the continent was that food production failed to keep up with population growth. While this conclusion might be plausible, it must be true by definition because the evidence is conditioned in that way.

The concurrence of introduction of new base years for the series, changes in the methodology and the inclusion of new benchmark data at the national statistical agency explain some of the extent of documented inaccuracies in growth reporting. The differences in the reported annual growth rates derive from extrapolations across missing years, and smoothing of data across changes in base years. There is an underlying contradiction between what the providers of national account statistics in the national agencies are aiming at, and the purpose of the growth time series of the international agencies. While the national agency strives each year to give the best estimate of economic change in that year in order to inform current policy makers, the users of international databases are interested in the comparison of economic change over time and space. When the time series disseminated by different international databases are constructed using different national account files and different price data these random growth effects appear.

IV. Conclusion. Lessons for Quantitative Interpretations of African Development

If one studies the comparative effect of the external economic shocks of the late 1970s on African economies, what should one do if one source reports 0.4 per cent growth from 1981–1985 and another reports 4.2 per cent for the same country? And what if, for the same period for another country one source reports a 2.2 per cent growth rate and another source 4.2? Did the first country experience rapid economic decline or did it cope fairly well? Did it perform better than the other country? These are precisely the questions one faces if one compares growth in Tanzania and Kenya between 1981 and 1985. Based on the available growth data it is not clear what the relative economic performances of African economies has been.

The study of accuracy in growth reporting for these countries shows that trusting any source at face value is unwise. In terms of a growth rate of any give year the data can indeed be described as random. It is very unlikely that the state of affairs is much better for most other African countries. It is evident that the variation across the sources of data, which are all in wide use, means that cross-country comparison cannot be conclusive based on growth rates alone. There is scope for wider work on this issue, covering more African economies. To improve the conduct of quantitative economic history in Africa it is critical to be open about which sources have informed the respective works, and it is advisable to double check with other sources for coherence.

Most of the accounting in the countries studied has been done according to convention, and therefore to consider the data 'random' would be wrong. While there are some methodological shortcomings, the foremost limitation of the estimates is the quality and availability of basic statistical data. This means the estimates could not easily be subject to a quick fix to make the estimates better. Such improvements would necessitate better basic statistical data, and it is clear that the national agencies have made the most of the data available. A major shortcoming is that the statistical methods, conditioned by the available data, are not fully standardised across the countries.

In general the Penn World Tables seem to be more often out of line compared to the other sources; this may in part be caused by the PPP adjustment which has some well established growth effects. The errors do seem to appear larger when there is gap in the official series, which indicates that there have been (apparent) growth effects when the different constant official series have been harmonised to one constant price series. Both WDI and PWT contain mistakes when there is a change of a base year in the official data. These two sources are evidently based on the official data series, but are not always successfully harmonised over time. In the evidence on Botswana and Kenya there is observed a trend towards better agreement as one get closer to the present. In the case of Zambia and Tanzania the onset of structural adjustment was far more disruptive both to economic structure and public administration resulting in confusion about which sources to use in compiling economic growth statistics.

The underlying evidence for all these sources is the national accounts data series. The sources differ in annual growth rates because of different methods of harmonising official series over different base years and different treatment of gaps in the series. The natural starting point to answer whether the growth evidence reflects actual economic change in these economies is to examine the national accounting methodologies.

The findings here imply that the definition of GDP changes significantly with the introduction of new base years, and that therefore the efforts of PWT and WDI to generate a harmonious series have been less than successful, and the resulting errors have already been subject to scholarly misunderstanding. While earlier research has hinted at the potential problems of the low quality of the African growth evidence this paper has factually established the extent of the problem. The implication is that a study of economic growth in Africa cannot rely on growth data alone without a serious study of the statistical methods used to assemble the growth time series for African economies.

Monographs on economic growth and development published in the 1970s and 1980s typically made use of national account statistics and other officially published data from statistical abstracts. With the appearance of the international databases, evidence has become readily downloadable, and very few researchers consult the actual publications of the statistical offices. Database data are frequently treated as primary evidence, but they are not. The main problem is the inability to directly check the source and the method used to obtain the data. Srinivasan (1992: 24–25) requested better documentation in the international databases in the interest of 'truth in data retailing' with a specific reference to the World Development Indicators and Penn World Tables. This call has not been heard, but perhaps it is also fair to call upon scholars to be more cautious data consumers. The last empirical work on the quality of African data was done by Blades (1980). One of the resulting reports was justified on the grounds that 'it is not possible to make intelligent use of the published statistics without knowing the estimation procedures used and the assumptions on which they are based' (Blades, 1975: 8). It follows literally that since such care has not been taken, most academic work on economic growth in Africa has been unintelligent. That would perhaps be to draw the implication too far. It might suffice to conclude that the subsequent research has not been properly informed.

Acknowledgements

I wish to thank friends and former colleagues at the Economic History Department at London School of Economics and Political Science for many helpful and critical comments on previous drafts of this paper, an anonymous referee and the journal Editor. In addition I received useful feedback on the paper when I presented versions of it at the annual African Economic History Workshop at LSE 2006, The Sound Economic History Workshop 2007 at Lund University, Economic History Society Annual Conference 2008 at University of Nottingham, the 11th Conference of Africanists in Moscow 2008 , the 2008 UK Biennial Conference of African Studies Association in Preston and at the Annual Conference at the Centre for the Study of African Economies in Oxford 2009. All the shortcomings of this paper are my responsibility.

References

Acemoglu, D., Johnson, S.H. and Robinson, J.A. (2003) An African success story: Botswana, in: D. Rodrik (ed) *In Search of Prosperity: Analytic Narratives on Economic Growth* (Princeton: Princeton University Press), pp. 80–122.

Anderson, E. and Morrissey, O. (2006) A statistical approach to identifying poorly performing countries. *Journal of Development Studies*, 44(2), pp. 289–310.

Arbache, J.S. and Page, J. (2007) Patterns of long term growth in Sub-Saharan Africa. World Bank Policy Research Paper, 4398, World Bank, Washington, DC.

Arbache, J.S. and Page, J. (2008) Hunting for leopards. Long run country dynamics in Africa. World Bank Policy Research Paper, 4715, World Bank, Washington, DC.

Ariyo, A. (1996) *Quality of Macroeconomic Data on Africa: Nigeria as a Case Study* (Nairobi: African Economic Research Consortium).

Arkadie, B. van (1973) National accounting and development planning: a review of some issues. *Development and Change*, 4(2), pp. 15–31.

Barkan, J. (ed.) (1994) *Beyond Capitalism vs. Capitalism in Kenya and Tanzania* (London: Lynne Rienner).

Bates, R.H. and Collier, P. (1995) The politics and economics of policy reform in Zambia. *Journal of African Economies*, 4(2), pp. 115–143.

Bigsten, A. and Durevall, D. (2008) Factor proportions, openness and factor prices in Kenya 1965–2000. *Journal of Development Studies*, 42(3), pp. 469–489.

Blades, D. (1975) *Non-Monetary (Subsistence) Activities in the National Accounts of Developing Countries* (Paris: OECD).

Blades, D. (1980) What do we know about levels and growth of output in developing countries? A critical analysis with special reference to Africa, in R.C.O. Mathews (ed) *Economic Growth and Resources: Proceedings of the Fifth World Congress, International Economic Association, Tokyo, Vol. 2, Trends and factors* (New York: St. Martin's Press). pp. 68–75.

Collier, P. (2000) *The Bottom Billion: Why the Poorest Countries Are Failing and What Can Be Done About It* (New York: Oxford University Press).

Deaton, A. and Heston, A. (2008) Understanding PPPS and PPP-based national accounts. NBER Working Paper No. 14499, NBER, Cambridge MA.

Durlauf, S., Johnson, P. and Temple, J. (2005) Growth econometrics, in: P. Aghion and S. Durlauf (eds) *Handbook of Economic Growth* (Amsterdam: Elsevier). pp. 555–667.

Heston, A., Summers, R. and Aten, B. (2006) Penn World Table Version 6.2, Center for International Comparisons of Production, Income and Prices at the University of Pennsylvania.

Kpedekpo, G.M.C. and Arya, P.L. (1981) *Social and Economic Statistics for Africa: Their Sources, Collection, Uses and Reliability* (London: Allen & Unwin).

Maddison, A. (2003) *The World Economy: Historical Statistics* (Paris: OECD).

MacGaffey, J. (1991) *The Real Economy of Zaire: the Contribution of Smuggling and other Unofficial Activities to National Wealth* (London: James Currey).

Maipose, G.S. and Matsheka, T.C. (2008) The indigenous development state and growth in Botswana, in: B. J. Ndulu, S.A. O'Connell, J.P. Azam, R.H. Bates, A.K. Fosu, J.W. Gunning and D. Njinkeu (eds) *The Political Economic of Growth in Africa 1960–2000: Case Studies* (Cambridge, UK: Cambridge University Press), pp. 325–368.

Mwanawina, I. and Mulungushi, J. (2008) Zambia, in: B.J. Ndulu, S.A. O'Connell, J.P. Azam, R.H. Bates, A.K. Fosu, J.W. Gunning and D. Njinkeu (eds) *The Political Economic of Growth in Africa 1960–2000: Case Studies* (Cambridge, UK: Cambridge University Press). Appendix (CD-ROM).

Mwase, N. and Ndulu, B.J. (2008) Tanzania: explaining four decades of episodic growth, in: B.J. Ndulu, S.A. O'Connell, J.P. Azam, R.H. Bates, A.K. Fosu, J.W. Gunning and D. Njinkeu (eds) *The Political Economic of Growth in Africa 1960–2000: Case Studies* (Cambridge, UK: Cambridge University Press), pp. 426–471.

Mwega, F.M. and Ndung'u, N.S. (2008) Explaining economic growth performance: the case of Kenya, in: B.J. Ndulu, S.A. O'Connell, J.P. Azam, R.H. Bates, A.K. Fosu, J.W. Gunning and D. Njinkeu (eds) *The Political Economic of Growth in Africa 1960–2000: Case Studies* (Cambridge, UK: Cambridge University Press), pp. 325–369.

Ndulu, B.J. and Mutalemwa, C.K. (2002) *Tanzania at the Turn of the Century – Background Papers and Statistics* (Washington DC: World Bank).

Ndulu, B.J., O'Connell, S.A., Azam, J.P., Bates, R.H., Fosu, A.K., Gunning, J.W. and Njinkeu, D. (eds) (2008a) *The Political Economic of Growth in Africa 1960–2000: An Analytic Survey* (Cambridge UK: Cambridge University Press).

Ndulu, B.J., O'Connell, S.A., Azam, J.P., Bates, R.H., Fosu, A.K., Gunning, J.W. and Njinkeu, D. (eds) (2008b) *The Political Economic of Growth in Africa 1960–2000: Case Studies* (Cambridge UK: Cambridge University Press).

Republic of Zambia, Central Statistical Office (1973–1978) *Annexes to Provisional Estimates. Consolidated National Accounts 1973–1978* (Lusaka: Central Statistical Office).

Samatar, A.I. (1999) *An African Miracle State and Class Leadership and Colonial Legacy in Botswana Development* (London: Heinemann).

Seers, D. (1952) The role of national income estimates in the statistical policy of an under-developed area. *The Review of Economic Studies*, 20(3), pp. 159–168.

Srinivasan, T.N. (1994) The data base for development analysis: an overview. *Journal of Development Economics*, 44(1), pp. 3–27.

World Bank (1981) *Accelerated Development in Sub-Saharan Africa: An Agenda for Action* (Washington DC: World Bank).

World Development Indicators (2003) Washington DC: World Bank. [CD-ROM].

GDP Revisions and Updating Statistical Systems in Sub-Saharan Africa: Reports from the Statistical Offices in Nigeria, Liberia and Zimbabwe

MORTEN JERVEN, YEMI KALE, MAGNUS EBO DUNCAN & MOFFAT NYONI

School for International Studies, Simon Fraser University, Vancouver, Canada, National Bureau of Statistics, Abuja, Nigeria, Statistical Services, Accra, Ghana, National Statistics Agency, Harare, Zimbabwe

ABSTRACT   *The quality of economic statistics in Africa has been likened to a statistical tragedy. Currently many statistical systems in Africa are being updated. This report from the statistical offices in Nigeria, Liberia and Zimbabwe documents that base year, data and methods used to generate GDP estimates currently date from 1990, 1992 and 1994. There is a growing need for macroeconomic statistics, but a rebasing of GDP estimates is costly and time consuming. The work to update economic statistics in Nigeria and Zimbabwe is still ongoing, while efforts to generate an authoritative estimate of the Liberian economy have proved unsuccessful.*

Recent publications have drawn attention to a key problem in the provision of macroeconomic statistics in countries in sub-Saharan Africa, namely that many GDP estimates are unreliable, out of date and likely to change dramatically upwards when revised (Jerven, 2013a, 2013b, 2013c), and that therefore current data may underestimate and misrepresent GDP for many countries. In response to such recent publications and the significant upward revision of GDP in Ghana (Jerven & Duncan, 2012), some commentators have gone as far as to declare the situation a statistical tragedy (Deverajan 2013).

In the light of the many recent improvements made in the provision of most social statistics, it may seem unfair or misleading to call the current state of affairs a tragedy. The importance of economic statistics in particular and the role of the statistical offices in general was neglected in the 1980s and 1990s. With the Millennium Development Goals, measurability came into focus, and with many African countries seeking to enter capital markets and attract investors. The data situation in African countries is changing rapidly. It may still be too early to declare that an 'African statistical renaissance' has fully occurred (Kiregyera, 2013). As a recent wave of GDP revisions have signalled, there is increased activity in the provision macroeconomic statistics from statistical offices in response to this growing demand, but the progress has been uneven.

The upward revision in Ghana, almost doubling GDP, was caused by an update of the statistical methods and the data basis for aggregating GDP. Until 2010, the Ghanaian economy had been accounted for using a 1993 base year, and data sources were growing increasingly out of date and were not capturing changes in the Ghanaian economy. When the base year was changed to 2006 in 2010 and new data sources were used to get a more accurate picture of the Ghanaian economy, GDP in Ghana almost doubled. As a result, in 2011 Ghana moved from the status of a low-income economy to the status of a lower-middle-income economy. Preliminary figures from Nigeria indicate a similar large jump in GDP there (*The Economist*, 2014), while recent reports from Kenya and Zambia signal increases in the order of 25–30 per cent as benchmark years are being updated across the region (*Financial Times*, 2014; The Africa Report, 2014).

Recent reports that have assessed trends in growth and poverty in Africa and have sought to portray an accurate picture of economic conditions on the continent show an increasing awareness of the problems of outdated statistical systems and the fact that GDP estimates between African economies are not comparable (African Development Bank, 2013a; International Monetary Fund [IMF], 2013a). This report from the statistical offices in Nigeria, Liberia and Zimbabwe highlights that there is a growing demand for statistics, accompanied by increased attention to the importance of updating economic statistics, particularly the data and methods used in national accounts to calculate GDP and other important economic development metrics. However, a rebasing of GDP estimates for a country is a costly exercise that consumes much time and many resources.

Currently, the work to update economic statistics in Nigeria and Zimbabwe is still ongoing, while the last effort to generate an authoritative estimate of the Liberian economy ultimately proved unsuccessful. Currently, the base years for calculating GDP in Nigeria, Liberia and Zimbabwe are 1990, 1992 and 1994 respectively. The preliminary new base year estimates for Nigeria were announced in April 2014, and the change caused an upward revision of the current price estimates of 89 per cent (National Bureau of Statistics [NBS], 2014). While these reports speak mainly to the situation in the country concerned, it may be noted that on the Statistical Capacity Indicator published by the World Bank, Nigeria, Zimbabwe and Liberia scored 76, 53 and 43 on a scale from 0 to 100, where 100 is meeting all international standards on periodicity, methodology and source data in reporting (World Bank, n.d.). For 2012, the average overall score for 53 African countries considered was 59, while the average for the whole sample of countries was 66.

As noted above, the picture of benchmark years for the continent changes rapidly. However, in 2013 the IMF's Regional Economic Outlook for sub-Saharan Africa surveyed 45 countries, and found that only four countries met the five-year rule (having a base year of 2007 or newer) – Cape Verde, Malawi, Mauritius and South Sudan – while 28 countries had base years more than 10 years old and 13 countries were still using base years more than 20 years old (IMF, 2013b). Thus the question we discuss here applies widely.

Nigeria's National Bureau of Statistics and the Reset of the Nigerian Statistical System

Arguably, Nigeria is experiencing a statistical reawakening. This section highlights current drive to reset the Nigerian statistical system through four key activities; rebasing of the national account estimates; scaling up the use of administrative statistics where possible; increasing data generation from the ground up via surveys; and engaging various stakeholders at the subnational and local levels of government.

Since the enactment of the Statistics Act in 2007, Nigeria's national statistical system has embarked on a transformation (Akinyosoye, 2008).[1] Yet, like many other national institutions, it continues to struggle against perception problems, which are largely a carry-over from over two decades of military rule and perhaps a suspicion of government in general. In some cases, data users are genuinely unaware of the considerable improvements in both data availability and credibility, presupposing that the days of 'no-data' which was an attribute of the precedents of NBS still exist. Others simply choose to disbelieve official statistics because 'it doesn't match facts on the ground'. This typically arises when users are unable or have difficulty in appreciating how official statistics (usually at aggregate level) relate to them, as individuals or businesses. These are the very reasons enormous efforts have been expended toward transforming – and resetting – the national statistical system, as discussed in this article.

Throughout its history, the national statistical system, and in particular the National Bureau of Statistics (NBS), has played a strategic role in Nigeria's development policy and planning structure. As the nation has evolved, the statistical system has tried to keep pace. The extent to which the system has been able to track and report on Nigeria's socio-economic development progress over the last century has been well documented – and an objective assessment would suggest a mixed outcome. However, it is useful to keep in mind the challenge of economic development and Africa's history of unrepresentative governments. Failure of governments to respond to the public has hampered record keeping in many African countries, including Nigeria. Over time, this has led to the seeming preference for rushed policy-making and implementation of projects to achieve political ends rather than because of economic or social welfare considerations.

Over the history of the national statistical system, a number of reforms have been initiated. The most recent is the comprehensive overhaul of the national statistical system through the enactment of the Statistics Act in 2007. This represents the latest watershed in the history of statistical development in Nigeria. The Act is supported by a key statistical planning and strategy document called the National Strategy for the Development of Statistics (NSDS), an internationally recognised framework for fostering statistical development adopted by Nigeria and several other countries.[2] The NSDS seeks to deploy the tool of strategic planning to ensure a coordinated and coherent data production system within the country's statistical system, by bringing together all agencies involved in data production across the three tiers of government (federal, state and local). In essence, it provides a framework for development and ownership of statistics in the country, enabling participants in statistical production to generate and disseminate reliable and timely statistics that will assist in the formulation, implementation, monitoring and evaluation of government policies and programmes.

The National Bureau of Statistics and Nigeria's National Statistical System before the Statistical Act of 2007

In the late twentieth century and into the twenty-first century, data production in Nigeria proliferated at the federal and state levels as various political changes over the period led to the creation of 19, 21, 30 and eventually 36 states. These changes increased the number of state statistical agencies at those levels. Furthermore, a military decree, Decree 43 of 1988, which reorganised the Federal Civil Service, created further decentralisation as departments of Planning, Research and Statistics were established in all ministries and government agencies.

In Nigeria, efforts at development planning gained momentum in each successive year after 1999. Prior to the adoption of the NSDS, however, the most notable reform of the national statistical system during the period 1988 to 2005 was the creation of the Statistical Master Plan (SMP) in 2004. This plan was a five-year roadmap that included milestones, a framework for meeting user needs, mechanisms for feedback and learning, and a structure that harnessed and leveraged international and national resources, taking into account the three-tier government structure.

This process led to the development of the National Economic Empowerment & Development Strategy (NEEDS) at the federal level in 2004 and its state-level counterpart, State Economic Empowerment and Development Strategies (SEEDS). NEEDS evolved as Nigeria's poverty reduction strategy paper in 2004 that in part aimed to strengthen the country's progress toward the attainment of the MDGs, and was a pre-condition for the high-profile debt relief the country received in 2005. With such renewed focus on economic planning, the role of statistics naturally became an important consideration. Both the MDG and the NEEDS/SEEDS process revealed that the country's statistical system required an overhaul to support not only MDG planning and tracking, but also development planning at all levels.

The Partnership in Statistics Development in the 21st Century (PARIS21, 1999), put together by the OECD, the World Bank, the European Commission, the IMF, and the United Nations, and the World Bank's Marrakech Action Plan for Statistics (MAPS, 2004) were fortunate statistical developments. Both programmes highlighted the need for high-quality statistics in developing countries and also proposed a roadmap for overcoming a key development challenge. These frameworks also served as critical inputs for the development of Nigeria's National Strategy for the Development of Statistics (2010–2014).

So Where Exactly Are the Numbers? Challenges in Data Generation for Nigeria

The first challenge is geographical. In 2012, Nigeria had a population of 167 million people and an area of about 923,768 square kilometres. The country consists of 36 states, 774 local governments and a federal capital territory, Abuja. Current budgetary allocations for the collection and management of statistics at the federal level are disbursed across 37 state offices, three Schools of Statistics, and six zonal offices of the National Bureau of Statistics. Each receives less than $0.5million annually. Given the current population of the country, these resources are very thin. This fact, coupled with the challenging geographical environment within which data collection takes place, imposes constraints on data-gathering activities, especially in topographically challenging areas such as the Niger Delta, where staff must visit some areas via boats to gather data.

The second challenge is low literacy levels, a lack of appreciation for record keeping and a poor understanding of the benefit of data. These factors constantly hamper efforts to generate and coordinate data production activities. This ultimately means that the NBS needs more time than is necessary to process field data. The third challenge is the low priority accorded to statistical activities. Although allocations have recently improved, more funding is needed.

The fourth challenge is the lack of trust in the government in some communities. This prevents individuals from revealing accurate information about themselves, such as number of children, income and expenditure, or asset ownership. Only advocacy can change this. In the recent past, the Bureau has constantly implemented multiple initiatives to address the perception problem.

Rapid Economic Growth and an Increased Demand for Data

The resurgent demand for data from the national statistical system can be broadly classified as driven by both exogenous and endogenous factors. Exogenously, the global financial crisis that started in the United States in 2008 forced investors to look more toward emerging markets as alternative investment opportunities. Nigeria has been receptive to international investors coming into the country.

According to the World Economic Outlook (IMF, 2013a), global economic growth rates averaged 4.4 per cent in the period 2004–2012. During this period, developed economies – the United States, the euro area and Japan in particular – grew at 2.5 per cent, 2.0 per cent and 2.4 per cent respectively, while Nigeria recorded an average growth rate of 7.2 per cent. After the onset of the 2008 global financial crisis (2008–2012), growth in developed economies (particularly the United States and the euro area) slowed to an average of 2.1 per cent and 1.3 per cent respectively. In contrast, Nigeria's growth during the period recorded an averaged 7.0 per cent. Statisticians at the NBS have experienced an increase in requests for information from international investors and analysts looking for explanations or clarification on macroeconomic statistics produced by NBS.

Endogenous factors broadly refer to developments on the local front that have also spurred the demand for data. Since the country's return to strategic planning in 2007, the design and implementation of Nigeria's Vision 20:2020, as well as the growing emphasis on key performance indicators for measuring public service delivery, there has been a greater demand for reliable data by government ministries, departments and agencies.[3] The focus on strategic planning seeks to emphasise output and outcomes rather than solely relying on inputs or how much money has been spent. The Nigerian government is no longer satisfied with saying that it has built, for example, 100 hospitals; instead it focuses on how an increased number of hospitals is reflected in MDG indicators such as infant mortality or HIV prevalence.

The government has recognised that producing such data requires better funding for the National Bureau of Statistics; over the period 2006 to 2013, total allocations for the bureau grew from $17,173,630 to $30,734,641, an increase of nearly 79 per cent. While the recurrent budget for the organisation has improved over the years, these funds cover only salaries for personnel costs and day-to-day costs. The capital budget is what provides funding for key surveys and projects the NBS intends to carryout for the fiscal year. While the capital allocation was cut by almost 50 per cent in 2011, the current administration increased the capital allocation by 25 per cent in 2012 and by a considerable 280.7 per cent for 2013.

Rebasing the National Account Statistics: The Elephant in the Room

GDP estimates are expressed in both current prices and constant prices. Current prices are estimates expressed at prices of the prevailing accounting period, otherwise known as the nominal GDP.

However, a proper assessment of economic growth in a country demands the removal of the illusions created by the price effect (inflation). When this is done, the results are real (constant) GDP estimates. Real GDP is estimated by calculating GDP for each year at the prices of a particular year, called the base year. The base year provides the mathematical anchor, or the reference point to which comparisons are made. Currently, national account estimates for Nigeria use the base year of 1990. The rebasing of the estimates is long overdue, given the recommendation that national account estimates should be revised every five years. The Nigerian government has given full support to the rebasing project. Rebasing involves changing the price and quantity base for individual prices and quantity relatives, updating weights used to aggregate individual quantity relatives into sub-indexes, and aggregating these sub-indexes to aggregated indexes.

Rebasing is important to give a clear and up-to-date picture of an economy, because over time prices change, as does the structure of an economy in terms of production patterns. Changes occur due to the introduction of new products or alteration in the variety of products and services because of technological innovations and developments. Changes also occur in consumption patterns, structural changes in the acquisition of capital goods and in the openness of an economy over time. These changes imply that there are changes to the relative prices of commodities. As consumption and production patterns change over time, the price structure of the economy changes and the base year structure becomes less representative of the economy.

One example that shows the need to rebase the national account estimates in Nigeria is the results of the 2010 Survey Report on Micro, Small and Medium Enterprises (MSMEs). According to the report, the total number of enterprises was 17,284,671 (microenterprises 17,261,753, small enterprises 21,264 and medium enterprises 1,654). The ratio of the output of the MSMEs to overall GDP was at 46.5 per cent (see Table 1).

Table 1. Contribution of micro, small, and medium enterprises to nominal GDP by sector, Nigeria, 2010 (millions of naira)

Sector	GDP, micro	GDP, small	GDP, medium	Total MSME contribution to GDP	Total GDP by sector	Percentage MSME contribution to total sector GDP
Agriculture, hunting, forestry and fishing	7,174,496	2,605,244	325,377	10,310,655	10,310,655	98
Mining and quarrying	1,943	16,193	12,833	45,691	45,691	67
Manufacturing	47,023	188,092	174,809	643,070	643,070	63
Building and construction	1,934	7,738	32,777	394,666	394,666	10
Wholesale and retail trade: repair of motor vehicles and household goods	183,075	2,171,612	805,530	4,648,696	4,648,696	67
Hotels and restaurants	4,795	31,970	9,452	113,791	113,791	40
Transport, storage and communications	51,010	83,464	180,116	791,543	791,543	39
Financial intermediation	4,925	15,762	6,304	507,799	507,799	5
Real estate, renting and business activities	1,083,974	235,130	17,392	1,348,226	1,348,226	99
Education	4,487	8,413	14,022	56,091	56,091	48
Health and social work	2,950	3,058	3,195	12,470	12,470	73
Other community, social and personal service activities	308,578	59	62	308,764	308,764	99
Totals	8,869,195	5,366,741	1,581,875	15,817,812	19,181,468	
Total nominal GDP at current basic prices					33,984,754	46

Source: National Bureau of Statistics and Small and Medium Enterprises Development Agency of Nigeria (2010, Table 100).

The MSME study (otherwise known as the SMEDAN report) was the first national-scale study of its kind in Nigeria. However, the total MSME-to-GDP ratio is based on GDP values at the 1990 base year. It is more than likely that once the GDP values are revised and additional data sources from surveys and administrative data are added, the nominal values of GDP will increase. Preliminary values from the Harmonised Nigeria Living Standard Survey 2009/10 (National Bureau of Statistics, n.d.) indicate substantially higher private final consumption estimates, giving support to the likelihood that Nigeria's GDP is being understated.

The basis for the revision can be categorised into four broad aspects. First, there will be a change in conceptual treatment. In revising the national account estimates, Nigeria will move from its current use of the 1993 System of National Accounts (SNA) to the most current version of 2008, and update the base year from 1990 to 2010. SNA 2008 recommends a way of recording certain variables different from SNA 1993: for example, expenditure on research and development (R&D).

Second, there will be an update in the classification of economic activities. NBS will move from using the International Standard Industrial Classification Revision 3.1 for its base statistics to Revision 4. This will mean substantial changes in the classification of economic activity; a preliminary reclassification of the Nigerian economy by the National Accounts Division reflects a different economic classification for reporting purposes. For example, the information and communications sector is currently estimated based on the records of telecommunications firms only. After the rebasing process, the system of national accounts will incorporate other data services' providers in addition to phone services, and will expand to four economic sub-activities. Similarly, the manufacturing sector previously covered three economic activities, but going forward will be further disaggregated to 13. This change in classification will have an impact on both the sample size for the GDP estimates as well as the relative weights for each economic activity. Specifically, the business register, which is a list of establishments from which the samples are drawn, has been expanded from just over 80,000 firms to over 850,000 firms. This reflects the fact that more activities are being captured in the GDP compilation framework. Some activities that witnessed considerable update include wholesale and retail trade and so forth, which previously contained 16,583 firms but now has over 500,000 firms. Similarly, professional services included 4,593 firms, but now includes 125,482 firms, to name but a few. On the whole, while the NBS reports on the economy according to 33 economic activities at present, the new classification will report on 46 activities to highlight changes in the economy since 1990. In total, the new economic classification will contain 224 groups and 410 classes.

A third aspect of change will be a marked improvement in data sources, both in terms of the quality and quantity of base data. To date, NBS has relied on quarterly field surveys of establishments to elicit information regarding firm operations, output, intermediate consumption and other indicators needed for GDP computation. This process was expensive, and the survey returns were sometimes late and often incomplete or inaccurate. The rebasing exercise, however, provides an opportunity to improve data sources by placing greater reliance on a better organised system of administrative statistics. This involves obtaining data from the industry regulators, which typically mandates periodic reporting of industry operators. For example, the Central Bank of Nigeria provides relevant data on all the banks in the country (and other financial institutions it regulates). Similarly, the National Communications Commission and the Securities and Exchange Commission will provide data on the operations of telecommunications and publicly listed companies respectively, based on a reporting template pre-pared by NBS. Financial (tax) records from the Federal Inland Revenue Service, the audited reports of state corporations, the Office of the Accountants-General of the States and the Federation, as well as companies' annual reports, are all sources that will replace the traditional emphasis on establishment surveys. This greatly increases the quality and quantity of sector data, as well as the timeliness of reporting.

In addition to these data sources, the NBS is planning nine sector surveys for 2013: hotels and restaurants; real estate; transportation; mining and quarrying; business services; construction; education; health; and manufacturing. The Bureau will also conduct a national census on commercial and industrial establishments, as well as an agricultural census. Lastly, a detailed producer price index will be developed to help deflate nominal GDP estimates.

Fourth, the on-going development of a supply and use table (SUT) is expected to further enhance the integrity of the finalised GDP estimates.

In Ghana's most recent revision,[4] the major increase of GDP estimates came from including new data and rebasing the weight of the contribution of various sectors to GDP, taking account of structural changes in the Ghanaian economy. Nigerian statisticians feel that because of the likelihood of significant changes in classification and in the size of the economy since the current base year was 1990, communication to data users about the pending revision and likely changes must be very clear. Communication with data users must be constant throughout the process, and not only at the conclusion of the process. In addition, all stakeholders (including government agencies, private business, business membership organisations, trade associations, independent analysts, development partners and research institutions), have been constituted into various technical committees to ensure transparency and the incorporation of feedback and best practices along the way.

Lessons from the Attempted Revisions of National Income Accounts Estimates of Liberia in 2010

Liberia was involved in a long civil war from 1989 to 2003 that cost more than 250,000 lives and displaced nearly one million people. The country returned to democratic rule in January 2006, when Ellen Sirleaf Johnson was elected president. After 14 years of war, Liberians were ready for the development of basic services on peaceful terms, particularly electricity and primary infrastructure. Many businesses that fled the country, taking capital and expertise with them, began to return after the installation of a democratically elected government in 2006. In tune with these developments, the demand for macroeconomic statistics increased.

The World Bank estimated Liberia's per capita GDP as US$130 in 2005, according to data from the African Development Indicators database (World Bank, 2007).[5] An updated database on all economic activities was needed for the post-conflict economy. National accounts had previously been rebased to 1987, on the basis of National Accounts Survey conducted by the Department of Statistics (now the Liberia Institute of Statistics and Geo-Information Services [LISGIS]). The results were published in December 1987. Another attempt to rebase national accounts was made 2001, but these results were not finalised because of a poor response rate. Therefore, GDP figures were derived from administrative and other related records. Additionally, where there were no data, guesstimates were made.

The evidence that the published GDP estimates for Liberia are highly underestimated is strong. First, the published GDP estimate for 2008 is USD919.9 million. This translates to a per capita GDP of USD262.83. This figure is well below the poverty lines set by two different approaches for rural and urban areas in 2007 using the results of a Core Welfare Indicators Questionnaire survey that was conducted that year. The first approach set the poverty line at USD344.60 for rural areas and USD376.55 for urban areas. This method puts the percentage of population living below the poverty line at 63.8 per cent. The second approach set the poverty line at USD402.30 rural area and USD567.16 for urban areas.

Another piece of evidence for underestimation of GDP is that imports of goods and services for 2008 were 83.3 per cent of GDP. According to available comparative statistics, this ratio was the highest in the ECOWAS subregion.[6] Because of the level of poverty and pace of development in Liberia, the import/GDP ratio looks overstated, likely because of a lower GDP estimate than is accurate. The question this statistic raises is: 'Are the majority of Liberians living on food aid?' The import data disaggregated by the Standard International Trade Classification (SITC) do not suggest that this is the case.[7]

Finally, the ration of tax revenue to GDP in Liberia was as high as 28 per cent in 2008. In a country with a large informal sector, a country that has the lowest tax rate in the ECOWAS subregion, who was taxed to achieve that revenue? Given that the average for low-income sub-Saharan African countries is 17 per cent, it is unlikely that Liberia had such an effective tax revenue system and even more unlikely that such high revenues could be collected at such low levels of income.

Macroeconomic statistics that paint a fairly adequate and accurate picture of the Liberian economy are of course useful for planners, advisors, and analysers occupied with the development of the Liberian economy. Having comparable methods and comparable validity of the estimates is important, particularly for international comparisons. Most macroeconomic indicators used to measure the health of an economy use GDP as a denominator. Two of the benchmark indicators in the convergence criteria for the implementation of a single currency for the countries in the West Africa Monetary Zone (WAMZ) use GDP as the denominator, fiscal deficit/GDP ratio and tax revenue/GDP ratio. This means that if a country's GDP estimate is far from reality, a wrong assessment will be about whether a country is meeting its convergence criteria.

The following report is a based on observations made when Magnus Ebo Duncan was on a mission to rebase national accounts in Liberia in 2010. The mission was part of the technical assistance programme of the World Bank country office in Liberia to help the country build a good databank for policy and decision-making. The first visit to Liberia under the contract was made to conduct a data audit to establish the adequacy of data for the review of the national income accounts estimates. Four subsequent visits of durations between six and fifteen days each were made to help the LISGIS to re-benchmark the national income accounts estimates. What follows is Magnus Ebo Duncan's estimate of the tasks that needed to be completed if the revision was to be completed in 2010.

In 2010 there was no institutionalised mechanism for routine data collection for national accounts in Liberia. In addition, the existing database was not sufficient for comparing and triangulating data in order to assess the quality of information from different sources. There was also no documentation of the methodological procedure for compiling national accounts. It was thus difficult to review the compilation procedures for published estimates and compare those estimates with newly generated estimates to ascertain reasons for disparities. There was no effective coordination between different divisions in LISGIS to ease data collection, and there were no clear systems to make data from government departments available for data collection. In sum, the compilers of national accounts faced data gaps in available statistics which made it difficult to compile good national accounts. LISGIS lacked the human capacity to build a strong national accounts unit and to produce key economic indicators.

In order to rebase the national accounts for 2010, the basic data needed were data from businesses and economic activities. In order to aggregate national accounts, detailed demographic data were also needed. It would have been preferable to have data showing the population in each socio-economic group, more detailed information on activity by sector (for example, public, private formal, private informal) and industry (for example, agriculture, manufacturing, transport) . In addition to such an overview of the demographic profile of the country, it was necessary to have data equivalent to a household budget survey. This would be needed to calculate consumption and to then distinguish between consumption needs that were met by purchased goods and services and those that were met through own production. It was also essential to have access to government fiscal data, which covers sources of public income (for example, income tax, sales tax) and incidence of public expenditure (for example, wages and salaries, expenditure on education and health) To account for the external sector it was necessary to have itemised balance-of-payments data from the central bank covering import and export statistics; factor payments such as direct investment income (profit remittances); current transfers, including unrequited transfers; and capital transfers. Finally, other administrative data from government ministries, departments, and agencies and financial statements of public and private institutions would have made the task of compiling national accounts much easier.

The Liberian data that actually existed consisted of two surveys that provided some basic information, both of which originated from important data collection activities that occurred in 2007 – a Core Welfare Indicators Questionnaire survey and an economic survey that listed all identifiable economic units in major towns in Liberia. The latter served as a sampling frame for the national accounts annual survey that was conducted in 2009. In addition, in 2008 national population and housing census had been conducted, as had an agriculture survey that concentrated on the input–output structure of crop production in the different counties. In 2009, a full-scale agriculture census began that collected information on crop output, farm gate prices and consumption, among other variables. Data on balance of payments, education, public finance, exports, output of selected commodities, and the financial statements of some large companies were also available.

Using these resources, it was possible to compile national accounts, but some problems were identified with the census and survey data. First all, complete enumeration of some variables is always needed to obtain raising factors when totals of variables in a sample survey are required. In order to raise the value added from the survey data to arrive at the national totals, value added per worker was to be raised using number of workers in that sector as recorded in the population census. Since value added per worker differs between employees in the formal and informal sectors for the same activity, workers classified by formal and informal should be used as the raising factors for the value added per worker. The 2008 population and housing census did not categorise employees as such, making it difficult to correctly raise the values to arrive at national aggregates.

In addition, the 2009 national accounts annual survey questionnaire followed the standard approach for surveys of this type. The key problem here is that informal enterprises do not typically keep business records. As a result, the survey depended completely on a combination of the ability of operators to recall revenue and expenditure and the ingenuity of field staff. The recall periods varied from one week to 12 months, depending on the expected frequency of the item in question. The questions also include the 'number of months operational'. This use of short recall periods – although necessary – can create a problem. When two-week recall periods are used, it is quite possible that an accurate response could show that there were sales but little or no expenditure in the period (maybe purchases are typically made monthly) or even expenditures but no sales. Such extremes are possible. Of course, if the sample size is adequate, such responses would cancel each other out. However, in this survey it was unlikely that the sample size for some activities was sufficient to cover these situations, so it was important to closely check each response for common sense at the time of enumeration. Both enumerators and supervisors failed to do this, leading to wide disparities between information provided by establishments with similar characteristics. Most of the problems encountered during data collection that affected the quality of the data could have been avoided. First, because of financial constraints, the five-day training of field staff was not adequate. Second, both the calibre of field staff that were recruited and their commitment to the task was not the best. Third, the built-in checks in the questionnaires were removed to reduce the size of the questionnaire to save cost, so consistency checks by the field officers could not be made. Finally, the consultant (Magnus Ebo Duncan) could not be with the field staff during the data collection period.

A serious gap in data existed because of non-response by some large companies during the 2009 national accounts annual survey. Although export data were available for some of them, information on their intermediate consumption was absent, thus making it hard to compute value added. In such cases, input–output ratios from Ghanaian data were applied, but of course this may not necessarily reflect the true structure of industry in Liberia.

The final estimates provided by Magnus Ebo Duncan estimated a per capita GDP of USD591.50.[8] Other indirect estimates of output were made from the data available in the Core Welfare Indicators Questionnaire survey. Willem van den Andel estimated a per capita GDP of USD578.6 from a supply and use table, while David Hughes estimated a per capita GDP of USD565.[9]

Because of the data gaps, the three experts who independently estimated Liberia's GDP used different methods to make indirect estimates; these accounted for the differences in the GDP estimates they made. In the end, the World Bank rejected all of these estimates, citing inadequate data sources as the reason for the high GDP estimates. The figures Liberian authorities currently use are still based on projections of the IMF.

The Exhaustiveness of GDP Estimates in Zimbabwe

There has always been reason to believe that the sources and methods used for estimating the gross domestic product in Zimbabwe could lead to underestimation. Various types of evidence have pointed in the same direction. Before independence in 1980, the commercial sector was adequately covered by both administrative sources of data and censuses and surveys. Where the economic activities of the subsistence sector, in which the majority of the population was engaged, were estimated, indirect methods and assumptions were used. For example, crop production estimates were not based on regular statistical surveys or reliable administrative records, except for deliveries to agricultural marketing authorities.

After 1980, under the auspices of the United Nations Household Capability Programme, a number of surveys were embarked upon in Zimbabwe to address the deficit of data that was needed for socio-economic planning. These household-based surveys included the annual Agriculture and Livestock Survey; the Labour Force Survey, taken every five years; and the Income Consumption and Expenditure Survey (ICES), also taken every five years. These three data sources could be used to complement establishment-based economic surveys in order to improve the exhaustiveness and accuracy of GDP estimates. Zimbabwe statisticians did not take advantage of this opportunity until 1998, when some estimates of the contribution of the informal sector were made using ICES data. However, even after this, evidence of underestimation persisted.

The underestimation seems to have been made worse by the near-collapse of the statistical system during the decade that began in 2000, coincident with the country's economic deterioration. This near-collapse of the system, which included poor responses to statistical inquiries, seems to have added the undercounting of the formal sector to the country's statistical deficits.

In addition to the work begun in 1998, the Zimbabwe National Statistics Agency (ZIMSTAT) has introduced other measures and methods to address these problems. These include the labour input method to gauge and correct for undercounting. It has also restarted work on supply and use tables and the construction of a central business register.

Preliminary results of some of this work indicate a possibly significant but declining underestimation of GDP, particularly in recent years. The activity sectors that are most underestimated include transport, storage, communications, community, social and personal services, finance, real estate and business services, mining and manufacturing, in that order.

An A Priori Case for the Existence of Non-exhaustiveness

The Eurostat tabular approach to exhaustiveness, which was recommended by the 2011 International Comparison Programme (ICP) to ensure exhaustiveness in the estimation of GDP, lists seven types of non-exhaustiveness, labelled N1 to N7. Under the category 'not registered', it includes the underground economy or those who deliberately do not register to avoid certain obligations (N1), those involved in illegal activities (N2), and those not required to register because of size or lack of market input (N3). Under the category 'not surveyed', it lists two types of non-exhaustiveness, both of which involve the exclusion of registered producers from surveys because of inadequacies of the statistical business register (N4 and N5). The third category includes misreporting in order to avoid tax and social security obligations (N6). The fourth and final category involves statistical deficiencies of data that are incomplete or cannot be directly collected from surveys or data that are incorrectly compiled during survey processing (N7).

No empirical evidence can be given about to the extent that each of the types of non-exhaustiveness applies in Zimbabwe. However, a number of indicators point to a prevalence of most of the types. For example, since 2009, when regular economic surveys by ZIMSTAT resumed, response rates have been consistently below 50 per cent by head count. For example, the average response rates for the Quarterly Employment Inquiry (QEI) were only 36 per cent in 2009, 29 per cent in 2010, 46 per cent in 2011, and 48 per cent in 2012. The QEI covers all kinds of economic activity included in the International Standard Industrial Classification of all economic activities. The response rate in terms of contribution to employment is not as poor as the head count response rate indicates. For example, it is estimated that in 2012, of the 7,724 establishments in the QEI register, including public service establishments (part of special returns), 1,674, or 23.4 per cent, contributed 90 per cent to total employment of the establishments. High non-response rates indicate N7-type non-exhaustiveness. This is more the case when the period for the estimation for non-response is long and spans pronounced economic changes.

A number of establishments in ZIMSTAT's business register were reported as having relocated when the surveys resumed, but it was not possible to establish to where they had moved. The Registrar of Companies, which is the main source of information for ZIMSTAT's business register, had not been updated since the country's economic meltdown during the period 2005–2008. These deficiencies in the registers lead to N4 and N5 types of non-exhaustiveness, and this in turn leads to underestimation of the contribution of the formal sector to GDP.

Illegal economic activities, such as the panning and smuggling of gold, prostitution and the growing and selling of hemp, that are within the production boundary of the System of National Accounts (1993 SNA and 2008 SNA) take place in Zimbabwe but are not covered by the sources of data used for compiling GDP. For example, according to an article in *NewsDay*, one of Zimbabwe's newspapers, Transparency International Zimbabwe (TIZ) researchers estimate that illegal gold panners produce two tons of raw gold per month. 'Of the total gold output, licensed dealers buy 3% of the gold, 10% is sold illegally across the borders and 87% is bought by private buyers who can also be illegal' (Langa, 2013). The Zimbabwe Republic Police (ZRP) sometimes mount special operations to get rid of illegal gold panning or prostitution, and there are many court cases of people arrested for allegedly growing or selling or transporting hemp. These examples indicate that N2 type of non-exhaustiveness exists.

Traditionally, the communal lands, where the majority of the population lived and practised subsistence farming, were scantily covered by surveys or administrative records. The household sector in urban areas was similarly excluded, especially black African households. Notable exceptions were the population census, school enrolment data, data on numbers of cattle collected through the dipping system, statistics on sales of crops and animals to agricultural marketing authorities, and a 1978 budget survey for lower-income urban families. These data have been used to derive Consumer Price Index weights.

The integrated household surveys that the United Nations began sponsoring in 1982 generated rich new sources of data that were not initially mined to improve the exhaustiveness of GDP estimates. The exclusion of these household economic activities leads to N3 type of non-exhaustiveness.

In 1998, the revised national accounts estimates included estimates of the contribution of the informal sector, based on data from the 1995/96 ICES. The same percentage contributions were assumed to obtain before and after 1995. However, indications that the GDP was still underestimated persisted and increased after the economic meltdown referred to above. These indications include the high ratio of tax revenue to GDP, the high levels of fuel consumption compared to other countries in the region with purportedly bigger economies as measured by GDP, and supplies of certain inter-mediate inputs, such as cement, that outstrip accounted-for use.

The 1998 exercise was the first to measure and incorporate a significant portion of the excluded economic production. However, that type of work does not include the unrecorded formal sector activities. There are also issues of classification in household surveys such that some units that are in fact part of the informal sector may be classified in the formal sector and vice versa.

In 2013 an exercise to improve exhaustiveness by deriving GDP estimates as a sum of three components was undertaken. The three components were (1) the formal sector that is covered by establishment based surveys and administrative records, (2) the formal sector that is not covered by the surveys and records and (3) the informal sector. Both components (2) and (3) were based on the results of the 2011 Poverty, Income, Consumption and Expenditure Survey (PICES). Item (2), the only new component since the 1998 exercise, employed the labour input method using the difference between the total numbers employed in each kind of activity according to the PICES and the same number according to the establishment based surveys. This difference was multiplied by the informal sector gross value added per worker (GVAPW) for that kind of activity, obtained from the PICES, to get a conservative estimate of the under coverage.

Effects of Non-exhaustiveness

Preliminary results of the exercise show that there could have been a significant underestimation of the GDP (about 30% in 2011).[10] The most underestimated kinds of activity are construction, other services, distribution, hotels and restaurants, mining and quarrying, and manufacturing.

The effects of the non-exhaustiveness of the GDP estimates in Zimbabwe are the same as the effects we see in the literature for any other country. These include the fact that all targets denominated by the GDP may appear to be achieved, when in fact they are not. An example is listing Zimbabwe as having one of the highest ratios of revenue to GDP in the world. This may lead the revenue authorities to start congratulating themselves before they reach the requisite standards of performance in their work, depriving the nation of urgently needed government revenue.

Conclusion

All GDP statistics are approximations, and with varying degrees providing a guide to the economic realities. Recent revisions of GDP in sub-Saharan Africa have shown that the problem of outdated GDP statistics is acute in some countries (Jerven, 2013a). Non-exhaustive GDP estimates distort assessments of welfare. When the size of the economy is incorrectly measured, its ranking among other countries is wrong. Moreover, comparisons of the economic performance of the country across time and space are not reliable (Jerven, 2010a, 2010b). In general, non-exhaustiveness puts any analysis of the economic conditions of the country and thus planning and management on an unsecured footing, and leaves a range of other targets such as share of taxes in GDP in deep uncertainty. With increased economic activity and investment in the region, reliable macro-economic statistics are increasingly in demand, and after well-publicised large GDP revisions, it is important for African countries to provide a reliable and up-to-date picture of their economies to facilitate and plan for further economic growth.

The GDP revision in Ghana also meant that the structure of the economy changed. Ghana used to be an agricultural economy on the 1993 benchmark, but on the 2006 benchmark it has made the leap into being an economy where the largest share of value added is created in the services sector (Jerven & Duncan, 2012). According to the preliminary figures from the Nigerian National Bureau of Statistics, a similar transformation has occurred in Nigeria (NBS, 2014). This highlights the importance of timely updates of the structure of the economy. This may be particularly important for economies that are highly dependent on the price of a few commodities. The case of Zambia demonstrates this clearly. In the 1970s the GDP at constant prices for Zambia was derived using 1970 prices; however, in 1973 and 1974 the price of Zambia's main export commodity – copper – fell dramatically. On GDP on constant prices the Zambian economy was doing fine, while on national income at current prices the economy was in free fall (Jerven, 2014). The GDP measure does only in a limited way capture livings standards, but it is crucial to have updated measures to express simple but much needed comparative measures such as taxes or exports as a share in GDP.

One of the reasons that benchmark years matter so much for low-income countries is that there is a dearth of annual data, and therefore a lot of the economic activities are not recorded each year. Instead one relies on projections – using proxies such as population growth, growth in other sectors, import statistics or other alternatives from the benchmark year. To update the benchmark year one requires more reliable data to replace the current estimate with a new and more exhaustive measure, but that requires long-term consistent planning, and it is not just a quick methodological fix. In 2005, the Nigerian GDP series was rebased from a 1984 base year to the 1990 base year. At the time the IMF noted that there was a lack of data on the agricultural sector (IMF, 2005). The same was reported in 2012 regarding latest rebasing from 1990 to 2010 (IMF, 2012), and there is still no agricultural census that supports the new estimates for Nigeria. Similarly, in 2010 and 2011 there was a lot of talk about the new numbers from Ghana, but with a base year of 2006 the 'new' numbers for Ghana are becoming increasingly out of date. Furthermore, as the peer review conducted by the African

Development Bank, the estimates since 2006 have not been compiled with data on the informal sector (AfDB, 2013b).

Despite clear evidence and indications that the GDP estimates of Nigeria, Liberia and Zimbabwe currently underestimates GDP, there is not an easy fix to improve the statistics and provide a new benchmark for measuring economic growth in these economies. In the case of Ghana, the GDP rebasing was initiated in the 2002, but due to a stop–start process it was not completed until 2010 (Jerven & Duncan, 2012). The provision of economic statistics is a public good, and the provision of better GDP statistics ultimately has to be weighed up against the funding of other public services. Moreover, it is shown here that even when funds and political support to provide better and up-to-date statistics exist, there are many difficulties ahead. Most pertinently is the access to basic data on economic activities. While we know that GDP is underestimated because of the lack of data on many agricultural activities and small-scale mining activities, out of date business registers and the exclusion of information on most small- and medium-scale service industries, it is not straight-forward to collect, and design a system that routinely collects data on these economic activities.

Notes

1. For a longer historical view on the Nigerian Statistical System, see Jerven (2011) and a National Accounts document provided by the NBS (n.d.b).
2. It is an international framework/document promoted by PARIS21 for the development of statistical capacity in developing countries; see PARIS21 (2004).
3. Nigeria's Vision 20:2020 is a long-term strategic plan for the country to become one of the 20 largest economies (by size of GDP) by 2020. It is coordinated by the National Planning Commission.
4. In 2010 Ghana rebased national accounts from a 1993 base year to a 2006 base year.
5. Because there is no internationally recognised GDP estimate for Liberia, many estimates of Liberia's GDP per capita have found their way to the public sphere. These range from a high of USD1,000 for 2012 from National Geographic to the much lower USD339 from West Africa Monetary Zone (also for 2012).
6. Different versions of the Technical Committee Reports of the West Africa Monetary Zone (WAMZ).
7. SITC is a product classification of the United Nations that is used for external trade statistics (export and import values and volume of goods) that allows for international comparisons of commodities and manufactured goods.
8. All the estimates are in unpublished reports submitted to LISGIS.
9. Duncan's estimates can be found in the Executive Summary of his final mission report (2010), van den Andel's estimates in 'SUT-2008-final.xls,' and David Hughes's estimates are in his mission report.
10. See Nyoni (2013).

References

African Development Bank, Statistics Department. (2013a). Situational analysis of economic statistics in Africa: Special focus on GDP measurement. Retrieved from http://www.afdb.org/fileadmin/uploads/afdb/Documents/Publications/Economic per cent20Brief per cent20- per cent20Situational per cent20Analysis per cent20of per cent20the per cent20Reliability per cen-t20of per cent20Economic per cent20Statistics per cent20in per cent20Africa- per cent20Special per cent20Focus per cen-t20on per cent20GDP per cent20Measurement.pdf.

African Development Bank, Statistics Department. (2013b). Peer review of national accounts – The case of Ghana. Retrieved from http://www.afdb.org/fileadmin/uploads/afdb/Documents/Publications/Economic_Brief_-_Peer_Review_of_National_Accounts_-_The_case_of_Ghana.pdf.

The Africa Report, (2014). Zambia GDP adds 25 per cent after rebasing economy. Retrieved from http://www.theafricareport.com/Southern-Africa/zambia-gdp-adds-25-per cent-after-rebasing.html.

Akinyosoye, V. (2008). Repositioning the national statistical systems of African countries within the framework of international best practices: The case of Nigeria. The African Statistical Journal, 6, 191–220.

Deverajan, S. (2013). Africa's statistical tragedy, Review of Income and Wealth, 59, S9–S15.

The Economist. (2014). Nigeria. Africa's new number one. Retrieved from http://www.economist.com/news/leaders/21600685-nigerias-suddenly-supersized-economy-indeed-wonder-so-are-its-still-huge.

The Financial Times. (2014). Kenya to make wealth leap with new GDP statistics. Retrieved from http://www.ft.com/intl/cms/s/0/99ea0902-bfc1-11e3-b6e8-00144feabdc0.html?siteedition=intl#axzz3138dMih3.

International Monetary Fund. (2005). Nigeria: 2005 Article IV consultation – staff report; Staff supplement; and public information notice on the executive board discussions. Retrieved from http://www.imf.org/external/pubs/ft/scr/2005/cr05302.pdf.

International Monetary Fund. (2013a). Growing pains. World Economic Outlook Update. http://www.imf.org/external/pubs/ft/weo/2013/update/02/pdf/0713.pdf.

International Monetary Fund. (2013b). Sub-Saharan Africa: Building momentum in a multi-speed world. Retrieved from http://www.imf.org/external/pubs/ft/reo/2013/afr/eng/sreo0513.pdf.

Jerven, M. (2010a). the relativity of poverty and income: How reliable are African economic statistics? *African Affairs, 109*(434), 77–96.

Jerven, M. (2010b). Random growth in Africa? Lessons from an evaluation of the growth evidence on Botswana, Kenya, Tanzania and Zambia, 1965–1995. *Journal of Development Studies, 46*(2), 274–294.

Jerven, M. (2011). *Controversy, facts and assumptions: Lessons from estimating long term growth in Nigeria, 1900–2007* (Simons Papers in Security and Development, No. 13 [2011]). Vancouver: School for International Studies, Simon Fraser University.

Jerven, M. (2013a). *Poor numbers: How we are misled by African development statistics and what to do about it.* Ithaca, NY: Cornell University Press.

Jerven, M. (2013b). For richer, for poorer: GDP revisions and Africa's statistical tragedy. *African Affairs, 112*(446), 138–147.

Jerven, M. (2013c). Comparability of GDP estimates in sub-Saharan Africa: The effect of revisions in sources and methods since structural adjustment. *Review of Income and Wealth, 59*, S16–S36.

Jerven, M. (2014). *Economic growth and measurement reconsidered in Botswana, Kenya, Tanzania, and Zambia, 1965–1995.* Oxford: Oxford University Press.

Jerven, Morten, & Duncan, Magnus Ebo. (2012). Revising GDP estimates in sub-Saharan Africa: Lessons from Ghana. *African Statistical Journal, 15*, 12–24.

Kiregyera, B. (2013, April). The dawning of a statistical renaissance in Africa. Paper presented at the Conference on African Economic Development: Measuring Success and Failure, School for International Studies, Simon Fraser University, Vancouver.

Langa, Veneranda. (2013). Massive gold pilferage exposed. *NewsDay*, December 13. Retrieved from http://www.newsday.co.zw/2012/12/13/massive-gold-pilferage-exposed.

National Bureau of Statistics & Small and Medium Enterprises Development Agency of Nigeria. (2010). Survey report on micro, small and medium enterprises (MSMEs) in Nigeria: Preliminary report. Retrieved from http://www.nigerianstat.gov.ng/pages/download/67.

National Bureau of Statistics. (2014). Presentation of the results of Nigeria's GDP rebasing. Retrieved from http://nigerianstat.gov.ng/pages/download/201.

National Bureau of Statistics. (n.d.a). Harmonized Nigeria Living Standard Survey 2009/10. Retrieved from http://www.nigerianstat.gov.ng/pages/download/116.

National Bureau of Statistics. (n.d.b). National accounts. Retrieved from http://nigerianstat.gov.ng/pages/download/19.

Nyoni, M. (2013, April). Adjustments for GDP exhaustiveness in Zimbabwe. Paper presented at the Conference on African Economic Development: Measuring Success and Failure, School for International Studies, Simon Fraser University, Vancouver.

World Bank. (2007). *World Development Indicators: 2007.* Washington, DC: International Bank for Reconstruction and Development/The World Bank.

World Bank. (n.d.) Bulletin board on statistical capacity. Retrieved from http://go.worldbank.org/LP2D32CR70.

Index

abstract theoretical concepts 4
administrative data 2, 6–20
African Development Bank 117
African Economic Research Consortium (AERC)
    Growth Project 95
agricultural data 2, 23–30; policy relevance of 27–30
aid donors 7–10
Akilire, S. 72
anthropological research 53–5
Arbache, J.S. 96–7
Arya, P.L. 84
asset ownership 69–75, 79–81

Bagachwa, M.S.D. 41
Banerjee, Raka
Beegle, K. 32, 69
benchmark years 116
Blades, D. 102
Botswana 86–96, 100–1
Breman, J. 41, 46
Bryceson, D.F. 41
Burkina Faso 52, 55, 59
bus workers 45–7

Cameroon 20
Cape Verde 106
Carfagna, E. 35
Carletto, Calogero 2–3, 32–5
censuses, agricultural 26–7
Chinganya, O. 27–8
Collier, P. 97
comparability of statistics 8
computer-assisted personal interviewing (CAPI) 30–1
consumption data 69
Crawford, E. 34–5

daladala workers 45–8
Dar es Salaam 45, 56–8, 61
data quality 1–4, 6, 105; *see also* measurement errors

De Weerdt, J. 69
Deaton, A. 88
Deininger, K. 33
Demographic and Health Surveys (DHS) 6–12,
    15–17, 55, 61, 64, 68–70, 74, 78
dependents, accumulation of 60–1
Devarajan, Shanta 1, 6, 23, 25, 36
Diagana, B. 34–5
diphtheria, tetanus and pertussis (DTP3) 7, 10–14
disaggregation of data 8–9
dissemination of information 6
Duncan, Magnus Ebo 3, 112–13
Durlauf, S. 96

Easterly, W. 72
education, returns to 70, 79–81
education data 2, 6–9, 14–19
education management information system (EMIS)
    databases 8–9, 15–16, 19
Egypt 75–6, 80
Elepu, G. 26
El Salvador 54
Ethiopia 26, 33, 77–8
ethnic fractionalisation 69–70, 78–9
Eurostat 114

farm surveys 27
'fast commodities' 30
Fields, G.S. 41
Fold, N. 41
Food and Agriculture Organisation (FAO) 23–7,
    34–5
Foster, A.D. 24
Foster, J. 72
Fox, L. 39, 41
Friedman, J. 69

geo-referencing 29
Gerry, C. 41

119

Ghana 1, 54, 76, 80, 105–6, 111, 116–17
Gibson, J. 69
Glassman, Amanda 2–4
Global Alliance for Vaccines
    and Immunisation (GAVI) 7, 10–11, 14
global positioning system (GPS) technology 34–5
Global Strategy to Improve Agricultural and Rural
    Statistics 23–4, 29–30, 35
Gooptu, N. 40
gross domestic product (GDP) 1–2, 84–6, 89, 92, 97,
    100, 102, 105–17; for Zimbabwe 113–16
growth, economic 86–102; accuracy in reporting
    of 86–94; comparisons of 85; rates of 87–9;
    implications of data quality for analysis of
    94–100
'guesstimates' 9
Guyer, J.I. 53–4

harmonisation of conflicting evidence 100–1
Harriss-White, B. 40
Hart, Keith 40–1
harvest diaries 33
health data 2, 6–9, 14, 20
health management information system (HMIS)
    databases 9, 14
Heston, A. 88
Himelein, K. 32
household relationship grids 64
household surveys 9, 19, 27, 115
households: definitions of 2, 4, 52–5, 62–5; *open* and
    closed 52, 56–65; size in relation to resources
    59–61
Hughes, David 113
Huillery, E. 20

immunisation statistics 7–13
imputation of missing data 11
income distribution 3
India 29
informal economy 2, 39–49; definition of 42
Integrated Labour Force Survey (ILFS) 40–9
intercropping 33
International Comparison Programme (ICP) 86, 114
International Development Association (IDA) 19
International Labour Organisation (ILO) 42
International Monetary Fund (IMF) 116; Regional
    Economic Outlook for sub-Saharan Africa 106;
    World Economic Outlook 108
international organisations, reporting on data sources
    by 86
Irz, X. 23

Jerven, Morten 3, 9, 29, 41, 84
Johnston, Deborah 2–4, 27, 36
Jolliffe, Dean 23, 28
Jonssøn, J.B. 41

Kale, Yemi 3
Keita, N. 35
Kelly, V. 34–5
Kenya 7–9, 16–19, 86–96, 100–1, 106
kernel density 73–5
Kilama, Blandina 2
Kilic, T. 35
Kiregyera, Ben 23, 36, 105
Knack, S. 79
Kpedekpo, G.M.C. 84

labour force surveys 3; *see also* Integrated Labour
    Force Survey
land area measurement 34
LeBrun, O. 41
Levine, R. 72
Liberia 2, 105–6, 111–13, 117
Lim, S. 10–14
Lin, L. 23
livestock farming 28
Living Standards Measurement Study (LSMS) 3,
    28–30; Integrated Surveys on Agriculture
    (LSMS–ISA) 24–5
Loayza, N. 79

Madagascar 76–7, 80
Maddison, A. 86–91, 95–6
Maipose, G.S. 95–6
Malawi 26, 29, 32–3, 53, 106
Maliyamkono, T.L. 41
Maputo Declaration (2003) 24
Marrakech Action Plan for Statistics (MAPS) 107
Masset, E. 54
Matsheka, T.C. 95–6
Mauritius 9, 106
measles 10–14
measurement errors 30–4; *see also* data quality
middle class 68–81; cross-country variations in the
    size of 78–81; definition of 69–74, 77; evolution
    of 73–7; growth of 69, 73–5, 80; mobility into and
    out of 77–81
Millennium Development Goals (MDGs) 1, 3, 16, 52,
    55, 105
'misplaced aggregation' 40, 49
mis-reporting, incentives for 2, 4, 6–10, 14, 16,
    19–20

Moi-Ibrahim index 72, 79
multiple correspondence analysis (MCA) 71–2
Mulungushi, J. 96
Muwonge, J. 33
Mwanawina, I. 96
Mwase, N. 96

national accounts 85–8, 99–102, 115
Ncube, Mthuli 3
Ndulu, B.J. 86, 95–8
Nigeria 1–2, 9, 29, 105–11, 116–17
Nshimyumuremyi, A. 27–8
Nyoni, Moffat 3

Oladejo, A. 27–8
Organisation for Economic Cooperation
    and Development (OECD) 85–91
Ouagadougou district 56–8, 61

Page, J. 96–7
Participatory Rural Appraisal 53
Partnership in Statistics Development in the
    21st Century (PARIS21) 107
pay-for-performance initiatives 20
Penn World Tables (PWT) 1, 86–8, 101–2
Peters, P.E. 53–4
Pimhidzai, O. 39, 41
'policy-driven evidence' 3
povcalnet 70
poverty 2, 52–65, 106; at the houshold level
    53–5; reduction of 23, 25, 27, 29; in relation to
    household size 61, 63
principal–agent problems 7, 14
private schooling 16
productivity, agricultural 27, 30–1
pseudo-panels 72
public transport 45
purchasing power parities (PPPs) 87–8, 96, 101

Quinn, S. 41

Reardon, T. 34–5
resource allocation decisions 8–9
Riddell, A. 18
Rizzo, Matteo 2–4
root crops 30
Rosenzweig, M.R. 24
Rwanda 7, 16–19

Sandefur, Justin 2–4
Sarris, A.H. 41

Savastano, S. 33, 35
schooling 16, 57
Scoones, J. 54
Seban, J. 20
Seers, D. 84–5
self-employment 39–48; definition of 42
self-reported landholdings 34–5
Senegal 41, 64
Shimeles, Abebe 3
Singh, M. 25
smallholder agriculture 23–8, 31–2
South Africa 64
South Sudan 106
Srinivasan, T.N. 1–2, 102
statistical capacity 1–3, 9, 106
statistical inference 11
'statistical renaissance' 23, 36, 105
'statistical tragedy' 1, 6, 23, 25, 36, 40, 105
Stern, Nicholas 1
structural adjustment programmes 3, 101
Swahili language 40, 46–7

Tanzania 2, 4, 8, 16, 25, 28–9, 35, 39–42, 45, 48–9,
    52, 55–61, 69, 86–9, 92–101
Task Team on Food, Agriculture and Rural Statistics
    28–9
Teal, F. 41
Thirtle, C. 23
Tripp, A.M. 41

Uganda 26, 33–5
United Nations: Economic Commission for Africa
    (UNECA) 19; Educational, Scientific and Cultural
    Organisation (UNESCO) 15; High Level Panel
    on post2015 development goals 6; Household
    Capability Programme 114
United States Agency for International Development
    (USAID) 7, 10
user fees, abolition of 18–20

vaccination data 10–14
Van den Brink, R. 41

wage labour 39–41, 45–8; definition of 40; statistical
    invisibility of 39–40, 48
Wangwe, S.M. 41
'wealth in people' 54–5, 62–3
wealth-ranking techniques 54
wealth status as an indicator of class 69
Weeks, J. 41
welfare measures 70–1

Wells, J. 42
White, H. 54
Whitehead, A. 54
Wiggins, S. 23
Willis, H.P. 25
women-centred households 59
World Bank 19, 29, 70, 86–9, 92–3, 96, 100, 106–7; Bulletin Board of Statistical Capacity 9, 106; Health Results Innovation Trust Fund 20

World Development Indicators (WDI) 86–92, 95–6, 101–2
World Healh Organisation (WHO) 11
World Values Survey 72, 74
Wuyts, Marc 2

Zak, P.J. 79
Zambia 2, 86–9, 92–101, 106, 116
Zezza, A. 35
Zimbabwe 54, 105–6, 113–17

For Product Safety Concerns and Information please contact our EU representative GPSR@taylorandfrancis.com Taylor & Francis Verlag GmbH, Kaufingerstraße 24, 80331 München, Germany

Batch number: 08153807

Printed by Printforce, the Netherlands